The Second Language Classroom:

Directions for the 1980's

The
Second Language
Classroom:

Directions for the 1980's

Essays in Honor of

Mary Finocchiaro

Editors:

James E. Alatis
Howard B. Altman
Penelope M. Alatis

New York   Oxford
OXFORD UNIVERSITY PRESS
1981

Copyright © 1981 by Oxford University Press, Inc.

Library of Congress Cataloging in Publication Data
Main entry under title:

The Second language classroom.

   Bibliography: p.
   1. Language and languages—Study and teaching—
Addresses, essays, lectures. 2. Finocchiaro, Mary
Bonomo, 1913–   I. Finocchiaro, Mary Bonomo
II. Alatis, James E.   III. Altman, Howard B.
IV. Alatis, Penelope, 1930–
P51.S32   418′.007   80-27236
ISBN 0-19-502928-3
ISBN 0-19-502929-1 (pbk.)

Notes from the English Language Teaching Department

The English Language Teaching Department of Oxford University Press, New York, is staffed by professionals with classroom experience in the fields of English as a Second Language and Bilingual Education.

It is the policy of this department to publish books and audio-visual materials that are innovative as well as professionally sound. It is in keeping with this tradition that we present *The Second Language Classroom*.

We hope you enjoy our materials and find them useful for your classroom needs.

Because we value the insights and experience of classroom teachers in various parts of the world, we invite you to write to us with your comments and suggestions.

The English Language Teaching Department
Oxford University Press, New York

Manager: Marilyn S. Rosenthal, Ph.D.
Editors: Susan Kulick, Ph.D.   Laurie Likoff, M.A.
Associate Editor: Debra Sistino, M.A.
Assistant Editor: Debra Musiker
Educational Specialists: Connie Attanasio, M.A.
Genaro Bastos, M.Ed.

Printing (last digit): 98765432
Printed in the United States of America

Dedication

It is rare to be able to say of a teacher that she has made a difference in the professional and personal lives of hundreds, if not thousands, of others. And it is, in our view, the highest praise to be able to say of an educator that her keen mind and warm heart have shaped her profession for the better. Of Mary Finocchiaro these statements can be made without reservation.

To Mary Finocchiaro this volume is dedicated with the love and appreciation of the profession of language teaching which she has helped to build and guide; she has been a teacher of languages, an instructional supervisor, a school principal, a professor of education, a methodologist, a textbook author, and an ubiquitous lecturer and consultant for almost half a century.

Today, Mary is best known for her work in the teaching of English as a Second Language, a field in which she has been active for four decades. She began her career in 1932 as a teacher of foreign languages with the New York City Board of Education, and her speeches and publications over the years have demonstrated her continuing interest in the teaching of all languages to all kinds of learners in a variety of educational settings.

DEDICATION

...distinguished career in the teaching of English as a ...e in a New York City high school in 1940, when she ...each English to a newly arrived group of students ...different countries. She used her previous experience ...a teacher of Romance Languages to meet this formidable challenge. She was an outstanding success, and was quickly recognized as a brilliant and energetic professional with wide-ranging talents. Public demonstration classes, preparation of curriculum materials, an appointment as Supervisor of Instruction for Non-English-Speaking Children, and a workshop in teaching methods at Columbia University, which she co-conducted, all contributed to deepening her insights and shaping her theories about the nature of language teaching and learning.

Dr. Finocchiaro's extensive background in English as a Second Language includes: Fulbright professorships in Spain and Italy; assignment as an American specialist in language and linguistics for the U.S. Department of State; language-teaching seminars in Germany, Morocco, Poland, Spain, Turkey, Yugoslavia and elsewhere; a worldwide television series for the U.S. Information Agency; a consultancy on English-teaching programs for the education departments of Puerto Rico, Poland, and Spain; the directorship of the program for teachers of children of Puerto Rican origin at Hunter College of the City University of New York—to mention only some highlights. In 1972, upon her retirement from full-time teaching, she became Professor of Education Emeritus at Hunter College, where she had taught since 1957.

That Mary Finocchiaro has so richly combined scholarship with teaching is demonstrated in part by the selective bibliography which is appended to this volume. In an age when so many individuals steadfastly espouse a point of view and refuse to change it despite mounting evidence to the contrary, Mary has never been afraid of change, and her research interests have reflected this. She is currently engaged in studies of bilingual education, and the applications of functional/notional language teaching principles to the second language classroom.

But it is the *human* phenomenon of Mary Finocchiaro that has distinguished her throughout the years and has made her appearances at conference podiums around the world an occasion for both learning and joy. Her warmth, her abundant sense of humor, the love which she radiates to her audiences, her remarkable ability to share her knowledge and experience with teachers everywhere, have helped to make Mary Finocchiaro one of the most beloved teachers of language in modern times. Her principal concern is, and has always been, the classroom language teacher. Her respect and love for teachers of language are revealed in every speech and in every publication. Mary has never let us forget the indispensable contribution of the classroom teacher in bringing about foreign or second language learning. Each of us has witnessed the miracle of Mary Finocchiaro speaking to groups of teachers, and we have watched their eyes light up in response and their heads nod in agreement every time she speaks. More often than not, she has received standing ovations.

Mary served TESOL (Teachers of English to Speakers of Other Languages) first as a member of the Executive Committee, then as First Vice-President, as President in 1970–71, and then for two years as *ex officio* member of the Executive Committee. She has been ubiquitous in her appearances, indefatigable in her efforts, and thoroughly committed to the field. All who know her in TESOL consider it one of the great privileges of their lives to have been able to work with her.

Since 1972, Mary has lived in Rome and her years of "retirement" have overflowed with professional activity. She has been lecturing around the world, making appearances at and addresses to TESOL, writing numerous articles and books, and performing a variety of consultancies. She currently serves as special consultant on English Language Teaching to the American Embassy in Rome. Despite personal loss and failing health, she has continued to share her expertise and love with teachers throughout Italy and around the world.

This *Festschrift*, consisting of chapters by only a very small number of Mary's many friends and colleagues, is meant as a tribute to her undaunted professionalism and is in recognition of her incomparable service to a profession which, and to teachers whom, she has deeply loved. Long may she continue to lead us forward and to guide our judgments with the skill and devotion which she possesses in limitless quantity.

J.E.A., H.B.A., P.M.A.
August, 1980

Contents

Dedication   v

Introduction   xiii

Section I: Focus on Second Language Teaching   1

Introduction   3

What Is Second Language Teaching? *Howard B. Altman*   5

Effective Language Teaching: Insights from Research
  Robert L. Politzer   21

The Relationship of Second Language Learning to Second
  Language Teaching   *G. Richard Tucker*   37

The Preparation of Second Language Teachers in the
  1980's   *Helen L. Jorstad*   49

Section II: Focus on Second Language Learning   63

Introduction   65

The Holistic Approach to Second Language Education
  Renzo Titone   67

Language Learners as Individuals: Discovering Their Needs,
  Wants, and Learning Styles   *Wilga M. Rivers and
  Bernice J. Melvin*   79

Effective Second Language Acquisiton: Insights from
  Research   *Stephen D. Krashen*   95

Affective Factors in Second Language Learning
  H. Douglas Brown   111

Communicative Language Teaching and Learning: Toward
  a Synthesis   *H. H. Stern*   131

Learning for Communication: Practical Considerations
  Virginia French Allen   149
The Evaluation of Second Language Learning
  Rebecca M. Valette   159
Optimal Language Learning Environments   *Marina Burt and
  Heidi Dulay*   175

Section III: Focus on Second Language Teaching Materials   193

Introduction   195
Issues in Second Language Syllabus Design   *Henry G.
  Widdowson and Christopher J. Brumfit*   197
Learners' Needs and the Selection of Compatible
  Materials   *Frederick L. Jenks*   211
Materials Design: Issues for the 1980's   An American Point of
  View   *Robert Lado*   227
Materials Design: Issues for the 1980's   A European Point of
  View   *L. G. Alexander*   245
Media in the Second Language Program: Forms and Uses for the
  Eighties   *Reinhold Freudenstein*   267

Notes on the Contributors   281
A Selective Bibliography of Mary Finocchiaro   286

Acknowledgments

The publication of a book involves the efforts of many people. We would like to express our appreciation first of all to the authors of the chapters in this volume who agreed to meet impossible deadlines so that the book would be published in time for presentation to Mary Finocchiaro at the 1981 TESOL Convention in Detroit. We are also extremely grateful to the English Language Teaching Department of Oxford University Press for their advice at every stage and for their enthusiasm for publishing this collection of essays.

To Dr. Susan Kulick of Oxford University Press, who had final responsibility for editing this volume, we are especially grateful; her skill and patience have made this a far more readable volume than we could have done alone.

J.E.A., H.B.A., P.M.A.

Acknowledgments

Permission to reprint copyright material is hereby gratefully acknowledged:

p. 17. From *Will The Real Teacher Please Stand Up?*, second edition by Mary Greer and Bonnie Rubinstein (p. 125). Copyright © 1978 by Goodyear Publishing Co. Inc. Reprinted by permission.

p. 72. In Titone, R., 1973, "A psycholinguistic definition of the 'glosso-dynamic model' of language behavior and language learning," *Rassegna Italiana di Linguistica Applicata*, vol. V, 1973, no. 1, p. 19. Integrated for the present book. Reproduction by permission of the Editor, R. Titone, and by the Publisher, M. Bulzoni, Inc., Rome.

p. 113. From *Principles of Language Learning and Teaching* by H. Douglas Brown. Copyright © 1980 by Prentice-Hall, Inc. Portions of chapters six and seven reprinted, in adapted form, by permission.

p. 142. From "A Three-Level Curriculum Model for Second Language Education," an unpublished work by J. P. B. Allen. This slightly adapted form is reprinted by permission of J. P. B. Allen.

p. 163. From *Modern Language Performance Objectives and Individualization: A Handbook* by Rebecca M. Valette and Renée S. Disick. Copyright © 1972 by Harcourt Brace Jovanovich. Rights reverted to author. Reprinted by permission of Rebecca M. Valette.

p. 168. From *Test Guide to Accompany the Testing Program, French for Mastery 2* by Jean-Paul Valette and Rebecca M. Valette. Copyright © 1976 by D. C. Heath and Co. Reprinted by permission.

p. 172. From *Approaches to Self-Assessment in Foreign Language Learning* by Mats Oskarsson. Copyright © by Council of Europe. Reprinted by permission of Council of Europe. Copyright © 1978 by Pergamon Press. New edition by Pergamon, 1980.

p. 189. This is an updated version of the model presented in *Viewpoints on English as a Second Language* edited by Marina Burt, Heidi Dulay and Mary Finocchiaro. Copyright © 1977 by Regents Publishing Co., Inc. Reprinted by permission.

p. 209. From *Communicative Teaching at the Secondary School Level* by Henry G. Widdowson. Copyright © 1981 by Longman Group, Ltd., London. Reprinted by permission.

Introduction

In the literature on foreign and second language learning which appeared at the beginning of the 1970's, one is hard pressed to find a volume which states directions for the new decade.

Why, then, a volume at the beginning of the 1980's which seeks to chart the paths for language learning and language teaching in the present decade?

One answer is that the directions which language teaching and learning have taken in the 1970's have allowed us to predict that certain paths are probable in the 1980's. For example, the emphasis on communication as the primary goal in language learning leads inextricably to the development of methods and techniques for teaching for communication. That different roads lead to the same goal is illustrated by the successes in European and American classrooms and by their different assumptions about learner needs.

A second answer reflects the fact that we talk about the "language teaching profession" as if language teachers around the world were a monolithic group of like-minded invididuals with common goals and common needs. In reality, language teaching is a highly fragmented enterprise, and unifying leadership is sorely needed. In part this task is performed by the professional associations, and in part by the professional literature. It is the purpose of this book to carry on that tradition by suggesting reasonable courses of action for the years ahead. To that end, the twenty authors who have contributed to this volume represent some of the most perceptive and prolific scholars and educators in language teaching and learning today. While none of these scholars has access to a crystal ball, all are recognized authorities in their special areas of writing.

The third answer for compiling this book is a personal one shared by each of the contributors. Each has been influenced, in a variety of ways, by the person to whom this volume is dedicated. Mary Finocchiaro has demonstrated for almost five decades that the thoughtful and constructive planning of the future in language teaching and language learning is the most reliable way to see our dreams and aspirations realized. She has approached this task with a precept which all of us would do well to copy: If *we* don't dream, who will? If not *now*, then when?

SECTION I

FOCUS ON SECOND LANGUAGE TEACHING

INTRODUCTION

The teaching of foreign or second languages in classrooms around the world constitutes a significant educational enterprise. Although it is impossible to estimate the number of individuals worldwide who are engaged full- or part-time in the teaching of target languages, we know that more than 100,000 persons are so engaged in North America alone.

Language teaching means different things to different people, and in the 1980's this is how it should be. If the 1950's and 1960's gave us answers, the 1970's and, increasingly, the 1980's pose questions such as the following which the profession of language teaching needs to tackle:

What method(s) work(s) best with specific types of learners in specific situations?

How can and should teaching be made most responsive to individual needs?

What factors influence language teaching?

What skills and competencies should second language teachers possess? How can these skills and competencies be assessed in teacher candidates?

The four chapters in *Section I* of this volume focus on second language teaching and second language teachers in the 1980's. Altman defines second language teaching as a facilitative activity and distinguishes between its essential components and its many optional conventions. Politzer traces the research on language teaching from previous decades and suggests some different research paradigms for the future. Tucker describes the need for a new research agenda in second language teaching and learning which takes into account the specific purposes of the learning. Finally, Jorstad traces the progress which has been made in training second language teachers and suggests components of language teacher education programs for the rest of the decade.

ABSTRACT

What Is
Second Language Teaching?

HOWARD B. ALTMAN
University of Louisville

Second language teaching, expanding upon a definition of teaching by Gage (1978), consists of any activity on the part of one person intended to facilitate the learning by another person of a language which is not his or her native one. This represents the *essence* of second language teaching, and everything else—*e.g.*, methodologies, curriculum materials, performance objectives, audio-visual equipment, etc.—is a *convention* of second language teaching which may vary from one educational setting to the next. In the 1980's the essence of second language teaching should remain unchanged, but one can predict major changes both in conventions and in the role expectations for the classroom teacher. Some eighty-five different role expectations, culled from the program of the 1980 TESOL annual meeting, are offered as examples. Suggestions follow to assist the classroom teacher in coping with this pedagogical and curricular "overchoice" and to reach decisions about what to preserve and what to change in his or her classroom. Finally, some characteristics of a "real" second language teacher are offered, as seen from the eyes of students.

5

What Is
Second Language Teaching?

HOWARD B. ALTMAN
University of Louisville

I have a poster on my office wall which has often puzzled me.
Beneath an abstraction of a unicorn, the message reads: "As a
teacher, I am unique and powerful."

Unique and *powerful?* Beset as many teachers are by the realities of classroom existence, we often don't feel this way. In describing second language teaching, this chapter tries to resolve this
paradox.

Teaching has often been characterized, but has rarely been defined, perhaps because its definition seems so obvious, hence not
worth stating. It is interesting to speculate that teaching may be
the only profession which requires a recipient for its action, con-
veniently though not always appropriately labeled a "learner," as
part of its definition. Physicians practice medicine in research laboratories devoid of patients; attorneys pursue the law in library
archives; clergymen engage in prayer in the absence of a congre-
gation. But a teacher is not teaching something unless he or she is
teaching it to *someone*. A teacher who performs in the absence of
a "clientele" may be engaged in talking, illustrating, explicating,
theorizing, or even philosophizing, but he or she is not engaged in
teaching.

In a recent book, Gage (1978) defines teaching in a way which
highlights this essential dependence of teachers on learners: "By
teaching I mean any activity on the part of one person intended to
facilitate learning on the part of another." From this we may conclude that *good* (i.e., successful) teaching is any activity which fa-

cilitates learning, while *bad* (i.e., unsuccessful) teaching, by extension, is any activity which fails to facilitate learning (either by failing to affect learning at all or by affecting it negatively, by obstructing learning).

To carry this one step further and thereby define our own field: Second (or foreign) language teaching—the distinction depends upon language function—is any activity on the part of one person intended to facilitate the learning by another person of a language which is not his or her native one. *Good* second (or foreign) language teaching is thus any activity which facilitates this learning; *bad* second (or foreign) language teaching is any activity which fails to facilitate this learning, either by failing to affect this learning at all or by affecting it negatively (by obstructing it).

In their thought-provoking critique of American schooling, Postman and Weingartner (1973) differentiate between the *essential functions* of school and the *conventional ways* of carrying out those functions which may vary in different educational settings. For example, *evaluation* is an essential function of school. All schools evaluate learners. Any institution which does not evaluate learners cannot be called a school. The *conventions* of evaluation are numerous and varied, however. Different grading systems abound; different criteria for evaluation coexist. In some institutions, learners evaluate themselves, in others they evaluate one another, in still others (probably the majority) they are evaluated by teachers. Evaluation may be formal or informal, frequent or infrequent, objective or subjective, alterable or unalterable. But its *existence* is unalterable, if the institution is to remain a school.

This distinction between *essence* and *convention* is worth examining as it may be applied to second language teaching. If we apply this distinction to our definition of second language teaching above, then it seems clear that the *essence* of second language teaching consists of

A. a person (who may be termed a teacher), who performs. . .
B. any activity designed to facilitate the learning of another language by. . .
C. another person (who may be termed a learner)

and that's it! Everything else related to second language teaching falls into the large category of conventions which differ from country to country, city to city, school to school, and classroom to classroom. On that long list of alterable conventions of second language teaching we may include:

- all language teaching methodologies
- all learning materials
- all school schedules, whether flexible or inflexible
- all kinds of tests and evaluation procedures
- all types of drills and exercises
- all formulas for grouping students (large group, small group, choral response, the "boys," the "girls," the high-ability group, the low-ability group, etc.)
- all activities to personalize instruction
- all syllabuses, be they grammatical, situational, functional-notional, or some yet-to-be-discovered variety
- all language laboratories and all other audio-visual media
- all learning goals and objectives, and the activities designed to reach those goals and objectives
- all pedagogical techniques

This list could be practically endless since conventions in second language teaching are discovered or, as so frequently happens, *re*discovered, in classrooms worldwide at a frenetic pace.

It is perhaps a sobering thought that these many pedagogical and curricular principles which second language teachers have alternately worshiped and condemned, and which linguists and methodologists have alternately eulogized or excoriated from academic pulpits, are revealed to be neither commandments carved permanently in stone nor eternal truths. They are *customs,* selected and practiced differentially by different teachers in different educational settings. They can claim no eternal validity; indeed, the pedagogical truths of one decade prove to be the misconceptions of the next one. What is likely to remain immutable for decades, however, is the *essence* of good second language teaching as we have described it above.

How can we characterize the role of the second language teacher in the classrooms of the 1980's? Some of the challenges of the 1980's concern the objectives of language instruction, the pedagogical strategies to meet those objectives, the construction of suitable learning materials, and the means for measuring the outcomes of teaching and learning. There is little doubt that these challenges are making, and will continue to make, new demands upon the skills and competencies of second language teachers, and will continue to result in new conventions in the teacher's role. How dramatic future changes will prove to be remains to be seen. There is, however, cause to predict that the second language teacher a decade from now will be engaged in activities to develop in learners a level of communicative competence heretofore unknown in the classroom. "The times," as folksinger Bob Dylan put it, "they are a-changin'," and these changes are already being felt in the expectations imposed upon the second-language-classroom teacher.

In a world of rapid change, many second language teachers find themselves overwhelmed by the number of choices in what to teach and how to teach. This phenomenon of *curricular and pedagogical overchoice* has not always been the case. Prior to the 1970's, teachers as well as learners had relatively few options from which to choose. The "method" of language teaching ruled supreme and provided the "answer" to all pedagogical and most curricular questions. Textbook authors and course developers instructed teachers in what to do and in what order to do it. Students either accepted the system or ceased to be a part of it. Both the *curriculum-centered* course and the *teacher-centered* course provided remarkably little flexibility in means or ends.

With the blossoming of *learner-centered* instruction in second language classes in the 1970's, however, far more options in both materials and pedagogical strategies were realized. Teachers and learners could and did exercise more freedom of choice. The "answer" was no longer provided in the pronouncements of "experts." Indeed, an increase in freedom to choose carried with it an obligation to use that freedom—an obligation to make choices, to engage in decision-making about what ought to be—for *me* as a second language teacher, in *my* specific educational setting, with *my* specific students—and to decide upon the appropriate objectives, methods, materials, and pedagogical strategies.

If anything, the number of available options will continue to grow in the 1980's. Evidence of this is clear if one examines the contents of journal articles or conference programs in second language teaching. The variety of options posed for classroom teachers, each put forth with the conviction of its presenter that it is "good" for teachers, seems limitless. To take as an example the 1980 TESOL Convention in San Francisco, one discovers a veritable cornucopia of choice for defining the role of a "relevant" second language teacher. The list of role expectations below, culled from the 1980 TESOL program, is probably not complete. I present the items in no special order of significance. From the TESOL program one can conclude that an up-to-date, competent, enlightened second language teacher is one who . . .

1. is an expert in dealing with the problems of refugees
2. is trained in psycholinguistics
3. is trained in sociolinguistics
4. is a drama coach
5. is a creative writing specialist
6. is a designer of communicative syllabuses
7. is a proficient oral interviewer
8. is a skillful developer of communicative competence in the classroom
9. individualizes instruction
10. is an expert on vocational education
11. is an authority on mime techniques
12. is a classroom researcher
13. utilizes (and develops) computer-assisted language instruction
14. is an expert at "total physical response" techniques
15. is a dialectologist
16. is a motivator
17. is an evaluator
18. is a skillful discourse analyzer
19. is a specialist in nonverbal communication
20. is a conference coordinator
21. is an expert on functional-notional teaching
22. is a statistician
23. is a specialist in teaching culture
24. is an expert on intercultural communication
25. is a builder of dyads in the classroom

26. is silent (the Silent Way)
27. is a specialist in simulations and gaming
28. is an authority on bilingual education
29. is an applied linguist
30. is an educational programmer
31. is a master at error analysis
32. is a syntactician
33. is a specialist in cloze testing
34. is a values clarifier
35. is an expert in teaching scientific and technical language
36. is a connoisseur of translation
37. is a master of pronunciation techniques
38. is an authority on teaching listening comprehension
39. is a master at special-purpose language teaching
40. analyzes speech acts
41. advises language learners on employment possibilities
42. is a spelling coach
43. is a reading specialist
44. is a musician
45. is an expert on tone and register in language
46. is an authority on the hemispheres of the brain and their functions
47. is a grammarian
48. is a jazz chanter
49. is a hypnotizer
50. is a specialist in affective education
51. is a comedian
52. is a metalinguist
53. is a creolist and pidginist
54. is a team-builder
55. is an authority on confluent education
56. is a story teller
57. is a psychometrician (psychometrist?)
58. is a specialist in mixed-level classes (as well as heterogeneous and homogeneous classes)
59. writes successful grant proposals
60. develops materials
61. is a counselor

62. is an expert on language transfer
63. is an authority on communicative disorders
64. trains paraprofessionals
65. is a folksinger
66. is a public speaker
67. is a program administrator
68. monitors the "Monitor"
69. advises foreign students
70. is a drill master
71. supervises student teachers
72. is a film critic
73. is a cognitive psychologist
74. is a poet
75. is a photographer
76. is a language laboratory director
77. is a specialist in note-taking skills
78. is a master of role-playing techniques
79. is a curriculum evaluator
80. is a puppet-maker
81. personalizes instruction
82. is a multi-cultural specialist
83. is a specialist in the teaching of literature
84. is a lexicographer
85. is a communication catalyst

If I've left out anyone's favorite role, it's only because it didn't come up in this meeting, but there are lots of other meetings! By the way, there is a "fact of life" in the classroom which did not get mentioned in the 1980 TESOL program, perhaps because it casts doubt on the freedom to choose many of the eighty-five topics which did get mentioned:

> The second language teacher, in many cases, teaches more than 150 students in six different classes every day while trying to remain both sane and cheerful despite being overworked and underpaid.

How can the second language teacher decide which options to choose and which to reject? It is not sufficient for a teacher to say: "I must choose those options which best meet the needs and interests of the individual students in my classes." We need to remember—in the 1980's more than ever—that teachers are individuals, too, with individual needs and individual abilities. To attempt to fulfill even a small fraction of the role expectations in the above list would require the patience of Job, the strength of Tarzan, the endurance of Superman, and quite possibly the nine lives of a cat! Frankly, the reality of ordinary classroom life is sufficient to tax many teachers to the limits of their ability. Is it any wonder that the phenomenon of "teacher burn-out" has become a major theme in education today?

In making decisions about which pedagogical or curricular paths to follow, and when (indeed, whether) to change paths, we need to keep the following points in mind:

1. To change from the status quo means, by definition, that one has to give up something in order to get something. Some aspects of our second language programs are working as we want them to, and we would be loath to give them up. Other aspects may not be working so well, and we would gladly see them gone. We need to ask ourselves the following questions, and to try to answer them as honestly as possible from the perspective of our students as well as ourselves:

a. What is it in my program which is working well and ought to be preserved unchanged?
b. What is it in my program which is not working well and which I would like to see changed?
c. Of those things which I would like to see changed, which are *capable* of being changed?
   1. in the short run? in the long run?
   2. by me? only by others?
   3. for free? for additional expense?
d. If I make the changes which I desire and which I am capable of making, what will I be giving up?

This is the kind of "needs analysis" which teachers should undergo *before* considering the advantages or disadvantages of the latest pedagogical or curricular fad.

2. Innovations in the second language classroom specifically, and in education in general, have a strong likelihood of success *only* where

a. teachers are philosophically supportive of the innovation
b. teachers are trained *in advance* in the procedures required by the innovation
c. materials are available, clear, and usable
d. there is sufficient "pedagogical fit" for the innovation in the course

Innovations in the second language classroom specifically, and in education in general, are likely to fail where

a. the innovation is imposed upon teachers without their support and commitment
b. teachers are not trained in advance in the procedures required by the innovation
c. clear and usable materials are not available
d. there is insufficient "pedagogical fit" for the innovation in the course

3. Good (successful) second language teaching, as we defined it above, comes in all shapes and sizes. So, too, does bad (unsuccessful) language teaching. Teaching is an art, as Gage (1978) suggests, but it is an art with a scientific basis. Teaching is something we can all learn more about.

4. It is therefore incumbent upon each of us to:

a. stay up-to-date in our knowledge, to the fullest extent possible; to make pedagogical or curricular decisions unencumbered by the facts is to risk disaster
b. evaluate carefully the likely advantages or disadvantages of any change from the status quo
c. preserve what is working well
d. change only what needs to be changed and is capable of being changed, and do so in a way which allows us to back out if, despite all of our efforts and good intentions, the change proves to be harmful to ourselves or our students

In the spring of 1961, a team of five foreign language teachers and specialists undertook a qualitative assessment of language teaching around the United States under the auspices of the Modern Language Association of America, with funds provided by the U.S. Office of Education. Their published report (MLA: no date) bore the title, "Good Teaching Practices: A Survey of High-School Foreign-Language Classes." Team members visited 1,011 classes taught by 747 different teachers. While it is of course predictable that many of the conventions of sound second language teaching twenty years ago are no longer recommended in the classrooms of the 1980's, it is interesting to examine the conclusions of this report since they reflect on the timeless essence of good language teaching:

We conclude by listing the nine features that characterized most of the successful classes we observed: (1) The class is at ease in working with the foreign language, and seldom reverts to [the native language] to express an idea. (2) Interest is high and students come to class with a real desire to learn by participating. (3) Neither teacher nor student depends on the book. Materials fit the interests and abilities of the students and follow the principles of sound FL teaching. Because their cultural content is significant and accurate, they are not stereotyped. (4) The students do most of the speaking. The teacher gives the setting for discussion, asks key questions to direct it, gives cues in case of difficulty, and gradually subordinates his own participation. (5) Control of the class is with the teacher at all times. The students look to him for direction and timing. They are made aware of the objectives of the FL learning and of how a technique or exercise will help them learn. (6) Standards of performance are high. The teacher sees that students are neither over- nor under-challenged, and tests are designed to appraise what has been learned. (7) A variable, or unusual, seating arrangement often indicates that the teacher will be interesting to observe and that he is probably willing to experiment. (8) As the student enters the classroom the atmosphere encourages him to use the FL and to assume his foreign role. Throughout the learning process the teacher creates situations (or leads students to create them) which lead to appreciation and understanding of the foreign culture. (9) The teacher's personality—demanding, yet fair and patient—leads his students to a high level of performance. His lessons are well planned, and the techniques of presentation and drill are used strategically and correctly to achieve the purpose of each type of exercise. If desired results are not attained with one technique, the teacher tries another. The teacher's manner makes students want to learn the FL, not just because it presents interesting problems to solve or things to say, or because it is fun, but because working under his confident and enthusiastic direction is appealing in itself. (p. 243)

There is, I suspect, little if anything in the above description that we would change today, some two decades after these conclusions about good second language teaching were written.

It is fashionable today to consider the specific competencies which second language teachers are expected to possess, and in which they need to receive training as part of their teacher preparation programs. An excellent and highly practical list of such competencies is provided by Finocchiaro (1975) in a general session address to the 1974 TESOL Convention. Another useful list, written from a philosophic point of view, is provided by Stevick (1980). Indeed, such lists of competencies abound, and the movement labeled "competency-based teacher education" has been a major source of controversy in educational circles since the mid-1970's. Instead of offering my own list of such competencies, which would certainly fail to improve upon the lists of Finocchiaro or Stevick, I offer the following poem entitled "A Real Teacher" (Greer and Rubinstein, 1972, p. 125) which, for our purposes, I have revised to read "A Real Second Language Teacher." The point of view expressed is of importance to us, for it belongs to our clientele:

A REAL SECOND LANGUAGE TEACHER

What do you think a real second language teacher is? A real second language teacher ——————————————————————— .

A real second language teacher is on my side

A real second language teacher lets me be me and tries to understand what it's like to be me

A real second language teacher accepts me whether he or she likes me or not

A real second language teacher doesn't have expectations of me because of what I've been or what he or she has been

A real second language teacher is more interested in how I learn than what I learn

A real second language teacher doesn't make me feel anxious and afraid

A real second language teacher provides many choices

A real second language teacher lets me teach myself even if it takes longer

A real second language teacher talks so I can understand what he or she means to say

A real second language teacher can make mistakes and admit it

A real second language teacher can show his or her feelings and let me show mine

A real second language teacher wants me to evaluate my own work.

And so we return to that puzzling poster on my office wall with the message: "As a teacher, I am unique and powerful." The explanation is that the student whom we help to grow can and will never be the same again. Someone once wrote that a teacher affects eternity; it is impossible to measure where his or her influence stops.

Much has been said in the 1970's, and much more is being said in the 1980's, about the primacy of learning and of the learner, about the responsibility of teachers to tailor instruction to the needs of learners. Pendulums in education have a funny way of swinging back again, and in this "age of the learner," the teacher and the process of teaching must not and cannot be overlooked. Indeed, *only a teacher can develop a learner-centered classroom* (McKim, 1972, p. 86; italics added).

Only the second language teacher can facilitate the when, where, and how of learning another language—or can single-handedly thwart it. The responsibility is awesome; the power to affect people's lives very real. It is a responsibility we choose when we make the decision to become second language teachers. It is a power which comes with the job, whether we wish it or not. We can exercise this power and fulfill this responsibility most effectively in the 1980's by never forgetting the priority of our roles in the classroom: first, to be a human being; then, to be a teacher; and only third, to be a teacher of languages.

REFERENCES

Finocchiaro, Mary. "The Crucial Variable in TESOLD: The Teacher." In R. Crymes and W. E. Norris, eds., *On TESOL 74.* Washington, D.C.: TESOL, 1975.

Gage, N. L. *The Scientific Basis of the Art of Teaching.* N.Y.: Teachers College Press, 1978.

Greer, Mary and Bonnie Rubinstein. *Will the Real Teacher Please Stand Up?* Pacific Palisades, CA: Goodyear Publishing Co., 1972.

McKim, Lester W. "Planning for Individualization: A Necessary Look Before Leaping." In H. B. Altman, ed., *Individualizing the Foreign Language Classroom: Perspectives for Teachers.* Rowley, MA: Newbury House, 1972.

Modern Language Association of America. *Reports of Surveys and Studies in the Teaching of Modern Foreign Languages, 1959–61.* N.Y., no date.

Postman, Neil and Charles Weingartner. *The School Book.* N.Y.: Delacorte Press, 1973.

Stevick, Earl W. *A Way and Ways.* Rowley, MA: Newbury House, Inc., 1980.

ABSTRACT

Effective Language Teaching: Insights from Research

ROBERT L. POLITZER
Stanford University

While the decade of the 1960's produced some major studies comparing methodological and other teaching variables, the 1970's focused on research in language learning. A content analysis of research reported in four major U.S. journals dealing with foreign (second) language education documents the increasing emphasis on learning research during the 1970's. Discussion of selected articles published from 1970 to 1979 highlights the present state of the art in foreign language teaching research with reference to process-product studies, treatment/student characteristics interactions, and the cumulative evidence for the emphasis on comprehension as a key to language acquisition.

The specific nature of second language learning suggests that evidence from teaching in general may not always be applicable in the language classroom. However, foreign language teaching research can profit from examining sociolinguistics, or such qualitative approaches as art criticism or ethnography. Research on individual learner behaviors as a mediating process between what teachers do and learners learn is seen as leading to the next major advance in foreign language teaching research.

Effective Language Teaching: Insights from Research

ROBERT L. POLITZER
Stanford University

Scope of the Article: Research in Teaching

Research in effective foreign language teaching includes a great variety of concerns. It is not my intention to cover the broad spectrum of educational research in this article. Since some of it will be covered by other contributors to this volume, space restriction makes it advisable to concentrate on a relatively narrow aspect of foreign language education research: the one that studies the effect of teaching variables on student outcomes. The main focus of this article will be on studies that relate teacher-classroom behaviors or teaching processes to student outcomes, in other words, on the so-called process-product paradigm (Rosenshine, 1971).

INSIGHTS FROM THE 1960's: THE LARGE-SCALE METHOD COMPARISONS

Foreign Language Education research during the 1960's was dominated by major research efforts to determine the relative effectiveness of competing methods of language teaching. The first major study pinning audiolingualism against the traditional approach was undertaken by Scherer and Wertheimer (1964) and came to the conclusion that "the experimental group (audiolingual) was generally superior in some skills, but that the control group was superior in others" and that when "a combination score was computed to assess any grand total differences, . . . the two groups were not significantly different" (Scherer and Wertheimer, 1964, p. 244).

23

The next important research effort during the decade was undoubtedly the Pennsylvania study (Smith, 1970). It pinned a "functional skills approach" (audiolingual method) against a "functional skills and grammar" and a "traditional" (grammar-translation) method. The results of the research showed no statistically significant difference in listening, speaking and writing, and showed the superiority of "functional skills and grammar" and "traditional" method over "functional skills" alone in reading (Smith, 1970, p. 236).

An example of non U.S.A.-based major research efforts of the 1960's is the Swedish Gumé project reported by Levin (1972). Three types of audiolingual-oriented approaches to the teaching of English were compared: (a) inductive without generalizations (b) deductive with generalizations in English (c) deductive with generalizations in Swedish and comparisons of Swedish and English structures. The results of the project showed a fairly consistent pattern of (c) over (a) over (b): A deductive approach including explanation in Swedish seemed superior to pure habit formation (Levin, 1972, pp. 192 ff.).

Some ten years later, the main message and impact of these studies can perhaps be summarized as follows: (1) They caused or perhaps rather confirmed a healthy skepticism in the pure habit formation type of audiolingualism which had dominated language teaching in the 1950's and early 1960's. (2) They underlined the apparently trivial but nevertheless very important fact that students tend to learn what they are taught. (3) They raised some doubts about the possibility of obtaining conclusive results from large-scale research in comparing methods of foreign language teaching.

The reaction to the 1960's was most effectively summarized by Birkmaier (1973): "Effective strategies cannot be encapsulated in *a method*" (p. 1288). "Method fanaticism must yield to inquiry. We need intense empirical study of language acquisition in order to do justice to the complexities of the language problem . . . Attention needs to be focused particularly on the learner, with an eye to adapting teaching to his specific needs" (p. 1295). Birkmaier's 1973 statement was both prophetic and a call for change.

INSIGHTS FROM THE 1970's: A CONTENT ANALYSIS OF SOME U.S. JOURNALS

The decade just passed is still too close to allow for retrospection. But it is not only lack of historical perspective that makes the task difficult. The mass of research produced throughout the world defies summarization within the confines of a short article. I have set myself, therefore, a more modest task: What was the research in language teaching presented in some major U.S. journals published from 1970 to 1979? What are the major implications of this research? What was its message concerning the importance of research in language teaching?

I examined four major journals published in the U.S.A. and devoted to language teaching: *TESOL Quarterly, Language Learning, Foreign Language Annals* and *The Modern Language Journal. TESOL Quarterly* is the professional journal for Teachers of English as a Second Language. The other three represent the three major language teaching-oriented journals not devoted to specific foreign languages. The initial examination of the journals consisted of (1) counting the total number of articles presented in the journals during the first and the second half of the 1970–79 decade; (2) determining which of those articles dealt with research in foreign language teaching and which dealt with research in foreign language learning.

Only articles that presented some kind of data analysis and involved an independent teaching variable are included among the research articles. Included as research in learning articles were those that presented data related to learning processes (*e.g.*, pupil errors, aptitudes, learning style, etc.). A few research-oriented articles were not included in either the teaching or the learning category (*e.g.*, articles dealing with research in language testing).

The results of the analysis are shown in Table 1: *Language Learning* is definitely the most research-oriented of the four journals examined. During the second half of the decade the proportion of research articles in the journal passes the fifty percent mark. In the other journals, the proportion of articles devoted to research is much lower, though it should be noted that in 1976 the

TABLE 1   Quantity of Teaching and Learning Research in Four Major U.S. Language Journals: 1970–79

Journal	Period	Articles	Teaching Research	Learning Research
TESOL Quarterly	1970–74	145	4	4
	1975–79	145	5	12
(Research Notes)	1976–79	—	[3]	[24]
Language Learning	1970–74	81	5	24
	1975–79	97	4	46
Foreign Language Annals	1970–74	101	7	8
	1975–79	217	10	4
The Modern Language Journal	1970–74	204	16	5
	1975–79	156	5	8
Totals		1,146	56	111

TESOL Quarterly started to publish abstracts of research reports (Research Notes). With the exception of *Foreign Language Annals*, in which research-oriented articles are relatively rare, the data of Table 1 show a preponderance of learning- over teaching-oriented research. The emphasis of learning over teaching becomes increasingly pronounced during the second half of the decade: The 1970's were clearly the decade of the "focus on the learner." The overall message of the research effort of the 1970's is the importance of understanding the learning process.

Table 1 indicates that some fifty-six of the articles in the four journals were devoted to teaching variables. Eighteen of the articles looked at language teaching in the context of bilingual education and immersion; these suggested the advantage of an immersion/bilingual eduation approach. Ten of the articles' research variables related to individualized instruction and advocate, on the whole, the advantage of individualization over "lockstep" (inflexible) approaches. The central themes of the rest of the articles cover a wide range of topics and independent variables. Very few take a detailed look at teaching as a classroom process or isolate a very specific variable which is normally under the control of a classroom teacher.

1970–79: SOME SELECTED RESEARCH STUDIES

From the fifty-six research-in-teaching articles identified through the content analysis of four journals, I have selected eight for further comment. The articles chosen seemed to represent a good cross-section of the state of the art and of the type of evidence that research has furnished.

The first group of articles is representative of the process-product paradigm; they are also "correlational" since they report relations between teaching behaviors and outcomes observed in natural contexts. Politzer (1970) dealt with the teaching of French at the high school level, Ramirez and Stromquist (1979) with English as a Second Language in Elementary School Bilingual Programs. Both studies used observational systems which classify teaching and/or student behaviors. Politzer's observation system primarily counted types of drills and use of visuals. Ramirez and Stromquist counted similar behaviors in teacher and student utterances. In both studies, teaching effectiveness was defined by class mean scores on pre- and post-tests. Both studies identified "successful" and "unsuccessful" teaching behaviors related to desired student outcomes. It should be noted, however, that the findings are limited to the contexts in which they occurred. The studies were conducted in classrooms which used audiolingual methodology. Both report correlational findings based on a relatively limited (N = ca. 20) number of subjects. As Politzer (1970) and others (e.g., Krumm, 1973) have pointed out, there may be (in teaching behaviors) a point of diminishing returns when there is too much of a good thing. The relationship between frequencies of teaching behaviors and pupil outcomes is not always unambiguous. Neither study pays attention to the interaction of individual learner characteristics and teaching behaviors. Teachers reading the research reports can only speculate as to what the results may mean for improving their teaching.

A different approach to the process-product paradigm was taken by Moskowitz (1976). She compared behaviors of ten teachers identified as "outstanding" by former students to behaviors of "typical" teachers. The criterion in this study was not student learning but student affect. The study identified some thirty-five behaviors differentiating "outstanding" from "typical" teachers. As one might expect as a result of the criterion measure used, many of the successful behaviors are related to affect (*e.g.*, patience, laughter, smile). Still, a very clear and unmistakable profile of the "good teacher" as a competent, humane, but at the same time, task-oriented person emerges from the study.

The studies by Hauptman (1971) and Tang (1974) are both experimental. Hauptman dealt with teaching spoken Japanese to American children. Tang's study concerned the teaching of reading in English to Chinese children in the U.S.A.

Hauptman contrasted the effects of a structural grammatically-sequenced approach with that of a situational approach. Both approaches presented the same materials but the situational approach embedded them in meaningful dialogues, without regard to grammatical sequence. He found that the situational approach produced results equal to or better than the structural approach. Its superiority was due to significant gains made by high aptitude rather than lower aptitude children. Although Hauptman's findings are not widely generalizable, they show the advantage of an experimental design based on an hypothesis, and they carry the message that situational context is important in language teaching. Hauptman's research paradigm also introduces the consideration of *Aptitude-Treatment Interaction*. Perhaps students with higher ability are more successful than lower ability students in formulating their own correct hypothesis about the functioning of L_2. At least in the context of formal instruction, it may be the students of lesser language aptitude who need the help of a grammatically-structured syllabus and of overt explanation.

The originality and contribution of Tang's study lie entirely in the consideration of an *Attitude-Treatment Interaction*. She found that the use of the native language (Cantonese) in the ESL classroom interacted with pupil's attitude to Cantonese and English. Pupils with positive attitudes to and interpersonal motivation for the study of English and little desire to use Cantonese performed much better in classrooms in which only English was used. For students with opposite attitudes the reverse was true: they achieved superior results in a program that included the use of Cantonese.

Tang's study does not pretend to arrive at generalizable conclusions concerning any particular language pedagogy, and this is its real message. As Fishman (1976) has pointed out, good language pedagogy and methodology may not be absolute but may be embedded in a social context which, in turn, affects individuals in different ways. Effective language teaching has to consider both the individual and the society outside the classroom.

The last three articles to be discussed in this section illustrate a common research result. The studies reported by Asher and his collaborators (Asher, 1972; Asher et al., 1974) and by Postovsky (1974) deal with different languages and methods. Asher reports the success of a method requiring physical responses to verbal stimuli. Postovsky deals with delayed oral practice within an audiolingual approach. Both studies, however, share the conviction that in initial instruction the delaying of verbal response is advisable and that learning is promoted by emphasizing comprehension over production, at least in the initial stage of instruction. Both approaches conclude that languages are acquired not as the result of the reinforcement of verbal responses but because the learner's "Language Acquisition Device" goes to work on linguistic input. Regardless of how one might evaluate the details of these particular research efforts, the overall message that comprehension may be the key to language acquisition is quite convincing. It is a message that has been confirmed by other researchers not included in the sample on which the discussion is based (*e.g.*, Asher 1969; Winitz and Reeds, 1973). During a decade which has been preoccupied with learning rather than teaching, the stress on comprehension as an important aspect of good teaching has probably been the major research development (see Gary, 1978; Benson and Hjelt, 1980).

GENERAL RESEARCH ON TEACHING: NEW DIRECTIONS

Foreign language classroom research can never entirely echo the research done in teaching in general. But the new directions suggested by generalists (Gage, 1978; Doyle, 1978) may have considerable impact. These new directions point to new and different ways of looking at classroom processes. That teaching is a "linguistic process in a cultural setting" is stated in the title of a conference organized by the National Institute of Education (Gage, 1974). The linguistic analysis of classroom discourse has already received considerable attention (*e.g.*, Sinclair and Coulthard, 1975) and the sociolinguistic study of teachers' classroom behavior is an expanding field (*e.g.*, Heath, 1978). Sociolinguistics and discourse analysis are making impressive impacts on the development of foreign language teaching syllabi or curricula, but so far they have been used only sporadically for the purpose of looking at the foreign language teaching process itself. Surely, foreign language teachers and researchers should be in the avant-garde in interpreting teaching sociolinguistically as speech events and interactions.

Some of the new directions follow qualitative rather than quantitative approaches. One of these qualitative approaches advocates the application of the methods of art criticism to the description and evaluation of classroom processes (Eisner, 1977). The possibility should not startle foreign language educators, many of whom have close affiliations with departments of language and literature which devote much of their efforts to criticism. Another major new direction in the study of classroom processes is also close to home for foreign language teachers, who have always felt that the teaching of culture was an almost inevitable part of the foreign language curriculum. The application of ethnographic anthropological techniques to the study of teaching has been a rapidly developing movement. One of its proponents even tried to warn against "Blitzkrieg Ethnography," which is the thoughtless overapplication of ethnographic techniques to educational research (Rist, 1980). There can be no doubt, however, that ethnographic studies hold out considerable promise for a real understanding of what happens in classrooms. Ethnographic research leading to understanding of the cultural processes of second language teaching and learning and a resulting increase of second language teaching efficiency should be among the attainable goals of the 1980's.

FOREIGN LANGUAGE TEACHING: A UNIQUE TEACHING ACTIVITY?

Carroll (1963) commented on the fact that for various reasons foreign language teaching should or could be the ideal laboratory for general teaching research. In what other subjects do individuals at various age levels start their learning experience "from scratch" and attend multiple-section courses that can be used for research purposes? Are there many other subjects in which achievement can be measured in relatively clear-cut behavioral terms? In 1963 there were relatively few well-trained researchers in foreign language education. Two decades later, language teaching research specialists abound.

There is some truth to the statements that (1) foreign language teaching researchers do not utilize the sophisticated paradigms that have been developed by the generalists and that (2) the generalists do not utilize the language teaching field for their research. With occasional and rare exceptions the fields of general teaching research and foreign language teaching research tend to ignore each other. However, the reason for this phenomenon is not simply mutual ignorance or narrowmindedness.

Researchers in teaching have occasionally pointed to the possibility that different school subjects may have their own peculiar psychology of learning and teaching (*e.g.*, Shulman, 1974). The value of a teaching behavior or strategy may vary with the subject. The value of some, but perhaps relatively few, behaviors may be nearly universal. Others may have only very reduced applicability (Gage, 1979). I should like to suggest that researchers have sensed for quite some time that the psychology of language learning and teaching may be so unique that there may be only very little in common between foreign language teaching research and research in teaching in general. Indeed, for what other school subject can one claim that it may be acquired most effectively *outside* of school? What other subject is acquired by an "acquisition device" perhaps identical or similar to the one responsible for first language acquisition as a maturational process?

The goal of teaching is learning. Hypotheses concerning teaching must ultimately be related to hypotheses about how learning takes place. Are foreign languages "learned" like other school subjects or are they acquired informally by processes identical to the ones involved in first language acquisition? The learning-monitoring-acquisition debate (Krashen, 1978, and this volume) may not be resolved in the near future. However, it seems that any research on language teaching must relate to a theory of learning. If general learning theory has only limited applicability to language acquisition, then the paths of general teaching research and of research in foreign language teaching may occasionally cross, but they will never be the same.

THE MEDIATING PROCESS PARADIGM

The process-product paradigm research in teaching has been criticized for various reasons, among them that it does not make sufficient allowance for the study of the learner. To remedy this shortcoming, a "mediating process" paradigm has been proposed (Gage, 1978, pp. 70 ff.; Doyle, 1978, pp. 172 ff.). Instead of simply studying the effects of teaching procedure or teacher-pupil interactions on learner outcomes, the researcher must also take into account the specific pupil behaviors or reactions that account for pupil learning. This particular paradigm for teaching research holds out great promise for progress in foreign language education. After a decade of focus on the learner, foreign language education research may now be ready to start refocusing on teaching procedures, but this renewal of concern with teaching must take into consideration all that can be learned about language acquisition processes. We should put behind us the dichotomy between learning and teaching research. Research in teaching is closely related to research in learning if we think of teaching behaviors as ways of verifying the models of learning that are emerging from the research of the past decade (Dulay and Burt, 1978; Schumann, 1978).

Before setting up a teaching experiment, researchers could then ask the following types of questions: (1) Will the proposed experimental intervention affect learning or acquisition? (2) How will it influence specific factors related to learning? (3) Will the experiment measure not only students' language learning but also the intermediate responses or reactions that account for learning within a learning model? Teaching research related to a model of learning is the next logical step in foreign language education. It holds out the promise of arriving at cumulative results. Series of relatively small-scale experiments can be related to each other from within the same model of learning. In the 1980's we look forward to experimentation in teaching that should give us further knowledge about how and why teaching brings about effective learning.

REFERENCES

Anderson, L.; Evertson, C.; and Brophy, J. 1979. "Experimental Study of Effective Teaching in First Grade Reading Groups." *Elementary School Journal* 79: 193–223.

Asher, J. J. 1969. "The Total Physical Response Approach to Second Language Journal." *The Modern Language Journal* 53: 3–17.

———. 1972. "Children's First Language Learning as a Model for Second Language Learning." *The Modern Language Journal* 56: 133–139.

———, Kusado, J. A., and de la Torre, P. 1974. "Learning a Second Language through Communication: The Second Field Test." *The Modern Language Journal* 58: 24–32.

Benson, P. C. and Hjelt, Ch. 1980. "Listening Competence: A Prerequisite to Communication." Oller, J. W. and Perkins, K. (eds.) *Research in Language Testing*, 1973. Rowley, MA: Newbury House Publishers, Inc., 59–65.

Birkmaier, E. M. 1973. "Research in Teaching Foreign Language." M. W. Travers (ed.) *Second Handbook of Research in Teaching*. Chicago: Rand McNally and Co., 1280–1302.

Brophy, J. 1979. "Advances in Teacher Research." *The Journal of Classroom Interaction* 15: 1–7.

Carroll, J. B. 1963. "Research in Teaching Foreign Languages." N. L. Gage (ed.) *Handbook of Research in Teaching*. Chicago: Rand McNally and Co., 1060–1100.

Doyle, W., 1978. "Paradigms for Research on Teacher Effectiveness." L. S. Shulman (ed.) *Review of Research in Education*, 1977, Vol. 5. Ithaca, IL.: F. E. Peacock Publishers, Inc., 163–198.

Dulay, H. and Burt, M. 1978. "Some Remarks on Creativity in Language Acquisition." W. C. Ritchie (ed.) *Second Language Acquisition Research: Issues and Implications*. New York: Academic Press, 65–89.

Eisner, E. 1977. "On the Uses of Educational Connoisseurship and Criticism for Evaluation of Classroom Life." *Teachers College Record* 78: 345–358.

Fishman, J. A. 1976. *Bilingual Education. An International Sociological Perspective*. Rowley, MA: Newbury House Publishers, Inc.

Gage, N. L. (ed.) 1974. *Teaching as a Linguistic Process in a Cultural Setting. NIE Conference on Studies in Teaching, Panel 5.* Washington, D.C.: National Institute of Education.

————. 1978. *The Scientific Basis of the Art of Teaching.* New York: Teachers College Press.

————. 1979. "The Generality of Dimensions of Teaching." P. L. Peterson and H. J. Walberg (eds.) *Research on Teaching: Concepts, Findings, and Implications.* Berkeley, CA: McCutchan Publishing Corporation, 214–288.

Gary, J. O. 1978. "Why Speak if You Don't Need to: The Case for a Listening Approach to Beginning Foreign Language Teaching." W. C. Ritchie (ed.) *Second Language Acquisition Research: Issues and Implications.* New York: Academic Press, 185–199.

Hauptman, H. C. 1971. "A Structural Approach vs. Situational Approach to Foreign Language Teaching." *Language Learning* 21: 235–244.

Heath, S. B. 1978. *Teacher Talk: Language in the Classroom.* Arlington, VA: Center for Applied Linguistics.

Krashen, S. 1978. "The Monitor Model for Second Language Acquisition." R. C. Gingras (ed.) *Second Language Acquisition and Foreign Language Teaching.* Arlington, VA: Center for Applied Linguistics, 1–26.

Krumm, H. J. 1972. *Analyse und Training Fremdsprachlichen Lehrverhaltens.* Weinheim and Basel: Beltz Verlag.

Levin, L. 1972. *Comparative Studies in Foreign Language Teaching: The Gumé Project.* Stockholm: Almquist and Wiksell.

Medley, D. M. 1979. "The Effectiveness of Teachers." Peterson, P. L. and Walberg, H. J., (eds.) *Research in Teaching: Concepts, Findings, and Implications.* Berkeley, CA: McCutchan Publishing Corporation, 11–27.

Moskowitz, G. 1976. "The Classroom Interaction of Outstanding Foreign Language Teachers." *Foreign Language Annals* 9: 135–157.

Politzer, R. L. 1970. "Some Reflections on 'Good' and 'Bad' Teaching Behaviors." *Language Learning* 20: 31–43.

Postovsky, V. A. 1974. "Effects of Delay in Oral Practice at the Beginning of Second Language Learning." *The Modern Language Journal* 58: 229–239.

Ramirez, A. G. and Stromquist, N. P. 1979. "ESL Methodology and Student Learning in Bilingual Elementary Schools." *TESOL Quarterly* 13: 145–160.

Rist, R. C. 1980. "Blitzkrieg Ethnography: On the Transformation of a Method into a Movement." *Educational Researcher* 9: 8–10.

Rosenshine, B. 1971. *Teaching Behavior and Student Achievement*. Windsor, England: National Foundation for Educational Research in England and Wales.

Scherer, G. A. C. and Wertheimer, M. 1964. *A Psycholinguistic Experiment in Foreign Language Teaching*. New York: McGraw-Hill Book Company.

Schumann, J. H. 1978. "Social and Psychological Factors in Second Language Acquisition." J. C. Richards (ed.) *Understanding Second and Foreign Language Learning: Issues and Approaches*. Rowley, MA: Newbury House Publishers, Inc., 163–178.

Shulman, L. S. 1974. "Psychology of School Subjects: A Premature Obituary." *Journal of Research in Science Teaching* 11: 319–339.

Sinclair, J. M. and Coulthard, R. M. 1975. *Towards an Analysis of Discourse: The English Used by Teachers and Pupils*. London: Oxford University Press.

Smith, P. D. Jr. 1970. *A Comparison of the Cognitive and Audiolingual Approaches to Foreign Language Instruction*. Philadelphia: The Center for Curriculum Development, Inc.

Tang, B. T. 1974. "A Psycholinguistic Study of the Relationship between Children's Ethnic Linguistic Attitudes and the Effectiveness of Methods used in Second Language Reading Instruction." *TESOL Quarterly* 8: 233–251.

Winitz, H. and Reeds, J. A. 1973. "Rapid Acquisition of a Foreign Language (German) by the Avoidance of Speaking." *International Review of Applied Linguistics in Language Teaching* 11: 295–317.

ABSTRACT

The Relationship of
Second Language Learning
to Second Language Teaching

G. RICHARD TUCKER
Center for Applied Linguistics, Washington, D.C.

In this paper, I argue that the encouragement of second language teaching and learning and, consequently, of bilinguality, is desirable from both personal and societal perspectives. Furthermore, encouragement and opportunity for such study should come from within a country's formal educational system. I describe the necessity to develop and implement a research agenda which takes cognizance of the move toward Language-for-Special-Purposes programs; and I allude to the changing nature of the demands which will be faced by language teachers during the coming decade.

The Relationship of Second Language Learning to Second Language Teaching

G. RICHARD TUCKER
Center for Applied Linguistics

In this paper, I shall briefly examine the changing pattern of available background evidence or knowledge that relates to whether our society should actively encourage bilingualism and second language learning; the ways in which such learning could be facilitated more effectively within the context of the public educational system; and selected areas to which increasing thought and attention must be given by teachers and researchers working in tandem during this decade.

WHY SHOULD WE ENCOURAGE SECOND LANGUAGE LEARNING?

During the period from 1900 until approximately 1960, there were three major research threads which purported to provide data indicating that the goal of developing bilinguality for as broad a segment of the population as possible was not desirable. A number of research studies during that time seemed to indicate that the attainment of bilingualism was associated with cognitive deficit or some type of mental retardation; others suggested that the encouragement of bilingualism and biculturalism (in this case, the nurturance or maintenance of one's mother tongue in a setting where this differed from the "official" language or the language of wider communication) was associated with ethnocentrism and with divisiveness; while others claimed that the fostering of societal bilinguality or multilinguality and hence of ethnolinguistic diversity was associated with economic stagnation or backsliding.

39

It is not my major purpose in this paper to focus in detail on each of these myths; but I do wish to clearly point out that the results of well-conceived and well-executed contemporary research conducted during the past twenty years point to exactly the opposite set of conclusions. Thus, for example, work conducted in settings as diverse as Canada, Israel, Singapore, South Africa and the United States has led to the conclusion that bilingualism is associated with an enhancement of individuals' creativity, cognitive flexibility or divergent thinking (e.g., Barik & Swain, 1976; Ben-Zeev, 1977; Ianco-Worrall, 1972)—a set of findings diametrically opposed to those reported in the earlier literature. The Canadian studies which lead to these recent, more optimistic conclusions are particularly noteworthy, for they constitute longitudinal studies carried out under conditions in which one group of carefully matched monolingual children are "caused" to become bilingual by virtue of their educational experience while their peers are not (Lambert & Tucker, 1978; Swain, 1978). In this particular educational setting, the act of becoming bilingual—of mastering another code—has had extremely positive cognitive repercussions.

Likewise, the results of research conducted during the past two decades to examine the social and affective correlates of bilinguality leads to the conclusion that children who attain sufficient facility in a second language so that they are able to learn new material, to form new friendships and to increase their occupational options via that language develop a more tolerant, open-minded and charitable view of others than do their peers who have not had the same opportunity (Cziko, Lambert & Gutter, 1979). Furthermore, these young adults develop a keen and positive perception of themselves, their primary reference group and their national identity while they simultaneously develop a broad and healthy appreciation for members of other ethnolinguistic groups (Cziko, Lambert, Sidoti & Tucker, 1980). There seems to be no support in recent social or psychological literature for the notion that the stimulation of language maintenance or language development through programs designed to encourage bilinguality leads to ethnocentrism which in turn spawns ethnic divisiveness.

In the same manner, a review of contemporary research fails to support the conclusion that the promotion of societal bilingualism or multilingualism is associated with economic disadvantage;

rather, the encouragement of second or foreign language study seems absolutely essential for the development of trade opportunities and continuing economic growth throughout the world (e.g., Fishman, Cooper & Conrad, 1977; Lambert, 1979; Lambert & Sidoti, 1980).

The major reason for focusing briefly on each of these three areas has been to try to convey the sense that the encouragement of second language learning and ultimately of bilinguality will have positive repercussions from a personal and from a societal perspective. The claim that second or foreign language study is a curricular frill when compared with other "hard" subjects and that it can and should be eliminated during times of budgetary retrenchment is without basis; but every opportunity must be taken to tutor and inform policy makers, educators, parents and prospective students that foreign or second language study can indeed have powerful personal and societal consequences.

HOW CAN WE FACILITATE
SECOND LANGUAGE LEARNING?

In keeping with the theme of the first section, one major purpose of this paper is to suggest that innovative instructional programs to encourage the development of second language skills should be implemented in the United States and elsewhere for as broad a spectrum of the population as possible. Although I shall focus my remarks on primary-, secondary- or tertiary-level students within the formal educational system, I do not wish to deny the overwhelming importance of these issues for those involved in diverse aspects of non-formal education.

Within the United States, there are four major student groups whose needs must be considered—students who are of non- or limited-English proficiency; students who are already at the time of school entrance "balanced" bilinguals; those who are English dominant but who come from some other ethnic background (e.g., Spanish ethnic origin but English mother tongue); and monolingual English-speaking students.

These four sharply distinct and divergent target groups bring different needs and different resources to any classroom; but for each, the goal should be similar. Educational options should be designed so that all students—from each of these four categories—have the opportunity to develop an ability to understand, speak, read and write English so that they can profit from instruction in that language and fully participate in all aspects of American society, while simultaneously developing or nurturing the ability to understand, speak, read, and write their mother tongue.

A variety of options is available to policy makers and educators for achieving this goal. They have been referred to as transitional, maintenance, restoration, and enrichment approaches. It is not appropriate in this paper to review or to renew the debate between transitional and maintenance programs of language education (cf., Tucker, 1979). Neither seems to take advantage of the fact that the language minority youngster represents a valuable natural resource who could be utilized in the classroom as a peer tutor by a patient and trained teacher to facilitate more effective second language learning.

I firmly believe that every opportunity must be sought to encourage the implementation of language-restoration or language-enrichment programs within the public school system. The first, emphasizing restoration, would be directed toward developing "lost" linguistic skills in a student's home or ancestral language. The popularity of this type of approach seems to be growing. This can be inferred from the numbers of native English speakers who are now choosing to participate in U.S. bilingual education programs, and from the enthusiasm in states such as California, Massachusetts, Maryland, New York, Ohio, and Wisconsin for so-called immersion programs. These educational options are not really so much programs or approaches as they are a philosophy which holds that monolingual English students are, in a curious sense, the most disadvantaged group of all. Adherents believe that transitional bilingualism is not a matter of compensation; it is rather a matter of enrichment which will ultimately benefit not only the individual student but society as well.

NEED FOR A FOCUSED RESEARCH AGENDA

With respect, then, to the question of how to best facilitate second language teaching and learning in the United States, I would like to suggest that we need first to acknowledge and then to probe in detail the very diverse needs of our student clientele and then develop a set of teaching options or programs that will provide every student with the opportunity to acquire facility in English and in at least one other language. However, this will be a very difficult, if not impossible, goal to achieve until there is a broader recognition of the many tangible and intangible values and benefits of being a bilingual individual in a society which comprises among its citizenry a large number of bilingual individuals (cf., President's Commission on Foreign Language and International Studies, 1979; Berryman, Langer, Pincus & Solomon, 1979).

I have tried, thus far, to argue that the encouragement of second language teaching and learning and consequently of bilinguality is desirable from a number of different perspectives, and that this encouragement and opportunity can and should come from within the formal educational system of a country such as the United States. In a recent paper (Tucker, 1978), I reviewed the profound effects which recent theoretical insights and empirical research results have had on pedagogical practice. I remain convinced that one of the major derivative insights is that the primary focus of activity in the second language classroom should be on communication—not just on simulated dialogue—but on genuine communication. I am much more convinced of this today than I was even three years ago and I find evidence for an increasing acceptance of this viewpoint from: (1) the adoption of objectives by many teachers which at least initially stress the development of communicative competence—even in some cases at the possible expense of grammatical correctness; (2) a continuing switch from structurally-graded to notionally-functionally-based syllabi with a concomitant development of English (or other language)-for-Special-Purposes (ESP) curricula and texts—for academic purposes, for technological training, or even for adult vocational language training (Crandall, 1979); and (3) a growing consideration and implementation of bilingual program options such as those referred to above. These innovations all capitalize on the fact that a student—whether at the primary, secondary or tertiary level—can effectively acquire a second language when the task of learning the language becomes incidental to the task of communicating with someone about something which is inherently interesting or desired. This shift in focus calls, of course, for a reassessment of the role and training of the second language teacher and it also calls for a broadening and intensifying of the research agenda with respect to examining different aspects of the role of language in education.

The proposed research agenda calls for an interdisciplinary approach and for a concerted effort involving practitioner and researcher. I believe that we must encourage diverse research programs in different enthnolinguistic, political, geographic and social settings: (1) to describe, measure or specify more precisely *what* is acquired during the course of foreign or second language teaching and learning; (2) to clarify further the course, causes, correlates and consequences of such teaching and learning as well as the personal and societal consequences of such learning or failure to learn; and (3) to describe the course, causes, correlates and consequences of language skill attrition. I am suggesting that for a teacher to be maximally effective we need to understand more clearly the discrepancy between what the student brings to the formal language learning situation—the form(s) and ranges of language functions controlled—and the demands imposed by teacher and by text, the demands placed by the examination system, and the linguistic expectations held by prospective content-subject teachers or employers. I believe that there exists a need for a much more broadly-focused research program than is currently underway. This research program would provide at least three types of useful information: (1) a clearer understanding of the background training and abilities that diverse primary-, secondary- or tertiary-level students bring to the language classroom; (2) empirical evidence concerning the growth *or* the attrition that occurs over time at different instructional levels as a function of methodology of language instruction and medium of content instruction (a crucial area for investigation if anecdotal report is any indication); and (3) information concerning the incipient bilingual's ability to process, store, operate upon, retrieve and produce information in either of two languages as circumstances demand. Results from research related to such questions would, I believe, serve to inform application in North America as well as in many areas of the developing world.

WHAT MAJOR PRESSURES WILL AFFECT THE LANGUAGE TEACHING PROFESSION DURING THE REST OF THE 1980's?

It is premature to speculate at length on directions for change within the language teaching profession for the rest of the decade; nevertheless, certain pressures or trends can already be observed which may exert major influence. With respect to our TESOL colleagues in the United States, I believe that there will be an increasing need for intensive or remedial English training for resident American students. This will result from the rapid increase in non-English mother tongue youngsters at the primary and secondary levels in the public school system (*e.g.*, current estimates indicate that more than fifty percent of the Los Angeles school population will be non-EMT by 1985). Rather than abating, pressures to develop innovative educational programs with well-integrated language arts components in English and a number of other languages will increase.

Likewise, the inevitable lowering of standards to allow the admission of foreign students to replace our declining number of native-born students, coupled with the move toward Universal Primary Education in many third world countries, and the replacement in these countries of expatriate teachers by nationals, all point toward a diminution of English skills on the part of foreign applicants for higher education. This will pose additional challenges for members of our profession in the United States.

Similarly, with the moves to replace English as the medium of instruction at secondary and even tertiary levels in many countries overseas, there will be a greater burden placed on teachers at the tertiary level who must prepare a much more heterogeneous group of students to pursue advanced studies via English—an increasingly unfamiliar subject for them. I mention these trends simply to note that the challenge faced by tomorrow's teachers will, I believe, be much greater than that faced by today's.

It is my belief that tomorrow's teacher will need to be broadly and eclectically trained and will need to work in close cooperation with subject-matter specialists in an integral partnership to develop curricula and to adapt materials responsive to the move toward a language for special purposes approach. I have complete confidence that tomorrow's teachers will meet this need.

REFERENCES

Barik, H. and Swain, M. "A Longitudinal Study of Bilingual and Cognitive Development." *International Journal of Psychology*, 1976, *11*, 251–263.

Ben-Zeev, S. "The Effect of Bilingualism in Children from Spanish-English Low Economic Neighborhoods on Cognitive Development and Cognitive Strategy." *Working Papers on Bilingualism*, 1977, *14*, 83–122.

Berryman, S. E., Langer, P. F., Pincus, J., and Solmon, R. H. "Foreign Language and International Studies Specialists: The Marketplace and National Policy." Santa Monica, Rand, R-2501-NEH. September 1979.

Crandall, J. A. (ed.) *English for Specific Purposes*. July 1979, Issue 28.

Cziko, G. A.; Lambert, W. E. and Gutter, R. "French Immersion Programs and Students' Social Attitudes; A Multidimensional Investigation." *Working Papers on Bilingualism*, 1979, *18*, 13–28.

―――, Lambert, W. E., Sidoti, N. and Tucker, G. R. "Graduate of Early Immersion: Retrospective Views of Grade Eleven Students and Their Parents." In R. N. St. Clair and H. Giles (eds.) *The Social and Psychological Contexts of Language*. Hillsdale, NJ: Laurence Erlbaum Associates, 1980, 131–192.

Fishman, J. A., Cooper, R. L. and Conrad, A. W. *The Spread of English*. Rowley, MA: Newbury House, 1977.

Ianco-Worrall, A. D. "Bilingualism and Cognitive Development." *Child Development*, 1972, *43*, 1390–1400.

Lambert, W. E. "The Social Psychology of Language: A Perspective for the 1980's." Paper presented at International Conference on Social Psychology and Language. Bristol, England. July 1979.

―――, and Tucker, G. R. "Graduates of Early Immersion: Retrospective Views of Grade Eleven Students and Their Parents." In A. Obadia (ed.) *Proceedings of the C.A.I.T. Second National Convention*. Ottawa: 1978.

―――, and Sidoti, N. "The Selection of Appropriate Teaching Languages and the Use of Radio for Education in Less Developed Countries." Multilithed paper for Department of Education of the World Bank. April, 1980.

President's Commission on Foreign Language and International Studies. *Strength through Wisdom: A Critique of U.S. Capability* Washington: Government Printing Office, 1979

Swain, M. "Home-School Language Switching." In J. C. Richards (ed.) *Understanding Second and Foreign Language Learning: Issues & Approaches.* Rowley, MA: Newbury House, 1978, 238–250.

Tucker, G. R. "The Implementation of Language Teaching Programs." In J. C. Richards (ed.) *Understanding Second & Foreign Language Learning: Issues & Approaches.* Rowley, MA: Newbury House, 1978, 204–217.

————. "Implications of Canadian Research for U.S. Bilingual Education: Setting the Record Straight." *NABE News,* 1979, 3, 1, 4, 5, 7.

ABSTRACT

The Preparation
of Second Language Teachers
in the 1980's

HELEN L. JORSTAD
University of Minnesota

Re-examination of the education of language teachers in the U.S. is focused on four sets of issues: (1) student issues: characteristics and needs of today's learners; (2) societal issues: the impact of other cultures on American life; (3) educational issues: curricular, instructional, and evaluation needs; and (4) teacher issues: professional needs and responsibilities.

Implications of these issues for teacher education programs and research include restructuring to include: (1) early and continuous involvement of every prospective language teacher in schools and second language communities; (2) cooperative planning of the entire teacher education program by psychologists, educators, linguists, and other professionals; and (3) a methodology sequence which provides a wide variety of alternative approaches and abundant opportunities for practice in real teaching situations.

The Preparation
of Second Language Teachers
in the 1980's

HELEN L. JORSTAD
University of Minnesota

Re-examination of the education of American language teachers is overdue. Such re-examination, carried out in light of vast societal changes, occasioned by an influx of refugees on all shores, by increasing needs for bilingual schooling, and highlighted by a Presidential Commission report (1979) on the dismal state of language and area studies, would lead one to conclude, inevitably, that teacher education programs are inadequate for today's needs. Our record is not a brilliant one, partly because of our own shortcomings and partly because the public is not convinced either of the importance of language study to our national interest or about what it takes for a student to learn a language well enough to function bilingually in America. It is time to ask ourselves whether teachers might do better in the 1980's. The response may be equally valid in other nations facing similar challenges.

This chapter will examine four sets of issues which must concern teacher educators if language teaching and learning are to improve: (1) student issues: characteristics and needs of today's learners; (2) societal issues: the impact of other cultures on American life; (3) educational issues: curricular, instructional, and evaluation needs; and (4) teacher issues: professional needs and responsibilities. Implications for teacher education programs and research will then be explored briefly and an alternative teacher education model suggested.

STUDENT ISSUES

Who are the students of the 1980's? U.S.-born students of elementary and secondary age are one of the best-informed generations we have had in schools. But they are also one of the least world-minded. They and their parents have not yet realized the importance of language study or the influence of other cultures on basic everyday life. When they do take language courses, they tend to need externally-supplied motivation, at least in beginning stages. They often seem either apathetic toward or afraid of new immigrant groups within their schools, as are some of their teachers—even language teachers.

Increasing numbers of immigrant children perplex teachers and administrators in almost every region of the U.S. Often illiterate even as teen-agers, they are usually highly-motivated to learn English and to succeed in school for economic and social reasons.

Parents of the immigrant children need to learn English quickly and efficiently to function in daily social situations and in order to succeed in a job or profession.

College and university students are increasingly older than the traditional 18-to-21-year-old population; often they are returning to school for job retraining. They are serious students, willing to work hard, especially on those courses and experiences leading directly toward their professional goals.

It is clear that a variety of foreign and second language needs exists. It should be equally clear that no single format for teacher education programs can be ideal for teachers in all situations. Better ESL teacher preparation is the most immediately crucial; many programs in schools and in adult education situations must use teachers with little or no training in teaching English or any other language, who know little about how language is learned, and who may know very little about the English language itself. Bilingual programs need vast numbers of teachers in many languages at both elementary and secondary school levels; few high-quality programs to train such teachers exist. For both ESL and bilingual situations, few states have licensure requirements; many "emergency" teachers hired for bilingual positions have little training for them. This is equally true in the case of adult education, where the rule often seems to be that if one can speak a language one can teach it to adults. In the case of foreign language teachers, there often is less than native ability to speak the language they are teaching; few states require a specific proficiency level in any skill area, especially in speaking, at this time.

We do not know enough about how a second or foreign language is learned at any age, and so we cling to teaching procedures which may be of dubious value. At the same time, even more deeply-entrenched teacher education models are not flexible enough to train teachers who can fill the variety of positions in which a teacher may be placed. For that matter, research findings on learning in general have been slow to affect language teaching. Some programs which train language teachers include little curricular content which might help them base their teaching on sound learning principles. There is little introduction to innovative language-teaching approaches or opportunities for students to reflect on how they might become involved in research on language learning. Focus on the middle school learner (see below) is often neglected, despite the fact that such programs are being developed in increasing numbers throughout the nation. They may offer unique opportunities to begin language and global studies.

Focus on the older learner is slow to develop, and the older foreign or second language learner has been largely ignored in the literature. Some university programs aimed at teaching adult students in other areas are being developed. Though programs in English for special purposes are beginning to make their appearance, programs in other languages for special purposes are not, despite a need for language-trained individuals through all areas of U.S. society. Language study rarely is included in professional programs aimed at the older worker returning for re-education.

SOCIETAL ISSUES

The impact of other cultures on American life is difficult to ignore today. Immigration of large numbers of individuals of all ages needing instruction in English and in their native languages is creating problems of staggering proportions in many areas of the nation. Programs to train teachers for work in bilingual and ESL situations of a wide variety of types for people with diverse language backgrounds are inadequate both in number and quality. While some use is made of minority individuals as resource teachers, many minority teachers are not trained to do much more than translate from native languages into English and vice-versa. Too many students still feel that their native language creates a handicap in learning English, and specific language resources are lost to the nation as a result.

In addition, large numbers of the majority English-speaking population presently demonstrate lack of understanding of other cultures and languages, believing that all should immediately learn English and abandon "foreign" ways and languages. At the same time as one group is to forget its native language, another is struggling to learn other languages. The result is the waste of a largely untapped national resource, often unrecognized even by language teachers in schools, who are sometimes reluctant to see minority children in their classes. In part, they may feel that the languages of minority children are somehow inferior to the quality of language which they are teaching to U.S.-born students. In part, they may be threatened by such individuals in their classes because (1) their own language skills may be weak; (2) they may not understand the cultures of the peoples who speak the language they are teaching; or (3) they do not know how to involve other language speakers in their classes, and they are unaware of the needs minority children have for additional training in their own home language. Teacher education programs have not generally faced these issues in an organized fashion.

EDUCATIONAL ISSUES

Faced with dwindling enrollments, public criticism, and lack of funds, public school districts in the U.S. are closing school buildings and combining grades in a variety of ways. The most common "new" approach is reorganization of grade levels which creates a middle school, usually grades five or six through grade eight. The National Society for the Study of Education devoted one of its 1980 Yearbooks to issues surrounding such middle school students, called "transcescents" (Johnson, 1980). Teachers generally need to

examine better ways of teaching such children; language teachers
in particular have not yet responded with innovative interdisciplinary programs of language and culture which fit well into the new
organizational structure. As development continues, much can be
learned about global education, motivation and attitudes of transcescents, and evaluation of learning in middle schools, as well as
articulation with secondary schools. Neither secondary school language programs nor "FLES" (Foreign Language in the Elementary
School) programs are appropriate for this situation. Extremely flexible, creative, and enthusiastic teachers must be identified, and
curricular designs, instructional procedures, and evaluation policies and procedures need to be developed.

Language teaching curricula based on functional/notional, situational, or topical organization are becoming increasingly accepted.
However, teachers are not prepared to teach using such curricula,
or to continue their development. Little research on the use of
such curricula for elementary, middle or secondary school situations has been done, and teacher education programs are often not
in a position to respond.

Varied and creative instructional strategies are needed to moti-
vate students for language study. The relationships between instructional strategies and learning in school situations have not
been adequately studied, partly because teachers have not been
trained to do research, partly because many language teachers and
teacher educators have been satisfied with a *status quo* approach,
and because many teachers have not had the time to go beyond
the textbook. Textbook programs, meanwhile, do not encourage a
variety of approaches suitable for adapting materials to different
situations. Continued development of computer and mini-com-
puter applications to language teaching and testing also awaits innovative teachers trained to use such technology.

Additional ways to evaluate language achievement and proficiency, dominance, aptitude, and attitudes are needed. There has
been considerable discussion in the profession about competency
levels and evaluation of competency, and there may be some progress in this area in the near future.

Research on language processing strategies and learning styles
also depends on teachers who are knowledgeable in the area and

who know how to vary methodology and approaches for a variety of learner needs.

Training in language skill development is needed; many teachers teach reading, for example, as though it could be learned by translation and structural analysis alone. Nor are we training teachers to develop the listening abilities of their students. There has been more emphasis on developing communicative abilities both in classrooms and in teacher education programs, yet many teachers are not confident in dealing with advanced students and fail to continue communicative activities at upper levels.

Many language classrooms still tend to be teacher-centered rather than student-centered despite the preparation of lists of student objectives, and despite literature in the field (e.g., Rivers & Temperley, 1978; Robinett, 1977, 1978; Stevick, 1976, 1980).

PROFESSIONAL ISSUES

Foremost among professional issues facing language teachers are issues which permeate public instruction in all U.S. schools: (1) a growing feeling of frustration about the possibility that education makes a difference. "Teacher burn-out" is a symptom which has received press attention. (2) Low salaries, large class sizes, and little money to spend for programs. These problems are certainly shared by language teachers; especially in cities where there are large numbers of new immigrants, ESL and bilingual classes are understaffed and under-supplied. (3) Lack of preparation of teachers for language programs. Again, bilingual and ESL teachers are often not trained for their special responsibilities. Licensure regulations are beginning to be adopted in more and more states; their spread can increase the professional status of the field and improve language programs.

MEETING THE CHALLENGES

Implications of these realities of teaching today for the education of teachers are serious and far-reaching. The issues demand immediate attention. It is clear that teacher preparation institutions cannot alone fill all of the nation's language needs; a cooperative effort by psychologists, linguists, educators, ethnographers, and the public might. If it is true that a teacher preparation program must contain four major components: "(1) the development of attitudes; (2) the development of skills; (3) the acquisition of knowledge; (4) the application of these in a real situation" (Blanco, 1976, p. 101), it is equally clear that educators alone cannot do the task. If, in addition, the development of personal characteristics in teachers is important, then "it is a herculean task that teachers face—one requiring not only knowledge and special skill but also enthusiasm, devotion, dedication, and love" (Finocchiaro & Ekstrand, 1977, pp. 217–18).

Teacher educators will need to reconsider both curricular content and organization of programs for second language teachers. More attention needs to be focused on (1) selecting persons with necessary personal characteristics for entry into a teacher education program; (2) providing courses or experiences designed to help teachers gain knowledge, skills, and undestandings in psychology of children, youth, and adults, the nature of language and how it is learned or acquired, the ethnic backgrounds of communities for which they are being trained; and especially (3) providing additional experiences in existing school programs as well as in neighborhood organizations and functions where prospective language teachers can learn more about total community language needs, both mother tongue and second language.

Selection of Prospective Teachers

The selection of the best-qualified prospective teachers is of vital importance. Some language teachers seem to be neither enthusiastic about the language they are teaching nor about their students. Robinett believes that "qualities like patience, tolerance, sensitivity, and warmth are innate" (1977, p. 36). While she believes that "they can be nurtured, developed, brought to the surface, even created—if teachers are *really* interested in their students, if they really want students to learn, and if they are willing to try everything in their power to help their students," it may be more realistic to seek ways of identifying individuals who already have such qualities in abundance, whether or not they are products of the target language community.

At the same time, prospective teachers must have abundant opportunities to interact with children and parents early in their training, so that those would-be teachers who may have interpersonal problems may be counseled appropriately. We are doing no service to students or to schools if we permit teachers without these essential qualities to enter the profession, no matter how strong their linguistic abilities or their knowledge of subject matter. This implies, for all teacher education programs, a need to strengthen and extend school and community experiences, and to place prospective teachers in schools as observers and as aides, or in communities as counselors, aides, or other helpers, with supervision by the teacher preparation institution and close guidance by school and community personnel. Inclusion of actual school and community persons as adjunct faculty should be attempted wherever possible. Such involvement would help prospective teachers to develop flexible attitudes and warm acceptance of people of all ages and language backgrounds.

Academic Program

The need for better knowledge and skills in psychology, linguistics, sociology, education, and other areas can best be met by the provision of multi-disciplinary teams for planning, executing, and evaluating content of the entire teacher education program. Provision of such teams would in most cases necessitate new ways of planning, especially in large universities where several "Schools," "Colleges," or departments would need to find flexible ways to cooperate. The fragmentation of a future language teacher's curriculum is part of the reason that teachers have had difficulty conceiving of total language needs and resources of students and of communities. Such fragmentation must be overcome if there is to be progress in language education. At the same time that a central core of courses which embrace a number of disciplines is mastered by the student, there should also be inclusion of such knowledge as native-culture and target-culture folklore, children's literature, games, music, and art. As a result of such a program, a prospective teacher would have had first-hand experience with cooperative learning, and would be more likely to transfer such learning into his or her own classes. We might more frequently see truly creative classrooms in which students feel safe to try out language to express what they really want to say, in which language is considered a vehicle to carry real messages rather than a subject to be dissected and isolated from human experience.

Interdisciplinary planning can also lead to cooperation among disciplines in carrying out needed research, with faculty members, students, and classroom teachers working as a team.

Other Community Experiences

When communities feel that they play a real role in the education of teachers for their schools, such teachers will tend to be more confident that (a) they can interact appropriately with students in those communities, and (b) they understand the role of children of all ages in a community. Teachers in schools can play a more important part in teacher education than they are now doing. A balance is still important, however, because there is also a danger that bad classroom practices may be emulated and perpetuated! At its best, close cooperation should lead to better in-service teaching, as teachers already in schools learn better ways to involve minority language aides and other personnel in their classes.

In addition, prospective teachers should have opportunities to observe at all levels of education, pre-school through secondary and adult classes, regardless of the level for which they may be training. Many problems of articulation among levels may be prevented by a fuller understanding of all levels by all teachers.

Finally, involvement with a pupil's community and home can lead to stronger likelihood that the prospective teacher will consider the student as the center of the teaching-learning process, and his or her progress in language learning as evidence not only of fuller cognitive growth but also of full human development.

A MODEL TEACHER EDUCATION PROGRAM

We might consider a model program for training language teachers with the following dimensions:

1. Early and continuous involvement in school and community by every prospective language teacher. Such involvement could begin as early as the freshman year, and could be part of core courses in anthropology, education foundations, psychology, and languages. Tutorial programs for migrant or other community children, youth, and adults could be carried out by language students.

2. Planning the training programs for ESL, bilingual, and foreign language teachers should be a cooperative venture including curriculum areas not traditionally involved in teacher education, with carefully planned and supervised practicum experiences for students as part of every course. Such experiences could provide opportunities for selection of students who demonstrate the best personal qualifications for teaching and who show promise of becoming passionate advocates for children and youth as well as for research in language teaching and learning.

3. A methodology sequence must provide the student with a wide variety of alternative approaches, as well as a base in evaluation and testing so that the most appropriate alternatives may be selected to meet identified pupil needs and learning styles. In addition, immediate opportunities should be provided for application first in non-threatening individual and small-group situations and later with larger groups of students. The methodology sequence should include consideration of a variety of classroom organization models (e.g. Johnson and Johnson, 1975), so that flexibility can be further encouraged.

The profession must focus on developing creative ways to meet the challenges of the multilingual situation, creativity described in part by Birkmaier (1971) as that which "allows students considerable latitude in their tasks and keeps the structure of situations open so that originality can occur" (p. 352). Such teachers could bring about vast changes in the attitudes of society. But first we must act together as a profession to promote a common-sense response to the problems we face, working vigorously for licensure requirements, and for a truly interdisciplinary attack on all phases of a potential problem which can also be the greatest opportunity that American education has faced.

REFERENCES

Birkmaier, Emma M. "The Meaning of Creativity in Foreign Language Teaching." *The Modern Language Journal* October, 1971, 55, 345–53.

Blanco, George M. "University Training for Developing Teacher Competencies in Bilingual Education," 101–104 in David P. Benseler, ed., *Second Language Teaching 77*. Corvallis, OR: Pacific Northwest Council on Foreign Languages, 1976. [Vol. 28, Part 2].

Finocchiaro, Mary, and Ekstrand, Lars. "Migration Today: Some Social and Educational Problems," 205–218 in Marina Burt, Heidi Dulay, and Mary Finocchiaro, eds., *Viewpoints on English as a Second Language*. New York: Regents, 1977.

Johnson, Mauritz, ed. *Toward Adolescence: The Middle School Years*. Chicago: National Society for the Study of Education, 1980. [79th Yearbook of the NSSE: Part I].

Johnson, David W., and Johnson, Roger T. *Learning Together and Alone: Cooperation, Competition, and Individualization*. Englewood Cliffs, N.J.: Prentice-Hall, 1975.

Rivers, Wilga M., and Temperley, Mary S. *A Practical Guide to the Teaching of English as a Second or Foreign Language*. New York: Oxford University Press, 1978.

Robinett, Betty Wallace. "Characteristics of an Effective Second Language Teacher," 35–44 in Marina Burt, Heidi Dulay, and Mary Finocchiaro, eds., *Viewpoints on English as a Second Language*. New York: Regents, 1977.

―――. *Teaching English to Speakers of Other Languages: Substance and Technique*. Minneapolis, MN: University of Minnesota Press, 1978.

Stevick, Earl W. *Memory, Meaning & Method: Some Psychological Perspectives on Language Learning*. Rowley, MA: Newbury House, 1976.

―――. *Teaching Languages: A Way and Ways*. Rowley, MA: Newbury House, 1980.

Strength Through Wisdom: A Critique of U.S. Capability. Washington, D.C.: U.S. Government Printing Office, 1979. (A Report to the President from the President's Commission on Foreign Language and International Studies).

SECTION II

FOCUS ON SECOND LANGUAGE LEARNING

INTRODUCTION

There are literally many millions of individuals engaged today in the learning of a language which is not their mother tongue. Some may pursue this activity independently, outside of formal classrooms, but most foreign or second language learners are enrolled in institutionalized instruction of some sort. Language learners are far from a monolithic group; they differ along many continua. They approach the study of another language for many different reasons, with highly different previous experiences, different aptitudes, attitudes, motivation, learning styles, and learning strategies. The 1970's has been called the "decade of the learner" in second language education, and this should continue into the 1980's. Researchers in second language acquisition in the 1970's and 1980's have explored and will continue to explore questions such as:

What factors (cognitive, affective, sociological, linguistic) influence second language learning?

How are the elements of a language acquired in natural and classroom settings?

How is second language learning to be evaluated?

What characteristics should a language learning environment possess?

How much of second language learning can be directly related to formal teaching?

The eight chapters in this section focus on second language learning and the second language learner in the 1980's. Titone defines second language learning based on psychological theories. Rivers and Melvin examine the second language learner's wants, needs, and styles of learning. Krashen considers recent research in second language acquisition and explores various hypotheses which attempt to account for the process of coming to know and use another language. Brown explores the role of affect in second language learning. Stern and Allen explore the learning of second languages for communicative purposes from theoretical and practical points of view respectively. Valette deals with the issue of evaluating second language production. Finally, Burt and Dulay investigate the optimal environments for second language learning and the features which such environments contain.

ABSTRACT

The Holistic Approach
to Second Language Education

RENZO TITONE

Centro di Linguistica Applicata, Rome

Psycholinguistic models of language learning and teaching have undergone radical changes in the last three decades. In this paper an "integrated" theory of language learning and teaching is described. This theory, called the Holodynamic Model (HDM), combines both behavioristic and cognitive learning principles, and fuses them to the view of personality developed by humanistic psychologists.

The HDM consists of a three-level hierarchy with personality structure at the core of the model. Personality is also considered to be the triggering mechanism for the language learning process. The proposed teaching model is derived logically from the psycholinguistic principles of the HDM.

The Holistic Approach to Second Language Education

RENZO TITONE

Centro di Linguistica Applicata, Rome

This chapter proposes an integrated, holistic theory of language learning. Its view that L_2 learning is holistic is based on the results of recent research. This showed that psychological considerations are of prime importance in L_2 learning.

PSYCHOLINGUISTIC MODELS OF LANGUAGE LEARNING

Psycholinguistic theory has undergone at least five radical changes in direction since its establishment as an autonomous discipline in the early fifties. The five stages may be summarized as follows:

Stage 1. During the 1950's and early 1960's, psycholinguistic theory was influenced primarily by the behavioristic views of psychologists such as Skinner, and by the linguistic theories of structuralist-taxonomic linguists such as Bloomfield.

Stage 2. During the 1960's and early 1970's, the mentalistic-cognitivist views of transformationalists such as Chomsky dominated all aspects of psycholinguistics.

Stage 3. The shift in emphasis toward the pragmatic, or communicative, aspects of language (*e.g.*, Chafe, Hymes, Labov,

Special thanks to Professor Marcel Danesi, University of Toronto, for reading and reacting to an earlier draft of this paper.

etc.)—still within the perimeter of transformational theory—deeply influenced psycholinguistic theory and L_2 teaching in the 1970's.

Stage 4. By the end of the last decade, the pragmatic or sociolinguistic viewpoint (emphasized by scholars such as Leontyev, Slama-Cazacu, Ervin-Tripp, Halliday and others) became mainstream.

Stage 5. In recent years, I have proposed an integrated model consisting not only of behavioral and cognitive components, but also of personality features.

Personality Features in Language Learning

The integrated, or holistic, model of language learning may be called the Holodynamic Model (HDM). It is based on the view that language learning consists of interacting components of a behavioral and cognitive nature which are controlled by the learner's personality structure. Consequently, it can be said that the L_2 learning process is marked by both operant conditioning (*à la* Skinner) and meaningful cognitive learning according to the particular type of skill that is being assimilated. In other words, the HDM combines behavioristic and cognitive theories, and amalgamates them with the personality theories of so-called "humanistic" psychologists. A similar view is expressed by Slama-Cazacu (1961).

The role played by personality in L_2 learning is, in fact, beginning to receive attention in the literature. As Matson (1971:9) states: "This recognition of *man-in-person,* as opposed to *man-in-general,* goes to the heart of the difference between humanistic psychology, in any of its forms or schools, and scientific psychologies." Humanistic psychologists such as Allport, Rogers, Fromm, Murray and Nuttin, to mention a few, have argued that personality is a cornerstone in the human organism. It must be stressed that personality is not equal merely to individuality. Rather, it is an open relational system that relates the individual's internal structure to the outside environment (physical, social, cultural). To paraphrase Nuttin (1968:205–206), personality is a mode of functioning involving the *Ego* and the *World.* The *Ego* is the sum of the individual's functions (perceptual, cognitive, etc.); and the *World*, or external environment, is simply the object of the *Ego*. The interconnection of personality and environment constitutes an open system in Bertalanffy's (1950) sense. Verbal communication is simply the linguistic expression of one's internal and external (social) personality.

A Holodynamic Model of L_2 Learning

Given that personality is a basic component of verbal behavior, it must be included in any theory of how language is learned. In the HDM, it is considered pivotal. This model consists of three interacting levels which are hierarchical. At the top is what may be called the *tactic* level. This corresponds roughly to what transformationalists call the surface structure of language. *Tactic operations* are ordering relations in the domains of language perception and production. In pedagogical terms, they correspond to the four skills (listening, speaking, reading, and writing). Since tactic operations clearly involve mental co-ordination and integration in order to become automatic, it is logical that the best teaching strategy at this level is one which focuses on habit formation.

The level below the tactic may be called *strategic*. It is at this level that rule-making, selection and programming operations occur. These are mentalistic, or cognitive, in nature. Thus, the rules of L_2 are assimilated by means of inductive and deductive generalization processes. Once these rules have been assimilated, the learner must be able to select and use the appropriate rules according to the context. Thus, the teaching of strategic operations must include not only rule-learning activities (as in cognitive-code techniques), but also contextualization ones (as in notional-functional approaches). As in the case of the tactics, true learning has occurred only when the learner is able to control the strategic operations in the flow of speech.

The strategic operations can be compared to the underlying, or deep, structure of transformationalists. However, in the HDM there is a deeper level which may be called *ego-dynamic*. This level consists of personality variables such as the learner's experience, world-view, attitudes, affective nature, cognitive learning style, metalinguistic awareness, etc. These features not only coordinate and control the tactic and strategic operations, but also relate them to the outside world. In other words, the ego-dynamic level relates the form of language to its use in actual communicative settings. The implications for language teaching are obvious. The learner's personality must always be taken into account in the selection of an appropriate teaching strategy or in the establishment of a student-teacher relationship.

The pedagogical implications of the HDM can be schematized as follows:

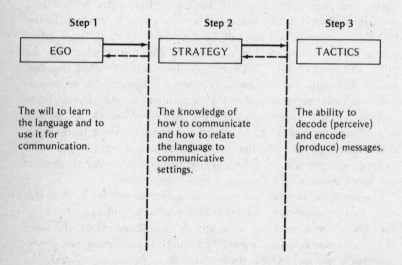

Step 1	Step 2	Step 3
EGO	STRATEGY	TACTICS
The will to learn the language and to use it for communication.	The knowledge of how to communicate and how to relate the language to communicative settings.	The ability to decode (perceive) and encode (produce) messages.

The language learning process can now be defined as the process that involves the simultaneous functioning of the ego-dynamic, strategic and tactic levels. This is an integrated, or holistic, process which consists of both instrumental and cognitive-code learning and which takes into consideration the personality variables of the learner.

FIRST LANGUAGE ACQUISITION AND SECOND LANGUAGE LEARNING

Before discussing the teaching model that may be derived from the HDM of language learning (in *Section 3*), we shall consider here very briefly the issue of how similar are L_1 acquisition and L_2

learning, so as to be able to determine if this teaching model is applicable to both children and adults.

The most obvious differences are, clearly, age and time. There are two schools of thought on this subject. Some scholars (e.g., Taylor 1974; Ervin-Tripp 1974) maintain that L_1 acquisition and L_2 learning are remarkably similar. Macnamara (1976) goes so far as to suggest that there are no differences between the two processes. This position has always been the central thesis of so-called "natural" methods of language teaching. On the other hand, some believe that the two processes are totally different. However, as I have previously argued (1964), it is probably more accurate to say that the two processes are *partially* similar. The most obvious differences between the two may be summarized as follows:

1. L_1 acquisition is spontaneous and rarely planned, whereas L_2 learning is to a large extent intentional and planned.

2. L_1 acquisition is conditioned by primary reinforcers (the need to communicate wants and desires, the need to establish an affective relationship with one's parents, etc.). L_2 learning, on the other hand, is often conditioned by weaker reinforcers such as a nod of approval, a grade, etc.

3. Unlike the infant who progresses from no knowledge through definite identifiable stages, the L_2 learner already knows his native language. This can, of course, be an asset since the learner can easily transfer some of his knowledge to the learning of L_2. However, in those areas where L_1 and L_2 contrast, his previous knowledge can become a source of interference.

4. The L_2 learner already has the ability to discriminate sounds and structures, while the infant starts "from scratch."

5. The L_2 learner already has certain perceptions and attitudes *vis-à-vis* the foreign culture which may influence the learning process.

However, despite such obvious differences, the fact that L_1 and L_2 learners are *human* implies that they inevitably share some learning characteristics. In both cases, motivation is the starting point of the learning process, and this occurs at the ego-dynamic level. Moreover, the strategic and tactic levels are operational in both L_1 and L_2 learning contexts, however in different degrees and in different ways.

L_2 Learning Characteristics

Motivation, language aptitude and the amount of time spent in learning are perhaps the three most significant factors that characterize L_2 learning. Motivational variables appear to be of prime importance to the learning task (see, for example, Burstall 1975). Some of these are as follows:

1. *"Integrative"* vs. *"instrumental"* *motivation*. Some studies have shown that students are most successful when they study a foreign language because they admire the culture and wish to become part of the society in which the language is used (integrative motivation). Instrumental motivation is, of course, the study of a foreign language for some utilitarian purpose.

2. *Contact with the foreign culture*. Students seem to develop a greater desire to study a foreign language if actual contact (through visits) with the foreign culture is made.

3. *Socio-economic factors*. Perhaps because of greater parental support and encouragement, it seems that a positive attitude toward the foreign language correlates positively with socio-economic status.

4. *Sex differences*. Some research has shown that female learners are better than male learners in specific language-learning tasks. However, this may be due to sociological rather than biological differences.

5. *The classroom situation*. The context and conditions of learning are clearly important variables. For example, a small class size seems to enhance achievement in learning.

6. *Teacher-student relationship*. The teacher's expectations of his students and his attitudes toward the foreign language and culture can definitely influence student success.

7. *The presentation of materials*. Clearly, the materials and activities in the classroom should be designed in such a way as to stimulate both interest and learning.

The role played by language aptitude has been studied extensively, especially by Carroll (*e.g.*, 1960) who has identified four basic features that characterize the good classroom language learner:

1. *Phonetic coding.* This is the ability to "code" phonetic stimuli in such a way that they can be stored and recognized easily.

2. *Grammatical sensitivity.* This is the ability to recognize the grammatical functions of words in sentences.

3. *Rote memorization.* This the ability to learn a large number of associations in a relatively short span of time.

4. *Induction ability.* This is the ability to generalize rules and patterns from linguistic data with only a minimum of help (Carroll 1961).

Carroll (1963) has also shown that the amount of time spent actively involved in the learning process can influence success in learning a foreign language. Simply put, the more time spent in learning, the better. Intensive (or immersion) curricula invariably produce the best results.

L₂ LEARNING AND TEACHING STRATEGY

What does an integrated model of language learning mean in pedagogical terms? Since the teaching process should reflect the learning process, the most obvious implication is that language teaching should also be "integrated" and "systematic." This approach implies a program of flexible steps or learning "modules" derived from a learning model. Recent studies have in fact shown that a systematic approach is desirable, if not indispensable, when teaching adults (see, for example, Krashen and Seliger 1976; and Krashen, Seliger and Hartnett 1976). However, its principles are applicable to teaching children as well.

There are three essential components of any systematic teaching model:

1. The teaching process is "reversible"; i.e., it is adaptive to the needs and abilities of the students.

2. The concept of reversibility is also extended to the area of teacher-student roles which should be interchangeable (the student learns from the teacher who learns from the student).

3. Teaching is "spiral" rather than linear. This means that the teaching modules should interact and overlap rather than be separated discretely.

This allows us to conclude that teaching consists of a series of acts which are integrated rather than discrete.

We can now view the L₂ teaching process as an integrated system of units. A large unit may be called a *macromatheme* and its components, *micromathemes*. These are teaching activities based on the HDM. The micromathemes of a teaching unit may be described as follows:

1. *Inchoation.* This micromatheme consists of perceptional and cognitive activities. The student is exposed to language material in a variety of forms. He performs comprehensive exercises based on this material. Then, he uses the known material to generate new utterances.

2. *Reinforcement.* Next, the teaching process must aim at strengthening what is learned by reinforcement exercises (pattern practice). However, pattern exercises should always be made meaningful by incorporating them into communicative settings (contextualization).

3. *Control.* The whole process is regulated by systematic testing of the learner as needed.

It should be made clear that the three phases described above are not necessarily sequential. Rather, the order of the teaching units is dictated by the learning conditions. Moreover, the teacher can "loop" back to any phase if it is found that certain things have not been adequately assimilated. It is also to be noted that this teaching model is an integrated one in the same sense of the HDM; i.e., it is based on both perceptual/cognitive and instrumental teaching strategies; and it is guided by feedback and control. It is, therefore, an applied psycholinguistic model since it is based on the view that language learning is governed by certain identifiable psycholinguistic processes (see also Titone 1970 and 1980).

REFERENCES

Allport, G. W. 1965. *Pattern and Growth in Personality.* New York: Holt.

Bertalanffy, L. von. 1950. "The Theory of Open Systems in Physics and Biology." *Science* 3.23–28.

Burstall, C. 1975. "Factors Affecting Foreign-Language Learning: A Consideration of Some Recent Findings." *Language Teaching and Linguistics Abstracts* 8.5–25.

Carroll, J. B. 1960. "Foreign Languages for Children: What Research Says." *The National Elementary Principal* 39.13 ff.

——. 1961. "The Prediction of Success in Intensive Language Training." In R. Glaser, ed. *Training Research and Education.* Pittsburgh: University Press.

——. 1963. "A Model of School Learning." *Teachers College Record.* 64.723–733.

Ervin-Tripp, S. 1974. "Is Second Language Learning Like the First?" *TESOL Quarterly* 8.111–127.

Krashen, S. D. and Seliger, H. W. 1976. "The Essential Contribution of Formal Instruction in Adult Second Language Learning." *TESOL Quarterly* 8.

——, Seliger, H. W. and Hartnett, D. 1976. "Two Studies in Adult Second Language Learning." *Kritikon Litterarum.*

Macnamara, J. 1976. "First and Second Language Learning: Same or Different?" *Journal of Education* 158.39–54.

Matson, F. W. 1971. "Humanistic Theory: The Third Revolution in Psychology." *The Humanist* 9.

Nuttin, J. 1968. *La Structure de la Personnalité.* Paris: Presses Universitaires de France.

Pask, G. 1964. "Adaptive Teaching Systems and a Minimal Cybernetic Model for Designing Them." *Cybernetics* 2.126 ff.

Slama-Cazacu, T. 1961. *Langage et Contexte.* The Hague: Mouton.

Taylor, B. P. 1974. "Toward a Theory of Language Acquisition." *Language Learning* 24.23–25.

Titone, R. 1964. *Studies in the Psychology of Second Language Learning.* Zurich: PAS.

——. 1970. *Psicolinguistica Applicata.* Roma: Armando.

——, (ed.) 1980. *Avamposti della Psicolinguistica Applicata.* Roma: Armando.

ABSTRACT

Language Learners as Individuals: Discovering Their Needs, Wants, and Learning Styles

WILGA M. RIVERS
Harvard University

BERNICE J. MELVIN
Austin College

I

Students' needs in language learning are dependent on political situations, societal demands, and career opportunities; their wants derive from their or their parents' perceptions of these factors (with some injection of personal preferences). The Council of Europe project is cited as an example of a well-planned and executed attack on the linguistic needs of a particular group in a well-defined situation. Student perceptions of their needs can be researched through a questionnaire, carefully drafted and sensitively interpreted; further indications come from student response to innovative course development. Above all, there should be choice.

II

It has long been known that students adopt distinctive styles of learning a foreign language. Systematic interest today in learning styles has been facilitated by advances in cognitive psychology and information processing models. The taxonomy of Hill (1971; 1977) termed "Educational Cognitive Style" is one approach to "cognitive mapping" of individual differences in styles of learning specific tasks. Another approach is that of Reinert (1976; 1977). Learning style information can be used to improve instruction through matching and remediation.

Language Learners as Individuals: Discovering Their Needs, Wants, and Learning Styles

WILGA M. RIVERS
Harvard University

BERNICE J. MELVIN
Austin College

PART I: DISCOVERING THE NEEDS AND WANTS OF LANGUAGE LEARNERS IN THE 1980's

In a recent novel entitled *At Sunrise, The Rough Music*, a landowner gives his foster-son the following advice as a guiding light in times of change: "There are times," he says, "when you must sit down, and take note, count the animals, find out what the harvest will be, and go clearly into time, never blindly, always ready to change course, as a good navigator must, when he finds the map wrong." The area of language teaching and learning is not static, set in some mold which represents an unchanging model of how things ought to be. The rapid shifts, vehement controversies, even recriminations, of the past fifty years make this quite clear (Rivers, 1980). The beginning of a new decade is a good time to ponder the possibilities for the harvest and to change course if we find our present direction is not leading us where we need to go.

Consideration of the harvest in modern terms implies market research, and market research presumes that there are consumers. Who are the consumers of what we have to offer in language teaching, and what will they be wanting from us in the 1980's? Our consumers are not only students, but also the society of which they are a part. As in all marketing research, we must not merely identify what we think our consumers need, but also what they want. As educators we must provide for a balance between these two if

Part I of this chapter was written by W. M. Rivers and Part II by B. J. Melvin.

students are to be motivated to learn what we offer (Rivers, 1976, pp. 256–57).

What our students need is dependent on political situations, societal demands, and the career opportunities that these create; what our students want derives from their or their parents' perceptions of these community factors, their final choices being influenced also by personal preferences. The decisions that determine educational programs are rarely made by earnest language acquisition researchers, teacher trainers, or theoreticians of language teaching methodology. Such people may have some effect on language learning through materials production, but even then the final word will come from the consumers, since books are accepted by publishers and flourish or fade according to their degree of response to the currently perceived needs of the wider society.

In support of this position we may consider the first result of the 1979 Report of the President's Commission on Foreign Language and International Studies: the creation of a National Council on Foreign Language and International Studies "to focus public attention on the nation's declining competence in foreign languages and the urgent need for improved understanding of international affairs" (*Chronicle of Higher Education,* June 2, 1980). Funded by private foundations and federal agency funds, the Council, which will be expected to make specific recommendations on such issues as "how many people should know what languages, where they should learn them, and how the learning should be made possible," does not have among its members one expert on language teaching. These policy decisions will be made by community representatives in response to an analysis of the needs of the nation in its relationships with other nations. Their recommendations, enhanced by the lure of possible funding and high-level support, will no doubt have a major impact on the direction foreign language study will take in the 1980's as their analyses and recommendations define career opportunities. As good navigators, we must be ready to change course if we find our map is wrong.

The most striking example in recent times of the implementation of high-level political decisions affecting language learning has been the work of the Group of Experts called together in 1971 by a Committee of the Council of Europe. This group of highly-respected applied linguists and language teachers was charged with creating "the conditions for the establishment of a suitable structural framework for the development, through international co-operation, of a coherent and progressive European policy in the field of adult language learning" (Trim, 1977, p. 1). The political and social need was created by the number of adult workers who were moving from their homelands to the more prosperous countries of the European Economic Community without speaking the languages of these areas. In 1977, the Parliamentary Assembly of the Council of Europe consecrated the efforts of the Group of Experts and their collaborators and opened the way for the application on a wide scale of their work as set out in *Systems Development in Adult Language Learning* (Trim et al., 1973), the *Threshold Level* (Van Ek, 1975), *Le Niveau-seuil* (Coste et al., 1976), and *Waystage* (Van Ek, 1977).

The European unit/credit system was developed on the basis of an analysis of the linguistic needs of adults in forty-four occupational categories. In the analysis, the actual activities in which persons of these specific occupations would need to use another language were studied and estimates made of the degree of proficiency they would require in each of the linguistic skills of understanding, speaking, reading, and writing. Some materials along notional-functional lines (Wilkins, 1976) have been developed to meet these needs and more are in production. (See also Van Ek, 1973; Richterich and Chancerel, 1978; Oskarsson, 1978; Rivers and Temperley, 1978, pp. 56–57; and Rivers, 1981, Ch. 8.)

The European notional-functional materials of the Council of Europe were developed to meet specific needs in the European context. They are not necessarily transferable to the American context where needs may be quite different. The closest American program for adult workers is Occupational English as a Second Language (also called Manpower ESL), a component of bilingual/ bicultural education which has been part of the training and technical assistance provided by the Area Manpower Institutes for the Development of Staff (AMIDS). (See Ramirez and Spandel, 1980.)

One fact that is already evident from the names of both the National Council, and that of the President's Commission mentioned above, is the close link that is assumed between foreign language and international studies. This association has not been strong in the past, so it behooves us to begin now to study the implications of this linkage for foreign language programs in the 1980's by building bridges of discussion and cooperation with our colleagues in international and global education.

All decisions, however, will not be made by experts or teachers. We must discover what students feel they need from us if their study of a language is to serve the purpose of developing an understanding of the ways of thinking and valuing of those of other nations, as well as an appreciation of their achievements, problems, and aspirations. This will be a new and untraveled path for many of our language teachers, who will themselves need re-education if they are to be successful in building cooperative programs in this area. They will need to seriously study the role of a foreign language as an auxiliary skill, rather than as a major focus of concentration. We are approaching a new frontier and this requires the flexibility and the innovative, untrammeled thinking of the frontier.

Leaving aside the broader political and social determinants of student needs, we come to the personal. Many students will have other interests than those of international affairs or even international trade. We must avoid the tendency of the past to see only one side of a multi-faceted problem at any particular moment. In the 1980's, we will have to accept the fact that there is no one pedagogical answer, only the answers of many individuals. Some language teachers will have to abandon the authoritarian approach of *"designing* the program to meet their students' needs," as they see them, in favor of discovering first how the students perceive their own needs and then considering what contributions they can make, as teachers and course designers, to meeting these needs. We must stop thinking that we know and start finding out.

We begin by seriously studying who our language learners really are. What age are they? Are they from the dominant culture? Are they learning a foreign or a second language (in the now generally accepted meaning of that term)? Are they learning this language for everyday intercourse? for job requirements? for personal enrichment and broadening of their educational experience? for reasons of ethnic curiosity or attachment? in order to understand and interact with a co-existent community? to fulfill school or college requirements? for study purposes (particularly through listening or reading materials)? as an additional skill to enhance a professional career? just for curiosity or love of language? because of a personal relationship? because they want to travel (for pleasure or business)? as a necessity for research? In this last sentence alone, we touch on twelve possible motivations, each indicating a somewhat different orientation to the learning task. We cannot continue to think in terms of one approach and one prototype course in the curriculum.

How then do we proceed? A questionnaire on students' perceived needs is a good start (Rivers, 1976), but cannot supply all the answers, since the questionnaire-constructor begins with certain assumptions which determine the questions the students will address. Even a section for free response may not provide sufficient information because not all students can articulate a clear idea of what they would like the language course to provide. There are many possibilities that do not occur to them. A questionnaire needs to be supplemented by teacher observation and attentive listening to students and community.

Sensitive teacher interpretation indicates many directions in which course design may develop, as is indicated by the extreme diversity of the following assessments from a 1979 survey of foreign language learners' goals in fifty countries and fifty states of the U.S.A. (Rivers, 1979).

"To gain an appreciative understanding of different modes of thought and to develop the ability to communicate within this framework." (Holland)

"To read—particularly scientific and technical English—so as to be able to extract information relevant to the practice of the student's profession and important to the development of the country as a whole." (Mexico)

"To be able to communicate with persons from other countries; to be able to read and understand newspapers; to be able to understand what is said on TV and radio." (Sweden)

"To form a harmony between academic learning and professional training or career education as contributing to the goals of liberal education, *e.g.*, to combine linguistic skills with a professional speciality—law, accounting, chemistry, etc., for a practical or utilitarian value." (Thailand)

"At a time when students are capable of understanding the global gestalt; are studying the intricate balances of nature and mankind in courses ranging through history through literature and beyond; and are firming up their philosophies of life, the foreign language class can—and should—center attention on the role of the human being in an interdependent collection of land/sea masses. Language is the vehicle that carries us down the multi-laned routes connecting people, all of whom are in motion. Language study can make the collisions on these byways meaningful rather than disastrous." (U.S.A.)

Perceptive interpretation of the articulated and implicit messages of students, parents, and community representatives can then be expressed in experimental course design (Rivers, 1979). The response of students to experimental courses will reveal clearly enough whether their needs are being met and enable them to express more concretely what they feel is still missing. Slowly, extra courses will be added and others modified to meet these needs. The proof of the pudding being in the eating, this more indirect approach will gradually lead to a viable diversified curriculum which allows for much student choice, without the chaos of an individual offering for each student.

What all of these motivations require, if the students are to feel their needs are fulfilled, is a solid, flexible basic course on which the student can later develop diversifications of language use for specific purposes. Without a serious general-purpose foundation, students can become locked into an approach which subsequent language experience causes them to realize they do not really want. The basic course must, however, provide for both the aurally- and the visually-oriented and introduce students to the various possible benefits of language study—interpersonal, cultural, expressive, global, humanistic (Rivers, 1979)—in such a way that the student is prepared to make a real choice of the direction in which to continue.

After the basic course, there should be choice, that is, courses with differing orientations that provide clear-cut options, even if these options go against the teacher's personal predilections. Even in a one-class situation options can be included and tests can be constructed which allow students choice in how they will be tested (Altman and Politzer, 1971). Unless teachers are trained or retrained, or retrain themselves through thoughtful reading and observation to recognize these potentialities, the promise of the 1980's will fade rapidly. Unless the students, with their needs and wants, become central to our planning and implementation, we will be re-echoing the old adage: the more things change, the more they stay the same.

PART II: THE COGNITIVE MAPPING APPROACH: DISCOVERING THE LEARNING STYLE OF LANGUAGE LEARNERS IN THE 1980's

There is nothing new about the notion that students vary widely in the particular set of aptitudes and abilities which they bring to the learning of a foreign language. It has been folk wisdom among language teachers for many years that some students are especially attentive to the spoken word, while others find the written word compelling; or that one student may be highly receptive to social interaction while others shun such interaction and prefer an impersonal relationship with the teacher and the other students.

What *is* new is the determination of researchers to get beyond casual observation in order to study and describe these individual differences in a systematic way. This interest in individual differences, which has undoubtedly been facilitated by a growing emphasis on cognitive psychology and information processing models, is not restricted to foreign language learning, but is directed toward the entire spectrum of learning activities. In psychology, the attempt to analyze individual differences falls under the rubric "structure of intellect." Work of Guilford (1967) and Carroll (1978) is typical of this approach, which involves two steps:

1. A wide variety of learning tasks are analyzed to isolate the particular cognitive activities involved. Carroll, for instance, mentions such things as association of meaning with sound; search through memory for particular graphemic or acoustic forms, and similar operations which have been invoked by the information-processing theorists to describe verbal behavior. The final result of

this, one hopes, will be a complete catalog of all possible cognitive activities. Any particular learning task can then be described by a sort of "recipe" which states the degree of involvement of each basic activity.

2. Once a catalog of basic cognitive activities exists, it is possible to see how individuals vary in their ability to perform these basic skills. Assessment instruments (generally paper and pencil tests) must be developed. When administered they should reveal a relatively stable profile of strengths and weaknesses on the various activities. This profile represents the individual's *learning style*.

Assessing Learning Styles

A truly dismaying number of cognitive activities, or aspects of activities, has been proposed as basic components to underpin task analysis and learning styles. Some early candidates, put forth in the context of personality theory, were variables such as field dependence/independence; convergent/divergent thinking; and impulsiveness/deliberation. These are all very general, high-level aspects of performance; so general, in fact, that their valid measurement for specific individuals and tasks remains problematic.

Under the label of "Educational Cognitive Style," Hill (1971; 1975) has presented a somewhat more task-oriented taxonomy (see Nunney, 1977, for a synopsis). In this approach, each task is analyzed according to the type of symbolic material (visual linguistic, visual quantitative, auditory linguistic, etc.); cultural determinants of symbolic meaning (self, family, peers); predominant type or modality of inferences (*e.g.*, differences, relations); and, finally, the aspects of memory required. The "Cognitive Preference Inventory," the assessment instrument developed by Hill, assigns a student a status on each variable referred to above, thus providing a "map" or profile of his particular strengths and weaknesses. Compared to the cognitive style variables, the educational cognitive style variables are relatively closely tied to actual task content. This makes the model attractive to those who research teaching and learning in the classroom; Lepke (1977), in fact, has applied it specifically to foreign language learning.

Reinert (1976; 1977) has developed an analysis of cognitive aspects which is narrower than Hill's model, but more directly relevant to foreign language learning. His approach starts out from the common belief that students and tasks invoke the various sensory modalities to differing degrees. Reinert's measuring instrument, called ELSIE (Edmonds Learning Style Identification Exercise), provides for four modal categories: visual image of thing or action; visual image of the printed word; meaning direct from sound; kinesthetic (muscular or emotional) response. The result is a profile of modal biases.

Matching and Remediation

Once learning style profiles are available, how can they be used to improve instruction? There are two basic approaches to utilizing the information: *matching* and *remediation.*

Matching means that instruction is individualized for each student (or group of students with similar learning styles) in such a way that the student has the opportunity of utilizing those cognitive skills in which he or she is particularly strong. This will enable all students to perform the task more effectively, and learning, as a consequence, will be more efficient. This is the approach advocated by Nunney (1977) in general, and by both Lepke (1977) and Reinert (1976) for foreign language learning.

Lepke reports a study in which elementary German students were assigned to either conventional "teacher oriented" or "individualized, self-paced" instructional formats. Afterward, all students received the Cognitive Preference Inventory. An attempt was then made to find the cognitive preferences which discriminated high from low achievers in each format. Interestingly, the most effective discriminators were more social than purely cognitive. In the teacher-oriented class, those students who were sensitive to others and looked to peers and self for authentication, did badly, while the more authority-oriented students did well. Under the individualized regimen this pattern was reversed. Lepke interprets this as evidence that students do better when their cognitive preferences match the instructional format.

Reinert reports several cases where a closer match of instructional activities to the visual/oral bias of a class resulted in improved class performance.

The other way of incorporating learning style information into instruction is *remediation,* an approach advocated by Birckbichler and Omaggio (1978). Rather than tailor instruction to fit a student's particular strengths, the student is assigned special activities for those aspects of the learning task where his or her skills are weak. The descriptions of "learning problems" which they provide are, in fact, couched in terms of general cognitive style variables such as field dependence, impulsiveness, and convergent thinking. It is not clear if these activities are intended to develop the learning skill in question or simply provide enough practice so that even students with weak skills can master the language material.

A detailed knowledge of learning styles will, of course, be most valuable when it is possible to individualize instruction heavily, *e.g.,* by the use of strategy-intensive computerized instruction. But even when such extensive individualizing is not practical, it can still be valuable to know the "average" learning style profile for an entire class, as well as the profile of the instructor. This will allow teachers to become aware of their own biases with respect to mode and style of presentation, and could prevent a drastic mismatch between the instructional method and the style of the "typical" student in the class. Students, once aware of their own weak spots, may be able to consciously plan compensatory working strategies. As Reinert comments, our own learning styles seem so natural, are so automatic, that we are generally unaware of them, and we may be shocked to learn that someone else approaches the same task in a totally different way.

Conclusion

While the difficulties attendant on individualizing instruction may be practical obstacles to the systematic use of cognitive mapping, the greatest theoretical difficulty is the lack of precision in describing the cognitive skills actually involved in the language learning activity. The work of Hosenfeld (1976) should serve as a warning that there are no simple solutions in this area: her interviews with students who were asked to verbalize their thinking while doing textbook exercises reveal that the processing done depends much more on the student's perception of the exercise than on its content or the author's intent.

During the next few years there will, one hopes, be sustained work directed to analyzing and describing the specific cognitive activities involved in foreign language learning. Only in this way will the promise of individualized instruction become a reality.

REFERENCES

Altman, Howard B. and Politzer, Robert L., eds. *Individualizing Foreign Language Instruction. Proceedings of the Stanford Conference.* Rowley, Mass.: Newbury House, 1971.

Birckbichler, D. and Omaggio, A. "Diagnosing and Responding to Individual Learner Needs." *Modern Language Journal*, 1978, pp. 336–45.

Carroll, J. B. "Psychometric Tests as Cognitive Tasks: A New 'Structure of Intellect' " in L. B. Resnick, ed. *The Nature of Intelligence.* Hillsdale, N.J.: Erlbaum, 1978, pp. 27–56.

Coste, Daniel; Courtillon, Janine; Ferenczi, Victor; Martins-Baltar, Michel; and Papo, Eliane. *Un Niveau-Seuil.* Strasbourg: Council of Europe, 1976.

Finocchiaro, Mary. *English as a Second Language: From Theory to Practice.* New Edition. New York: Regents, 1974.

———, and Bonomo, Michael. *The Foreign Language Learner: A Guide for Teachers.* New York: Regents, 1973.

Guilford, J. P. *The Nature of Human Intelligence.* New York: McGraw-Hill, 1967.

Hill, J. *The Educational Sciences.* Bloomfield Hills: Oakland Community College, 1971.

———. "The Educational Science of Memory: Function X Concern X Condition." *Educational Scientist* I (1975), 3–11.

Hosenfeld, C. "Learning About Learning." *Foreign Language Annals* 9 (1976), 117–29.

Lepke, H. "Discovering Student Learning Styles Through Cognitive Style Mapping" in R. Schulz, ed. *Personalizing Foreign Language Instruction: Learning Styles and Teaching Options.* Skokie, Ill.: National Textbook Co., 1977, pp. 15–20.

Llewellyn, R. *At Sunrise: The Rough Music*. New York: Doubleday, 1976.

Nunney, D. "Educational Cognitive Style: A Basis for Personalizing Foreign Language Instruction" in R. Schulz, ed. *Personalizing Foreign Language Instruction: Learning Styles and Teaching Options*. Skokie, Ill: National Textbook Co., 1977, pp. 1–14.

Oskarsson, Mats. *Approaches to Self-Assessment in Foreign Language Learning*. Strasbourg: Council of Europe, 1978.

Ramirez, Alicia D. and Spandel, Victoria. "Occupational English as a Second Language." *Foreign Language Annals* 13:3 (1980), 169–77.

Reinert, H. "One Picture is Worth a Thousand Words? Not Necessarily." *Modern Language Journal* 60 (1976), 160–68.

———. "ELSIE is No Bull! or: On Utilizing Information Concerning Student Learning Strategies" in R. Schulz, ed. *Personalizing Foreign Language Instruction: Learning Styles and Teaching Options*. Skokie, Ill.: National Textbook Co., 1977, 21–28.

Richterich, René and Chancerel, Jean-Louis. *Identifying the Needs of Adults Learning a Foreign Language*. Strasbourg: Council of Europe, 1978.

Rivers, Wilga M. *Speaking in Many Tongues*. Expanded 2nd edition. Rowley, Mass.: Newbury House, 1976.

———. "Educational Goals: The Foreign Language Teacher's Response" in W. C. Born, ed. *The Foreign Language Learner in Today's Classroom Environment*. Middlebury, Vt.: Northeast Conference on the Teaching of Foreign Languages, 1979, pp. 19–51.

———. "Psychology and Linguistics as Bases for Language Pedagogy" in F. M. Grittner, ed. *Learning a Second Language*. 79th Yearbook of the National Society for the Study of Education, Part II. Chicago: University of Chicago Press, 1980.

———. *Teaching Foreign-Language Skills*. Rev. Ed. Chicago: University of Chicago Press, 1981.

———, and Mary S. Temperley. *A Practical Guide to the Teaching of English as a Second Language*. New York: Oxford University Press, 1978.

Trim, John L. M. *Report on Some Possible Lines of Development of an Overall Structure for a European Unit/Credit Scheme for Foreign-Language Learning by Adults*. Strasbourg: Council of Europe, 1977.

———, et al. *Systems Development in Adult Language Learning. A European Unit/Credit System for Modern Language Learning by Adults*. Strasbourg: Council of Europe, 1973.

van Ek, Jan A. *The Threshold Level in a European Unit-Credit System for Modern Language Learning by Adults.* Strasbourg: Council of Europe, 1975.

———. *Waystage.* Strasbourg: Council of Europe, 1977.

Wilkins, David A. *Notional Syllabuses.* Oxford: Oxford University Press, 1976.

ABSTRACT

Effective
Second Language Acquisition:
Insights from Research

STEPHEN D. KRASHEN
University of Southern California

This paper summarizes several current theoretical hypotheses in second language acquisition research, and then discusses their implications for teaching methods and materials. The hypotheses are as follows: (1) The Acquisition-Learning hypothesis: there is a difference between subconsciously *acquiring* language ("picking up" a language) and consciously *learning* a language ("knowing about" a language); (2) The Natural Order hypothesis: grammatical items are acquired in a predictable order; (3) The Monitor hypothesis: conscious grammar knowledge is only available as a Monitor, or editor; (4) The Input hypothesis: we acquire by understanding input that contains structure that is "a bit beyond" our current competence; (5) The Affective Filter hypothesis: the effect of affect is not directly on the LAD. Rather, affective variables may act to block input from the LAD. The most important "implication" of these hypotheses is that acquisition is central, and our pedagogical programs in FL and ESL should focus on supplying students with input that encourages acquisition and on helping the student get input outside of the classroom. Optimal input, it is hypothesized, has the following characteristics: it is comprehensible, it is interesting and/or relevant to the student, it is *not* grammatically sequenced, and it is supplied in great quantities. It should also be presented in a way that will not encourage a strong affective filter or put the student "on the defensive" (Stevick, 1976).

Effective
Second Language Acquisition:
Insights from Research

STEPHEN D. KRASHEN
University of Southern California

The purpose of this paper is to briefly summarize some current theoretical work in second language acquisition, and then to discuss what some of the practical implications of this work are; to show, in other words, how research results can help us encourage effective second language acquisition. Before proceeding, however, there are a few points that should be discussed concerning both theory and practice in second language acquisition.

First, I consider second language acquisition to be a part of theoretical linguistics. It is not to be confused with formal linguistics (syntax, phonology, etc.), but it is theory. It consists of a set of interrelated and testable hypotheses that attempt to predict experimental data. Because it is theory, it is always subject to challenge, always open to counterexample. The summary of theory I present below then, is not a set of immutable laws engraved in stone, but consists of current hypotheses that so far appear to be supported by empirical evidence.

Second, my position is that practice in second language teaching should not be based only on theory. We have made this mistake before. While practice should be in communication with theoretical work, it should also be based on what can be termed "applied linguistics research," defined as studies that attempt to show "what works" and "what doesn't work." It should also be based on the intuitions and insights of experienced teachers. What seems to be happening now, I think, is that all three of these sources are telling teachers similar things; they are all reaching similar conclusions.

A third comment that needs to precede this discussion of "theory to practice" is a point that I have become increasingly more aware of in the last few years. "Practice" is much harder than we linguists thought. It does not simply consist of applying our knowledge of the structure of language directly to teaching materials. What I will present in section II of this paper is a set of hypotheses concerning practice. These hypotheses are an implicit theory of practice, the claim being that methods and materials that follow the principles described in section II will be more successful than those that do not. While some principles may appear obvious to some readers, they were not obvious to me for a long time, and I do not think they are obvious to many practitioners and materials writers.

I. THE RESEARCH: SOME HYPOTHESES ABOUT SECOND LANGUAGE ACQUISITION

I present here those current hypotheses from second language acquisition research that are the most relevant to the discussion of practice that follows. The hypotheses are presented here without supporting evidence, since this evidence has already been described in many other papers and volumes.

The Acquisition-Learning Hypothesis

This hypothesis is perhaps the most fundamental, and has been extremely useful in explaining many experimental findings and everyday phenomena in second language use and acquisition. It states that adults have two different and independent means for "developing ability" in second languages. We can "acquire" and many of us can "learn." *Acquisition* is subconscious, and is the way children develop ability in first languages. The everyday term meaning "to acquire" a language is "to pick up" a language. Acquisition requires meaningful and communicative use of the target language (see discussion of the Input Hypothesis below).

In hypothesizing that adults acquire, I am hypothesizing that the "language acquisition device" does not disappear at puberty.

Adults still have access to the LAD, even though many adults "fossilize," or cease making progress before they reach native-like levels of proficiency in the second language (Selinker, 1972; Selinker and Lamendella, 1978).

Language *learning* is conscious knowledge "about" language. The everyday term for learning is "grammar." Other equivalent terms are "formal knowledge" of a language and "explicit knowledge." We learn by consciously attending to form, by reading about or listening to explanations of rules (deductive), figuring out rules (inductive), and by having our errors corrected.

The Natural Order Hypothesis

This hypothesis states that acquisition, as defined above, occurs in a predictable order. There are some grammatical forms that tend to be acquired early, and some that tend to be acquired late. We know, for example, that among the grammatical morphemes of English, the progressive marker *-ing* is nearly always among the first acquired, while the third person singular marker *-s* is among the last. In first language acquisition, these two may be separated by anywhere from six months to one year (Brown, 1973). The order of acquisition in first language is not quite the same as the order of acquisition in second language, but there are similarities (Krashen, 1977; 1981).

In addition to the predictable order of acquisition of "mature" forms, we also see predictable "transitional" or intermediate stages; the "errors" that acquirers make en route to acquiring correct grammatical form are also quite predictable in both first and second language acquisition. (See Dulay, Burt, and Krashen, forthcoming 1982, Oxford University Press, for a review.)

The Monitor Hypothesis

This hypothesis shows the interrelationship between acquisition and learning. It states that our fluency in second language performance is due to what we have acquired, not what we have learned. Learning is only available as a Monitor, or editor. We "initiate" utterances with our acquired competence, and refer to conscious rules only later, and we use conscious rules to correct the output of the acquired system. This can occur before we speak or write, or it can happen after, which is termed "self-correction."

I have recently posited that three conditions are necessary for successful Monitor use: we need *time* to access conscious knowledge about grammar and apply it to performance; we need to be focused on form, or thinking about correctness (Burt and Dulay, 1978); and we need to know the rule. These conditions are rarely met in the real world (they are met on grammar tests), and, appropriately, our research indicates that Monitor use is light or absent in most conditions involving communication.

We do not wish to avoid Monitor use entirely in communicative performance. Our goal, rather, is *optimal* Monitor use; using conscious knowledge of language to increase formal accuracy when it does not interfere with communication.

The Input Hypothesis

This hypothesis attempts to answer the important question of how we acquire language. It states that a necessary (but not sufficient) condition for language acquisition to occur is that the acquirer *understand* (via hearing or reading) input language that contains structure "a bit beyond" his or her current level of competence. In terms of the Natural Order, if an acquirer is at stage or level i, the input he or she understands should contain $i+1$.

By *understand*, I mean understanding for meaning, and not form, or focusing on the *message*. As Hatch (1978) has pointed out, much second language teaching assumes students should first master forms and then "learn how to use them." This hypothesis presumes that acquisition happens in the opposite way; we first "go for meaning," and acquire structure as a result of understanding the message. This is only possible if we utilize more than our knowledge (subconscious or conscious) of language in understanding, which is clearly the case; we use our knowledge of the world and extra-linguistic information.

It is important to note that while the input needs to contain $i+1$, it does not have to focus exclusively on $i+1$. A most interesting sub-hypothesis of the Input Hypothesis is that if there is enough comprehensible input, enough $i+1$ will be provided to allow for

successful acquisition. We do not, in other words, have to deliberately program in $i+1$. We return to this idea later.

According to the Input Hypothesis, we need not teach speaking
directly. Speech, rather, "emerges" after the acquirer has built up
sufficient competence via input. Generally, acquirers talk when
they are "ready," and there is some individual variation as to when
this "silent period" ends.

Evidence for the Input Hypothesis comes from the work of
Newport, Cross, Brown, Shipley, Smith, and Gleitman, Hatch,
MacNamara, Postovsky, Asher, and Winitz. For more detailed
presentations of my position, see Krashen (1978; 1981 in press).

The Affective Filter

The construct of the Affective Filter comes from Dulay and Burt
(1977), and is a hypothesis about the relationship between "affective variables" and second language acquisition.

The second language acquisition research literature identifies
several affective variables that relate to success in second language
acquisition. Briefly, researchers have concluded that certain personality characteristics predict success, such as self-confidence and
lack of anxiety. Also, certain types of motivation relate to success
in language acquisition, "integrative motivation" being more suitable for some situations and "instrumental" motivation for others.
The chapter by Brown in this volume explores affective factors in
second language acquisition in detail. In a previous paper
(Krashen, in press) I hypothesized that affective variables relate
more directly to acquisition than to learning. Acquirers with more
self-confidence and motivation will interact more and thereby obtain more input for acquisition. Also, their Affective Filters will be
weaker, or lower.

The hypothesis of the Affective Filter states that the effect of
affect is not directly on the Language Acquisition Device. Rather,
affective variables act to block input from the LAD. Two acquirers
receiving equal amounts of comprehensible input may acquire at
different rates depending on Filter strength, which can vary
according to personality, the relationship between the acquirer
and the source of the input, and on the acquisition situation.

I have hypothesized that Filter strength increases markedly at about puberty and that this event is a determinant of child-adult differences in attainment in second language acquisition (Krashen, in press). While the adult Filter is higher than the child's, Filter strength is quite variable, and we can do a great deal to keep the Filter as low as possible.

II. EFFECTIVE SECOND LANGUAGE ACQUISITION

Probably the most important application of the research hypotheses described above concerns the importance of acquisition, as opposed to learning. If acquisition is central, as the Monitor Hypothesis claims, the fundamental goal of pedagogy should be to encourage acquisition. Acquisition occurs, according to the Input Hypothesis, when the acquirer understands input that contains structures a bit beyond his or her current level of competence $(i + 1)$ and when the acquirer's Affective Filter permits the input to "strike deeply" (Stevick, 1976). Effective pedagogical programs, it follows, are those that provide at least two things:

1. comprehensible input, presented under conditions that encourage
2. a low or weak Affective Filter.

To be more specific, I will attempt to list, in this section, some characteristics of input that seems to me to be "optimal" for fostering language acquisition. As explained in the introductory page of this essay, these are not "rules to follow," but are themselves hypotheses. It is predicted that more acquisition will occur when input is provided which has three characteristics.

Characteristics of Optimal Input

Comprehensibility. We cannot acquire when we do not understand the message encoded in the input. Incomprehensible input is simply noise.

If comprehensibility is indeed a necessary condition for language acquisition, several very practical implications emerge. We can tell our beginning students not to waste time listening to the radio in the target language, or to try to eavesdrop on conversations that are clearly over their heads. It predicts, and I think correctly, that children will acquire very little from TV, "educational" or not, if they cannot understand what is going on. It also predicts that, for beginning stages, the second language classroom is potentially very useful for second language acquisition. The outside world is often quite reluctant to supply comprehensible input for adult second language acquirers (Wagner-Gough and Hatch, 1976), while the classroom can supply it quite well. Indeed, this may be its major function.

Interesting/Relevant. For input to be useful for language acquisition, it has to be processed for its meaning. The more interesting and/or relevant it is for the acquirer, the better the chances are that this will happen. A possible generalization is that the input should be so interesting that the acquirer is not even aware that it is encoded in a second language, so focused is he or she on the message.

In traditional terms, this means that even "meaningful" drills and exercises are not enough; only genuinely "communicative" activities will strike "deep" enough.

This is an extremely difficult requirement to meet, and is practically impossible to satisfy in beginning foreign language classes consisting of students with different backgrounds and interests, who often have no real interest in being in the class. It may be somewhat easier to meet in ESL, where students are more instrumentally motivated and need to learn new facts and concepts at the same time that they are acquiring English.

Not grammatically sequenced. In the "theory" portion of this paper, it was hypothesized that input for acquisition need not be focused on $i+1$. Given enough comprehensible input, $i+1$ will be supplied without a deliberate attempt to program it in. There are very good reasons, I think, not even to attempt to sequence. I am claiming, in other words, that grammatical sequencing is not only unnecessary, it is undesirable when the goal is acquisition and not learning.

Here, in brief, are the arguments against grammatical sequencing:

1. Grammatical sequencing assumes that we know the order of acquisition of all structures presented. We only have data on a few structures in a few of the better studied languages, enough to hypothesize that a natural order exists, but not enough to provide detailed information to syllabus designers for different languages. This is, however, the least serious of the criticisms of grammatical sequencing.

2. Not every student will be at the same $i+1$. Due to differences in background and strength of the Affective Filter, it is quite likely that in a given class we will find a significant percentage of students whose $i+1$ is well in advance of the "structure of the day," and a significant percentage whose $i+1$ is well behind. If the Input Hypothesis is correct, sufficient quantities of interesting, comprehensible input should supply enough $i+1$ for everyone, if, in other words, the topic is of some interest and everyone in the class can follow the discussion.

3. Grammatically sequenced syllabi traditionally present structures once. The student is given a certain amount of practice on the imperative form, and may not see it again until the "review" lesson. If the form is not "mastered" the first time around, the review lesson, in most texts, provides little additional help, and the student must wait until next year, when most foreign language courses work through the entire grammar again. Comprehensible, communicative input, on the other hand, provides built-in review; the student need not wait until next year, but is insured of constant exposure to a variety of structures.

4. A grammatically sequenced syllabus will distort any attempt at real communication. If the hidden agenda of a reading selection or discussion is the presentation of a particular structure, it is very hard to make it interesting. "Contextualization," as my colleague Steve Sternfeld has pointed out, is not the answer. The answer is using language to communicate real ideas. When we do this, grammar may take care of itself.

Sufficient quantity. The language teaching profession has seriously underestimated the amount of input it takes to promote even moderate levels of language acquisition. It requires more than a few exercises and more than a brief paragraph of input for the acquirer to fully acquire a new structure. It takes hours of extensive reading for content and/or pleasure, many, many conversations, and not a few exercises or just a handful of reading selections.

The chances of supplying $i + 1$ for a given student are vastly increased when input is supplied in quantity. In the non-sequenced language teaching program, it is unlikely that a single paragraph will contain a given student's $i + 1$. It is quite likely, however, that $i + 1$ will be contained in abundance in a short novel that the student can read for pleasure.

I do not, unfortunately, have definite statistics on just how much input is necessary to reach intermediate and advanced levels of proficiency (for some speculations, see Krashen, forthcoming). What seems evident, however, is that we are not taking full advantage of our potential. The foreign language classroom can be literally filled with comprehensible input; this potential of forty to fifty minutes per day is probably superior to what the outside world can provide the beginner, as we noted earlier. Some very successful newer approaches to language teaching do just this; they provide an input-rich classroom for the entire class period (Asher's Total Physical Response System and Terrell's Natural Approach are good examples), and owe, I think, much of their success to this fact.

We have also not met our potential outside the classroom. In my view, beginning foreign language students should be reading for pleasure a great deal, perhaps for an hour per evening. This means extensive reading, not what Newmark (1971) terms cryptoanalytic decoding of difficult texts. In most cases, the materials are simply not available.

Additional Points

My claim is that comprehensible input that is relevant or interesting to the acquirer, that is not grammatically sequenced, and that is supplied in sufficient quantity will be optimal in encouraging acquisition. These necessary requirements need to be supplemented by two additional characteristics of the teaching program, one focusing on the strength of the Affective Filter and the other on helping the student gain more input outside the classroom.

We should not put the student "on the defensive." The way the input is presented should not strengthen the Affective Filter. It should not, in Stevick's terms, put the student on the defensive. Our goal is not to test, not to reveal weaknesses, but to provide input for further language acquisition.

The profession is beginning to realize this. Indeed, several newer approaches seem to have, as an explicit goal, lowering the Filter (*e.g.* Counseling-Learning, Suggestopedia), and I think they owe much of their apparent success to this emphasis.

A considerable amount has been written on this topic, Stevick's *Memory, Meaning, and Method* being especially clear. I only wish to add this hypothesis: If we are "true" to the Input Hypothesis and its implications, we will do a great deal toward keeping the Filter as low as possible. If we provide relevant, interesting input, and keep our students focused on meaning and not form, if we allow production to "emerge" on its own and not force students to speak before they are ready, we will avoid much of the tension normally seen in language classes. If we avoid excessive error correction, and recognize that there is a natural order of acquisition, we will also avoid needless anxiety. Errors in early stages in Monitor-free performance are inevitable; the "cure," however, is not error correction, but more comprehensible input.

Helping the student obtain input on the outside. Our goal, I think, is to bring students to the point where they can improve on their own from the informal environment. We cannot, nor do we expect to, produce extremely high levels of competence in the classroom alone.

A very desirable goal of pedagogy, especially for second language teaching, is therefore to give beginning and intermediate students the tools they need to converse successfully, despite their less-than-perfect competence, and thereby obtain additional input. These students will have predictable problems in conversation. There will be problems in comprehension; there will be the need for "place holding" in conversation while searching for the right word; there will be the need for opening and closing conversations appropriately and politely. In short, they will need the means for controlling the quality and quantity of the input they receive (Scarcella, unpublished paper). Current research is revealing the gaps second language students have in "conversational competence," and materials writers are giving it more and more attention (Sternfeld, 1979).

What About Learning?

All of the discussion in section II has, up to now, been focused on language acquisition. While the research definitely gives acquisition the central role, it does not imply that learning should be rejected entirely. Learning only needs to be put in its proper place. As I have indicated in several other papers (See *e.g.* Krashen, 1978), learning has two possible roles in the second language teaching program.

First, conscious learning is available as a Monitor. The research indicates that some performers can raise the accuracy of their output a small, but significant degree by conscious Monitoring (for a review see Krashen, forthcoming). When conditions permit, learners can provide some items that they have not yet acquired, but have learned. They can, in a sense, "beat the system" and outperform their acquired competence, using learning as a supplement to acquisition.

For most learners, Monitor use is limited to "easy" rules, rules that are less complex in terms of syntactic operations and/or semantics. While adding these forms does not contribute greatly to communication, they do make written output look more "educated" or more polished.

With a great deal of "structure" teaching, however, it seems to me that we are really teaching linguistics, or "language appreciation." This occurs whenever students learn rules that they cannot utilize in performance. I personally support the study of linguistics as subject-matter, but wish to point out here that teaching complex rules, for all but a few "super Monitor users," is not language teaching but is linguistics. Giving detailed explanations of complex forms, such as the conditional *passé* for first-year French students, certainly falls into this category.

Some Conclusions

According to current theory, language *acquisition* occurs when we are not focused on language, but when we are using language—more specifically, it occurs when we are focused on *understanding* spoken and written messages. The formal study of grammar has value, but it is clearly peripheral. The language teacher is seen not solely as a grammarian, but as someone who can provide input in an environment conducive to acquisition (i.e. with a low filter), can help make the input comprehensible, and provide the student with the tools to get input on his own.

A real problem in language teaching today, in my opinion, is that in many cases the wrong people are teaching. Many of us become language teachers just because we are interested in the structure of language for its own sake, and derive pleasure from learning ("mastering") conscious rules. We enjoy conscious Monitoring, and relive the pleasure of learning each time we use a learned rule successfully! Our problem is that we think all of our students are, or should be, like us.

But most language students are not like us. They get their pleasures elsewhere, and their competence in second language will derive largely from what they acquire. It is our job to help them acquire, to provide them with the comprehensible input they cannot get from the outside world, and to help them develop to the point where they can improve *without* us, in the informal environment. This is our primary responsibility. Building the conscious Monitor is a desirable, but secondary goal.

REFERENCES

Brown, R. 1973. *A First Language*. Cambridge: Harvard Press.

Burt, M. and Dulay, H. "Some Guidelines for the Assessment of Oral Language Proficiency and Dominance." *TESOL Quarterly* 12:2 (June, 1978), pp. 177–92.

Dulay, H. and Burt, M. 1977. "Remarks on Creativity in Language Acquisition." In M. Burt, H. Dulay, and M. Finnochiaro (eds.) *Viewpoints on English as a Second Language*. New York: Regents, pp. 95–126.

————, Burt, M., and Krashen, S. *Language Two*. New York: Oxford University Press. 1982.

Hatch, E. 1978. "Discourse Analysis and Second Language Acquisition." In E. Hatch (ed.) *Second Language Acquisition*. Rowley, MA: Newbury House, pp. 401–435.

Krashen, S. 1977. "Some Issues Relating to the Monitor Model." In H. D. Brown, C. Yorio, and R. Crymes (eds.) *Teaching and Learning English as a Second Language: Trends in Research and Practice. On TESOL '77* Washington, D.C.: TESOL, pp. 144–158.

————. 1978. "Adult Second Language Acquisition and Learning: A Review of Theory and Practice." In R. Gingras (ed.) *Second Language Acquisition and Foreign Language Teaching*. Washington, D.C.: Center for Applied Linguistics, pp. 1–29.

————. 1981. *Second Language Acquisition and Second Language Learning*. Pergamon Press.

————. *Second Language Acquisition in Theory and Practice*. Forthcoming.

————. "Attitude and Aptitude in Relation to Second Language Acquisition and Second Language Learning." In K. Diller (ed.) *Individual Differences and Universals in Language Learning Aptitude*. Rowley, MA: Newbury House, in press.

Newmark, L. D. "A Minimal Language-Teaching Program." In P. Pimsleur and T. Quinn (eds.) *The Psychology of Second Language Learning*. Cambridge, Eng.: Cambridge University Press, 1971, pp. 11–18.

Scarcella, R. "Developing Conversational Competence in a Second Language." Unpublished paper.

Selinker, L. 1972. "Interlanguage." *International Review of Applied Linguistics* 10: pp. 209–231.

————, and Lamendella, J. 1978. "Fossilization in Interlanguage Learning." In C. Blatchford and J. Schachter (eds.) *On TESOL '78: EFL Policies, Programs, Practices*. Washington, D.C.: TESOL, pp. 240–249.

Sternfeld, S. 1979. M.A. Paper, Dept. of Linguistics, University of Southern California.

Stevick, E. 1976. *Memory, Meaning, and Method*. Rowley, MA: Newbury House.

Wagner-Gough, J. and Hatch, E. 1976. "The Importance of Input Data in Second Language Acquisition Studies." *Language Learning* 25: pp. 297–308.

ABSTRACT

Affective Factors in Second Language Learning

H. DOUGLAS BROWN
University of Illinois

The affective domain of human behavior, crucial to the successful learning of a second language, will be the focus of continued research in the 1980's. Self-esteem and inhibition are components of a "language ego" which second language learners develop, and the extent to which that ego is healthy will have a bearing on success in learning a second language. In our transactions—reaching out beyond ourselves to others—optimal levels of empathy and extroversion are necessary. A person's motivation to acquire a language and attitudes toward the language are inextricably bound up in both egocentric and transactional factors of personality. In the 1980's research findings on affective factors will need to be carefully but cautiously applied to teaching materials and methods.

Affective Factors
in Second Language Learning

H. DOUGLAS BROWN
University of Illinois

The process of learning a second language is one that involves a total commitment from the learner. A total physical, intellectual, and emotional response is necessary to successfully send and receive linguistic messages. Language is inextricably bound up in virtually every aspect of human behavior. It is therefore difficult to isolate the component parts of second language acquisition; it is even more difficult to treat one of those components—the affective domain—without reference to other domains, many of which are dealt with in other chapters in this volume. Nevertheless, we can speak of affective, or emotional, factors in second language learning with some degree of precision, as long as that precision presupposes the inter-relationship of the dynamics of human behavior.

It would be easy to claim that of the major facets of human behavior, the affective domain is the most important in governing a person's success in second language learning. After all, human behavior in general is dominated by emotion. And a good deal of research in the past decade points to the crucial nature of affective factors in second language acquisition. It appears at least that *un*successful language learning can be attributed largely to affective blocks of various kinds. It is important, then, to understand those affective factors that either facilitate or prevent second language

Grateful acknowledgment is made to Prentice-Hall, Inc., for permission to adapt for use here portions of chapters six and seven of H. Douglas Brown, *Principles of Language Learning and Teaching* (1980).

learning, and then to learn how such factors may be optimally controlled within learners, enabling them to construct pathways to success.

In the 1980's we will surely learn much more about the affective domain in second language acquisition. We have only begun to discover how such variables as self-esteem and empathy can be defined, let alone applied systematically to our knowledge of the second language acquisition process. The past decade has given us a *global* picture of the affective nature of second language learning. The 1980's will give us a more *specific* picture of the factors of affectivity that influence second language learning. Methods of measurement will become more refined. We will learn more about individual variation across learners. And we will more successfully incorporate research findings into methods and materials.

In examining some selected areas of interest in the pages that follow, we will look principally at what we know now, but we will also attempt to chart some directions for the 1980's.

EGOCENTRIC FACTORS

It could easily be claimed that no cognitive or affective endeavor could be carried out successfully without a considerable degree of self-confidence, knowledge of one's self, and belief in one's own capabilities for that endeavor. Malinowski (1923) noted that all of us have a need for *phatic communion*—defining ourselves and finding acceptance in expressing that self in relation to valued others. Personality development universally involves the growth of a person's concept of self, acceptance of self, and reflection of self as seen in the interaction of self and others.

The worth that persons place upon themselves is commonly referred to as self-esteem. People derive a sense of self-esteem from the accumulation of experiences with themselves and with others, and from assessments of the external world around them.

General, or *global* self-esteem is thought to be relatively stable in a mature adult, and is resistant to change except by active and extended therapy. But since no personality or cognitive trait is predictably stable for all situations and at all times, self-esteem has been categorized into three levels, only the first of which is global self-esteem. *Specific* self-esteem is a second level of self-esteem, referring to one's appraisals of one's self in certain life situations, such as social interaction, work, education, home, or on certain relatively discretely defined traits—intelligence, communicative ability, athletic abilities, or personality traits like gregariousness, empathy, and flexibility. The degree of specific self-esteem one has will vary, depending upon the situation or the trait in question. The third level, *task* self-esteem, relates to particular tasks within specific situations. In the case of second language learning, global self-esteem would refer to classroom contexts in general; specific self-esteem might refer to second language acquisition itself; and task self-esteem might appropriately refer to one's self-evaluation of a particular aspect of the process: speaking, writing, a particular method of learning a second language, or even a special kind of classroom exercise.

Little research has been carried out on the relationship between self-esteem and second language acquisition. Most recently Heyde (1979) studied the effects of the three levels of self-esteem on performance of an oral production task by American college students learning French as a foreign language. She found that all three levels of self-esteem correlated positively with performance on an oral production measure, with the highest correlation occurring between task self-esteem and performance in oral production. Brodkey and Shore (1976) and Gardner and Lambert (1972) both included measures of self-esteem in their studies of success in language learning; both studies concluded that self-esteem is an important variable in second language acquisition.

We do not at this time know the answer to the classic chicken-or-egg question: does high self-esteem cause language success, or does language success cause high self-esteem? Clearly, both are interacting factors. It is difficult to say whether teachers should try to "improve" global self-esteem or simply improve a learner's proficiency and let self-esteem take care of itself. Heyde (1979) found that certain sections of French 101 (sections made up of randomly-assigned students) manifested better oral production and self-esteem scores than other sections—after only eight weeks of instruction. This finding suggests that teachers really can have a positive and influential effect on both the linguistic performance and the emotional well-being of the student. Perhaps those "good" teachers succeeded because they gave optimal attention to linguistic goals *and* to the personhood of their students.

Closely related to, and in some cases subsumed under the notion of self-esteem, is the concept of inhibition. All human beings, in their understanding of themselves, build sets of defenses to protect the ego. Newborn babies have no concept of self; gradually, they learn to identify a self which is distinct from others. Then, in childhood, growing degrees of awareness, responding, and valuing begin to create a system of affective traits identified with self. In adolescence, the physical, emotional, and cognitive changes of the pre-teenager and teenager bring on mounting defensive inhibitions to protect a fragile ego, to ward off ideas, experiences, and feelings that threaten to dismantle the organization of values and beliefs on which appraisals of self-esteem have been founded. The process of building defenses continues on into adulthood. Some persons—those with higher self-esteem and ego strength—are more able to withstand threats to their existence, and thus their defenses are lower. Those with weaker self-esteem maintain walls of inhibition to protect what is self-perceived to be a weak or fragile ego, or a lack of self-confidence in a situation or task.

The human ego encompasses what Guiora et al. (1972a, 1972b) have called the *language ego* to refer to the very personal, egoistic nature of second language acquisition. Meaningful language acquisition involves some degree of identity conflict as the language learner takes on a new identity with his newly acquired competence. An adaptive language ego enables the learner to lower the inhibitions which may impede success. Guiora et al. (1972a) produced one of the few studies on inhibition in relation to second language learning. Claiming that the notion of ego boundaries is relevant to language learning, Guiora designed an experiment using small quantities of alcohol to induce temporary states of less than normal inhibition in an experimental group of subjects. Performance of the alcohol-induced subjects on a pronunciation test in Thai was significantly better than the performance of a control group. Guiora concluded that a direct relationship existed between inhibition (a component of language ego) and pronunciation ability in a second language.

Some have facetiously suggested that the moral to Guiora's alcohol experiment is that we should serve cocktails before foreign language classes! While many students would certainly take delight in such a proposal, the experiments have highlighted a most interesting possibility: that the inhibitions, the defenses, which we place between ourselves and others can prevent us from communicating in a foreign language. Since Guiora's experiments were conducted, a number of giant steps have been taken in foreign language teaching methodology to create methods which reduce these defenses. Current language teaching methods will give rise to methods in the 1980's which will successfully create contexts for meaningful classroom communication such that the interpersonal ego barriers are lowered to pave the way for free, unfettered communication.

Anyone who has learned a foreign language is acutely aware that second language learning really necessitates the making of mistakes. We test out hypotheses about language by trial and many errors; children learning their first language and adults learning a second can only make progress by learning from mistakes. If we never ventured to speak a sentence until we were absolutely certain of its correctness, we would likely never communicate productively at all. But mistakes can be viewed as threats to one's ego. They pose both internal and external threats. Internally, one's critical self and one's performing self can be in conflict: the learner performs something "wrong," and he becomes critical of his own mistakes. Externally, learners perceive others exercising their critical selves, even judging their very person when they blunder in a second language. Earl Stevick (1976) spoke of language learning as involving a number of forms of *alienation*, alienation between the critical me and the performing me, between my native culture and my target culture, between me and my teacher, and between me and my fellow students. This alienation arises from the defenses that we build around ourselves. These defenses do not facilitate learning, rather, they inhibit learning, and their removal therefore can promote language learning, which involves self-exposure to a degree manifested in few other endeavors.

TRANSACTIONAL FACTORS

It is already apparent that our egocentricity cannot be easily differentiated from transactions—the process of reaching out beyond self in communication with others. We are "social animals" whose identity is an integral part of the way we interpret others' responses to us. Language provides us with the means of making the transactions necessary for shaping that identity. Nevertheless, some highly sophisticated methods of language teaching have failed to accomplish the goal of communicativeness in the learner. We have either overlooked the social nature of language, oversimplified it in our reluctance to deal with the complexity of the relation between language and society, or considered socially-oriented problems in language learning as a simple matter of "acculturation." Research and methodology in the 1980's will more carefully address the sociocultural nature of human transactions.

A variety of transactional variables can be related to second language learning: imitation, modeling, identification, empathy, extroversion, aggression, styles of communication, and others. Empathy and extroversion are perhaps the most interesting and promising variables to consider in an effort to understand transactional affectivity in second language learning.

Empathy, like so many personality variables, defies adequate definition. Empathy is commonly thought of as "putting yourself in someone else's shoes"—an appropriate metaphor to express the process of reaching beyond self to the understanding and feeling of what another person is understanding or feeling. It is probably the major factor in the harmonious co-existence of individuals in society. Language—especially nonverbal language—is the primary means of empathizing.

In more sophisticated terms, empathy is usually described as the projection of one's own personality into the personality of another in order to understand that person better. Psychologists generally agree that there are two necessary aspects of the development and exercising of empathy: first, a self-awareness and self-knowledge of one's own feelings, and second, identification with another person or persons (Hogan 1969). In other words, one cannot fully empathize—or know someone else—until one adequately knows oneself.

Communication requires a sophisticated degree of empathy. In order to communicate effectively, one needs to be able to understand the other person's affective and cognitive states; communication breaks down when false presuppositions or assumptions are made about the other person's state. From the very mechanical, syntactic level of language to the most abstract, meaningful level, we assume certain structures of knowledge and certain emotional states in any communicative act. In order to make those assumptions correctly, we need to transcend our own ego boundaries, or, using Guiora's term, to "permeate" our ego boundaries so that we can send and receive messages clearly.

Oral communication is a case where, cognitively at least, it is easier to achieve empathic communication, since there is immediate feedback from the hearer. A misunderstood word, phrase, or idea can be questioned by the hearer, and then rephrased by the speaker until a clear message is interpreted. Written communication requires a special kind of empathy, a "cognitive" empathy in which the writer, without the benefit of immediate feedback from the reader, must communicate ideas by means of a very clear empathic intuition and judgment of the reader's state of mind and structure of knowledge.

So in a second language learning situation the problem of empathy becomes acute. Not only must the learner-speaker correctly identify cognitive and affective sets in the hearer, but he must do so in a language in which he is insecure. To make matters even more complex, the learner-hearer, attempting to comprehend a second language, often discovers that his own states of thought are misinterpreted by a native speaker, and the result is that linguistic, cognitive, and affective information easily passes "in one ear and out the other."

If indeed a high degree of empathy is predictive of success in language learning, it would be invaluable to discover how one could capitalize on that possibility in language teaching. It is one thing to claim to be able to predict success, and quite another matter to cause success by fostering empathy in the language classroom. We would need to determine if empathy is something one can "learn" in the adult years, especially cross-culturally. If so, then it would not be unreasonable to incorporate "empathy-building" in language teaching methods. What kinds of drills and exercises could be devised which require a person to predict or guess another person's response? How worthwhile is it to attempt to organize foreign language classes which operate on a high empathy basis, as in Community Language Learning, where principles of T-group therapy are used to aid the language learning process? These and other questions give rise to some creative issues in language teaching methodology, issues that form an exciting agenda for the 1980's.

Extroversion, and its antithesis, introversion, are also interesting and salient variables in the acquisition of a second language. Again, the construct is beyond adequate definition, but there is general intuitive consensus on what is meant by extroversion. It is a common belief among teachers in general, particularly in Western society, that extroversion is a desirable behavior. The outgoing, amiable, talkative personality tends to be held up as axiomatically ideal. This valuing of extroversion carries over into the language classroom as well. Quiet, reserved personalities are treated as "problems," and language teachers seek ways of encouraging extroversion. The syndrome is further complicated by the tendency in modern language teaching to emphasize speaking in the classroom with all too little emphasis on aural comprehension.

Educational psychologists tend to agree that a child's introversion and extroversion may be "a grossly misleading index of social adjustment" (Ausubel, 1968:413). The role of introversion and extroversion may also be misinterpreted in language classes. Is it indeed true that the "proficiency" of more introverted persons is qualitatively lower than their extroverted counterparts? And do those students whom a teacher assumes to be introverted actually classify as such, if cultural variations are taken fully into account? Teachers are prone to stereotype certain people as introverted or extroverted without regard for cultural differences in behavior. However, a careful analysis of the sociolinguistic expectations of different cultures could significantly change such judgments.

Extroversion is commonly thought to be related to empathy, but such may not be the case. The extroverted person may actually behave in an extroverted manner in order to protect his own ego, with extroverted behavior being symptomatic of defensive barriers and high ego boundaries. At the same time, the introverted, quieter, more reserved person may show high empathy—an intuitive understanding and apprehension of others—and simply be more reserved in the outward and overt expression of empathy.

It is not clear, then, that extroversion or introversion helps or hinders the process of second language acquisition. Naiman, Fröhlich and Stern (1975) found no significant effect for extroversion in characterizing the "good" language learner. It is quite conceivable that extroversion may be a factor in the *speaking* of a foreign language, but not in aural and reading comprehension, or in writing. On a practical level, the facilitating or interfering effects of certain methods which invoke extroversion need to be carefully considered. How effective are methods which incorporate drama, pantomime, humor, role playing, and overt personality exposure? The teacher of the 1980's needs to be acutely aware of the role of kinesic and other nonverbal factors in communication and the degree of extroversion that is optimal within the context of a particular culture and particular communicative situations.

MOTIVATION

Motivation is probably the most frequently used term for explaining the success or failure of virtually any complex task. It is easy to figure that success in a task is due simply to the fact that someone is "motivated." It is easy in second language learning to claim that a learner will be successful with the proper motivation. Such claims are of course not erroneous, for countless studies and experiments in human learning have shown that motivation is a key to learning. But these claims gloss over a detailed understanding of exactly what motivation is, what the subcomponents of motivation are. What does it mean to say that someone is motivated? How do you create, foster, and maintain motivation?

Motivation is commonly thought of as an inner drive, impulse, emotion, or desire that moves one to a particular action. More specifically, humans universally have needs or drives which are more or less innate, yet their intensity is environmentally conditioned. Six desires or needs of human organisms are commonly identified (see Ausubel 1968:368–379) which undergird the construct of motivation: (1) the need for *exploration*, for seeing "the other side of the mountain," for probing the unknown; (2) the need for *manipulation*, for operating—to use Skinner's term—on the environment and causing change; (3) the need for *activity*, for movement and exercise, both physical and mental; (4) the need for *stimulation*, the need to be stimulated by the environment, by other people, or by ideas, thoughts, and feelings; (5) the need for *knowledge*, the need to process and internalize the results of exploration, manipulation, activity, and stimulation, to resolve contradictions, to quest for solutions to problems and for self-consistent systems of knowledge; (6) finally, the need for *ego-enhancement*, for the self to be known and to be accepted and approved of by others.

There are other possible factors that could be listed in accounting for motivation. Maslow (1970) listed hierarchical human needs, from fundamental physical necessities (air, water, food) to higher needs of security, identity, and self-esteem, the fulfillment of which leads to *self-actualization*. Other psychologists have noted further basic needs: achievement, autonomy, affiliation, order, change, endurance, aggression, and other needs. The six needs listed above appear to capture the essence of most general categories of needs, and are especially relevant to second language acquisition.

Examples abound to illustrate the sixfold concept of motivation. Consider the child who is "motivated" to learn to read. He is motivated because certain needs are important to him, perhaps all six of the needs mentioned above, particularly exploration, stimulation, and knowledge. The child who is not motivated to read sees no way in which reading meets the needs which he has. The adult who learns to ski and learns to do so well, no doubt is motivated by a need for exploration and stimulation and activity, and maybe even ego-enhancement. The foreign language leaner who is either intrinically or extrinsically meeting needs in learning the language will be positively motivated to learn. Motivation, as the fulfillment of needs, is closely connected to behavioristic reinforcement theory. Inasmuch as certain needs are being satisfactorily met in a person, reinforcement occurs. If learning to speak a foreign language enhances one's ego, for example, the ego-enhancement is in itself an internal reinforcer of the desired behavior.

Motivation, then, is an inner drive or stimulus which can, like self-esteem, be global, situational, or task-oriented. Learning a foreign language clearly requires some of all three levels of motivation. For example, a learner may possess high "global" motivation but low "task" motivation to perform well on, say, the written mode of the language.

Why do second language learners persevere in their task? Or how can the less intelligent person appeal to inner needs and enhance motivation? How can a language teacher provide extrinsic motivation where intrinsic motivation is lacking? These are questions for the 1980's. Answers to these questions necessitate probing the fundamental nature of human psychology, and such probing will ultimately lead to a deeper and richer understanding of both motivation and the second language learning process in general.

One of the best known studies of motivation in second language learning was carried out by Gardner and Lambert (1972). Over a period of twelve years they extensively studied foreign language learners in Canada, several parts of the United States, and the Philippines, in an effort to determine how attitudinal and motivational factors affect language learning success. Motivation was examined as a factor of a number of different kinds of attitudes. Two different clusters of attitudes divided two basic types of motivation: instrumental and integrative motivation. *Instrumental* motivation refers to motivation to acquire a language as a means for attaining instrumental goals: furthering a career, reading technical material, translation, and so forth. An *integrative* motive is employed when a learner wishes to integrate himself within the culture of the second language group, to identify himself with and become a part of that society. Many of Lambert's studies (see Lambert 1972), and one study by Spolsky (1969), found that integrative motivation generally accompanied higher scores on proficiency tests in a foreign language. The conclusion from these studies was that integrative motivation may indeed be an important requirement for successful language learning. And some teachers and researchers have even gone so far as to claim that integrative motivation is absolutely essential for second language learning.

In recent years evidence has begun to accumulate which challenges such a claim. Lukmani (1972) demonstrated that among Marathi-speaking Indian students learning Engish in India, those with higher *instrumental* motivation scored higher in tests of English proficiency. Kachru (1977) noted that Indian English is but one example of a variety of English*es*, which, especially in Third World countries where English has become an international language, can be acquired very successfully for instrumental reasons alone.

The more recent findings, coupled with Gardner and Lambert's, point out once again that there is no single best means of learning a second language: some learners in some contexts are more successful in learning a language if they are integratively oriented, and others in different contexts benefit from an instrumental orientation. The findings also suggest that the two types of motivation are not necessarily mutually exclusive. Second language learning is rarely motivated by attitudes which are exclusively instrumental or exclusively integrative. Most situations involve a mixture of each type of motivation.

The instrumental/integrative construct helps to put some of the recent interest in affective variables into perspective. It is easy to conclude that second language learning is an emotional activity involving countless affective variables, or to assert that learning a second language involves taking on a new identity or language ego. But the studies of Lukmani and Kachru warn us that, while perhaps some contexts of foreign language learning involve an identity crisis, there are a good many legitimate language learning contexts in which that identity crisis may be minimized, or at least seen as less of a personal affective crisis and more of a cognitive crisis. Does the child in French-speaking Africa, who must learn French in order to succeed in educational settings, and who is quite instrumentally motivated to do so, meet with an identity crisis? Must he take on a "French" identity? It is possible that he does not, just as the child learning English in India tends to learn Indian English as an integral part of his own culture: in some cases, then, the foreign language does not carry with it the heavy affective loading that some have assumed to be characteristic of all language learning contexts.

ATTITUDES

Attitudes, like all aspects of the development of cognition and affect in human beings, develop early in childhood and are the result of parental and peer attitudes, contact with people who are "different" in any number of ways, and interacting affective factors in the human experience. Such attitudes form a part of one's perception of self, of others, and of the culture in which one is living.

Gardner and Lambert's (1972) extensive studies were systematic attempts to examine the effects of attitudes on language learning. According to Gardner and Lambert, the most important of these attitudes is group-specific, the attitude that the learner has toward the members of the cultural group whose language he or she is learning. In their model, a positive attitude toward French Canadians—a desire to understand them, and to empathize with them—will lead to high integrative motivation to learn French in Canada. That attitude is a factor of attitudes toward the learner's own native culture, the degree of ethnocentrism, and the extent to which he or she prefers the native country over the country whose language is being learned. Among the Canadian subjects measures were taken of their attitude toward French-Canadians as distinct from attitudes toward people from France.

John Oller and his colleagues (Oller, Hudson, and Liu, 1977; Chihara and Oller, 1978; Oller, Baca, and Vigil, 1978) conducted several large-scale studies of the relationship between attitudes and language success. They looked at the relationship between Chinese, Japanese, and Mexican students' achievement in English and their attitudes toward self, the native language group, the target language group, their reasons for learning English, and their reasons for traveling to the United States. Each of the three studies yielded slightly differing conclusions, but for the most part, positive attitudes toward self, the native language group, and the target language group enhanced proficiency. There were mixed results on the relative advantages and disadvantages of integrative and instrumental motivation. In one study they found that better proficiency was attained by students who did not want to stay in the United States permanently.

It seems clear that the second language learner benefits from positive attitudes and that negative attitudes may lead to decreased motivation and in all likelihood unsuccessful attainment of proficiency. Yet the teacher needs to be aware that every learner has both positive and negative attitudes. The negative attitudes *can* be changed, often by exposure to reality and by encounters with actual persons from other cultures. Negative attitudes usually emerge either from false stereotyping or from undue ethnocentrism. Teachers can aid in dispelling what are often myths about other cultures, and replace those myths with a realistic understanding of the other culture as something that, although different from one's own, is to be respected and valued.

SOCIOCULTURAL VARIATION

Culture, the context within which persons exist, think, feel, and relate to others, is the collective identity of which each of us is a part. Larson and Smalley (1972:39) described culture as a "blueprint" which

> guides the behavior of people in a community and is incubated in family life. It governs our behavior in groups, makes us sensitive to matters of status, and helps us to know what others expect of us and what will happen if we do not live up to their expectations. Culture helps us to know how far we can go as individuals and what our responsibility is to the group. Different cultures are the underlying structures which make Round community round and Square community square.

Culture establishes for each person a context of cognitive and affective behavior, but we tend to perceive reality strictly within the context of our own culture, a reality which we have "created," not necessarily "objective" reality, if indeed there is any such thing as objectivity in its ultimate sense. "The meaningful universe in which each human being exists is not a universal reality, but a 'category of reality' consisting of selectively organized features considered significant by the society in which he lives" (Condon, 1973:17). Although opportunities for world travel in the 1980's are increasing, there is still a tendency for us to believe that our own reality is the "correct" perception. Perception, though, is always quite subjective. Perception involves the filtering of information even before it is stored in memory, resulting in a selective form of consciousness. What appears to one individual to be an accurate and objective perception of a person, a custom, an idea, is sometimes "jaded," or "stilted," in the view of someone from another culture. Misunderstandings are therefore likely to occur between members of different cultures. We will probably never be able to answer the question of how perception came to be shaped in different ways by different cultural groups; it is another chicken-or-egg question.

It is extremely difficult, with such sociocultural variation at work in human behavior, to adequately define or understand many of the affective variables which have been discussed here. While egocentric, transactional, motivational, and attitudinal factors are universally experienced by human beings, their expression and sources seem to be almost infinitely varied. Americans learn, within the context of American culture, to perceive and give empathy by means of certain nonverbal messages: eye contact, body posture, touching. A Japanese has different ways of expressing empathy—in a more "reserved" fashion—which can easily be read as *non*-empathic by an American. We must therefore be cautious in our eagerness both to categorize affective behavior and to relate affective factors to success in learning a second language. Teachers need to be sensitive to the possible (and probable) affective traits that may cause failure or success in students of a second language. But at the same time we need to be attuned to the critical features of affective expression cross-culturally. Never be too quick to judge a student's motivation, inhibitions, or attitudes. Carefully consider the cross-cultural learning experience that may be involved, particularly in the case of "second"—as opposed to "foreign"—language learning. However, once those caution signals have been heeded, then it behooves the teacher and researcher of the 1980's to attend most rigorously to the affective domain in second language learning.

REFERENCES

Ausubel, David. 1968. *Educational Psychology—A Cognitive View.* New York: Holt, Rinehart & Winston.

Brodkey, Dean, and Shore, Howard. 1976. "Student Personality and Success in an English Language Program." *Language Learning,* 26:153–159.

Brown, H. Douglas. 1980. *Principles of Language Learning and Teaching.* Englewood Cliffs, N.J.: Prentice-Hall, Inc.

Chihara, Tesuro, and Oller, John W. 1978. "Attitudes and Attained Proficiency in EFL: A Sociolinguistic Study of Adult Japanese Speakers." *Language Learning,* 28:55–68.

Condon, E. C. 1973. "Introduction to Culture and General Problems of Cultural Interference in Communication." *Introduction to Cross-Cultural Communication,* No. 1. N.J.: Rutgers University.

Gardner, Robert, and Lambert, Wallace E. 1972. *Attitudes and Motivation in Second Language Learning.* Rowley, MA: Newbury House Publishers.

Guiora, Alexander Z., Beit-Hallami, Benjamin, Brannon, Robert C. L., Dull, Cecilia Y., and Scovel, Thomas. 1972a. "The Effects of Experimentally Induced Changes in Ego States on Pronunciation Ability in Second Language: An Exploratory Study." *Comprehensive Psychiatry,* p. 13.

———, Brannon, Robert C. L., and Dull, Cecilia Y. 1972b. "Empathy and Second Language Learning." *Language Learning,* 22:111–130.

Heyde, Adelaide. 1979. "The Relationship Between Self-Esteem and the Oral Production of a Second Language." Unpublished doctoral dissertation, University of Michigan.

Hogan, Robert. 1969. "Development of an Empathy Scale." *Journal of Consulting and Clinical Psychology,* 33:307–316.

Kachru, Braj. 1976. "Models of English for the Third World: White Man's Linguistic Burden or Language Pragmatics?" *TESOL Quarterly,* 10:221–239.

Lambert, Wallace E. 1972. *Language, Psychology, and Culture: Essays by Wallace E. Lambert.* Stanford, CA: Stanford University Press.

Larson, Donald N., and Smalley, William A. 1972. *Becoming Bilingual: A Guide to Language Learning.* New Canaan, CT: Practical Anthropology.

Lukmani, Yasmeen. 1972. "Motivation to Learn and Language Proficiency." *Language Learning,* 22:261–274.

Malinowski, Bronislaw. 1923. "The Problem of Meaning in Primitive Languages." In Charles K. Ogden and I. A. Richards (eds.), *The Meaning of Meaning*. London: Kegan Paul.

Maslow, Abraham H. 1970. *Motivation and Personality*, 2nd ed. New York: Harper & Row.

Naiman, Neil, Fröhlich, Maria, and Stern, H. H. 1975. *The Good Language Learner*. Toronto: Ontario Institute for Studies in Education.

Oller, John W., Baca, Lori L., and Vigil, Alfredo. 1978. "Attitudes and Attained Proficiency in ESL: A Sociolinguistic Study of Mexican-Americans in the Southwest." *TESOL Quarterly*, 11:173–183.

————, Hudson, A., and Liu, Phyllis F. 1977. "Attitudes and Attained Proficiency in ESL: A Sociolinguistic Study of Native Speakers of Chinese in the United States." *Language Learning*, 27:1–27.

Spolsky, Bernard. 1969. "Attitudinal Aspects of Second Language Learning." *Language Learning*, 19:271–283.

Stevick, Earl. 1976. "English as an Alien Language." In John F. Fanselow and Ruth Crymes (eds.), *On TESOL 76*. Washington, D.C.: TESOL.

ABSTRACT

Communicative Language Teaching and Learning: Toward a Synthesis

H. H. STERN

Ontario Institute for Studies in Education

The concept of communication has been interpreted in language pedagogy in two different ways, but the distinction between them has been largely overlooked, and this has resulted in confusion and misunderstanding. In a linguistic frame of reference communication is analyzed for discourse features, notions, functions, and speech acts. In a psychological or pedagogic frame of reference it is treated non-analytically as an invitation to use language in a real-life context. The chapter outlines the pedagogical consequences of these two approaches. Taking up a suggestion by J. P. B. Allen to combine a functional and experiential approach with a grammatical one, the chapter proposes in its conclusion an extension of Allen's scheme by adding a cultural component. The first three—the grammatical, functional and cultural components—constitute the academic element and the fourth, the experiential-communicative element of proficiency and the language curriculum.

Communicative Language Teaching and Learning: Toward a Synthesis

H. H. STERN

Ontario Institute for Studies in Education

Introduction

During the last few years communication, communicative competence, and communicative language teaching have become key concepts in language pedagogy. A whole set of new terms clustering around the central theme of communication has come into use, such as notions, functions, speech acts and discourse. While these concepts appear to exercise an irresistible attraction in current discussions on language teaching, the wary practitioner must wonder whether "communication" or "notions and functions" are not fast becoming another new bandwagon replacing the audiolingualism and cognitivism of the 1960's and 1970's.

Communicative language teaching (CLT) is not interpreted uniformly. There is indeed a good deal of uncertainty, if not to say, confusion as to what it is all about. For some it is the Council of Europe's *Threshold Level* syllabus (van Ek, 1975; Coste et al., 1976). For others it is just an up-to-date way of talking about audiolingual teaching. For others again, it has the significance of a totally new, more personal and more humane approach to the language class. And this does not exhaust the different interpretations.

Several attempts have already been made to clear up some of the confusions.[1] Yet, a good deal of uncertainty remains, and it is not at all clear how different approaches to CLT hang together, if at all, and how they square with earlier developments such as audiolingualism or the cognitive approach. If CLT is to play a constructive role in the 1980's, its scope and place must be more clearly defined. It is the purpose of this chapter to attempt to do this.

TWO APPROACHES TO CLT

The different developments for which "communication" has become an umbrella term have one thing in common—the intention of bringing language learners into closer contact with the target language community. In spite of this common purpose CLT has become difficult to understand because, basically, two quite different underlying strands, both of which are perfectly legitimate, can claim to offer an approach to communication. But the differences between them have been largely overlooked, and discussions on CLT have switched from one to another, often without recognizing the change in the frame of reference. What is needed is a better understanding of the distinct contribution of these two approaches, one of which we shall call the L approach (L for linguistic) and the other the P approach (P for psychological or pedagogic), and of ways in which they can perhaps be reconciled and indeed combined.

The L approach. Primarily based on recent advances in linguistics, the L approach is linguistic, analytical, and "formal." It is the logical continuation of the efforts made by structural linguists to bear on prevailing views of language pedagogy. Thus the audiolingualism of 1950 to 1965 reflected the structural or taxonomic view of language first formulated by Bloomfield and the structuralists from around 1940.

Since the 1960's the study of language has freed itself more and more from self-imposed restrictions of American linguistics of the previous decades. Semantics, sociolinguistics, ethnomethodology, and pragmatics provided the intellectual climate for a more social or functional, and a less abstract or idealized, view of language. A characteristic expression of this change of outlook was Dell Hymes' development of the concept of communicative competence between 1967 and 1971 (*e.g.*, Hymes, 1970). Created deliberately in

contrast to Chomsky's concept of linguistic competence, it marks
a turning point in American linguistics.

To linguists in Britain and continental Europe, the move away
from a structural view of language was perhaps easier to make than
for American theoretical and applied linguists. British linguistics in
the tradition of Firth and Halliday had always taken a more semantic and more social view of language; it is therefore not surprising
to find that a number of British applied linguists over the last
dozen years or so have played a leading role in the growth of a
social and semantic approach to the study of language and to the
application of this view to language teaching.

The theoretical foundation for much of their work lies partly in
the linguistic philosophy of Austin (1962) and Searle (1969), who
formulated speech act theory, thus relating language use to the
intentions of the interlocutors, and partly in the sociosemantic
view of language expressed by Halliday (e.g., Halliday, 1973). On
this foundation, some linguistics at a few centres across Britain
have been prominent in developing British approaches to CLT.[2]
The focus of attention was the language "syllabus." This British
term is used in a dual sense. It usually refers to the curriculum
content of a language course of study. But it also indicates the
guiding principle for selecting and arranging the content of a language course. According to this point of view, a language syllabus
need not necessarily be based upon a principle of grammatical sequencing but could be founded on thematic, situational or semantic criteria. For example, Wilkins drew up what he called a "notional syllabus," in which "notional" can be regarded as a more
descriptive synonym for the word "semantic" (Wilkins, 1976). In
other words, he attempted to make meaning the main principle of
syllabus design. It is not always recognized that Wilkins' scheme
was put forward quite tentatively as a first sketch and was not intended as a definitive statement.

An outstanding example of the L approach to CLT is the well-
known Council of Europe Project which was initiated in the early
seventies and developed through the participation of a number of
applied linguists from different European countries who co-
operated across the frontiers of Western Europe. This impressive

international undertaking, described in Rivers in this volume, is still in progress. Besides advocating a communicative approach, it is also an attempt to offer to adult language learners across Europe a flexible scheme or "system" of well-defined objectives, that is, a number of graded levels of proficiency in different languages, applying the North American concept of educational "credit" as a useful unit for a system of European adult education.[3]

It should be noted that little has as yet been done to verify by empirical research the schemes and inventories that have appeared. The main concern of the project has been the determination of the linguistic content of language teaching objectives and the definition of stages of proficiency.

The L approach for which the Council of Europe scheme merely serves as a prominent illustration is different from the structural and audiolingual approach of the 1960's in that its emphasis has shifted from sounds and structures to one on meaning, discourse and speech acts. But like earlier approaches the curriculum is based on a linguistic analysis. The expectation is that a careful diagnosis of the language needs of learners can provide directions for a curriculum of notions, functions, and discourse features.[4]

These new principles and the inventories that have emerged are beginning to affect language programs and are likely to be of increasing importance in the coming years. What these new developments mean in terms of classroom teaching and materials is only beginning to emerge. Several attempts have already been made in working out the implications of these challenging ideas for the classroom at the adult and the school level (e.g., Widdowson, 1978).[5]

It should, however, be made clear that most writers are firm in the view that the L approach to CLT has not superseded a structural or grammatical treatment of language in the language class (e.g., Canale and Swain, 1980; Brumfit, forthcoming; Allen, 1980).

The P approach. The other approach to CLT can best be described as experiential. It operates in a psychological and pedagogic framework.

What are the underlying assumptions of this approach? In ordinary language use, that is, when we talk to someone, read a letter or the newspaper, listen to the news on the radio, our attention is usually focused on the message itself, not on its formal linguistic properties. We are involved in communication, and are not paying much attention, if any, to the forms of language or the "code" in which we communicate. This intuitive use of a language for communication is characteristic of the full competence of the native speaker. Indeed, for a native speaker it may be difficult to focus on isolated formal features of the code. Learning to read and write and other aspects of schooling provide to some extent a training in paying attention to language features. But to focus on code and communicate at the same time is difficult, if not entirely impossible. One of the central problems of second language learning that has interested investigators over the past ten years has been this "code-communication dilemma": to what extent should language teaching be a formal study of the language or simply involve the learner in natural communication?

It is a common observation that children learn their first language in the process of communication, and if they are exposed to more than one language in their environment, they become bilingual and even multilingual. By contrast, the experience of learning a second language by first learning the code, as is commonly done in the language class, has been far less successful. This is why empirical research on language learning over the last ten years has begun to study specifically the conditions and processes of free, "natural," or undirected language learning and the outcome of such learning. Particular attention has been paid by some investigators to the interlanguage that develops and by others to the communication strategies of second language learners: how does someone who knows a language imperfectly make himself understood and come to understand his interlocutors?

Two main criticisms that can be leveled against language teaching which emphasizes the formal structure of the language and not communication are: (1) *the Humpty Dumpty effect*—the difficulty of making the structures studied one by one coalesce into a serviceable instrument (it is easier to pull a language apart than to put it together again); and (2) *the transfer problem*—what is learned consciously in the classroom is not automatically applied under conditions of real use (Stern, forthcoming). These deficiencies of classroom instruction have of course been known for a long time, and pedagogical practice has always tried to compensate for them. The direct method of the late nineteenth century was partly an attempt to introduce communicative experiences into the language class. Residence abroad or exposing the learner to the reality of language use by contact with native speakers have been widely recognized as necessary to an advanced knowledge of a second language.

What has characterized recent pedagogical experimentation is communication as an authentic direct experience which is deliberately and systematically built into the curriculum at a very early stage of language learning and not delayed to a "never-never" stage of advanced proficiency. According to this point of view, communication, then, is not a late phase that follows language instruction; it must be part of that instruction. Around 1970 the emphasis on communication as part of pedagogy was, for example, advocated by Jakobovits (1972) in the preface to a seminal experimental study by Sandra Savignon (1972) which pioneered a communicative approach as a technique of language teaching. Around the same time, Wilga Rivers, in a well-known paper entitled "Talking off the Tops of Their Heads," argued that the *skill-getting* practices of the audiolingual method were insufficient. They must be associated with *skill-using* opportunities.

On similar grounds, Dodson (1978), in the context of bilingual schooling in Wales, advocated a combination of medium-oriented (i.e., formal) and message-oriented (i.e., communicative) practice.

French immersion programs in Canada which had first been introduced in the mid-sixties in Montreal and which, since the early 1970's, had spread to other parts of Canada, demonstrate a radical form of a communicative approach to language learning. In an immersion class young children experience the second language in use as a medium of communication and instruction, well before it is studied as a subject. While in immersion a conscious and self-conscious study of the target language is not excluded, the emphasis must be on message, and not on medium. Otherwise, the immersion approach would lose its point. Immersion can therefore be described as the deliberate and artificial creation of a second language environment in which the second language has to be used for communication in the expectation that it provides a near approximation of conditions which a learner would face in the natural target setting.[9]

Other out-of-school ways of placing the learner into the second language environment such as residence abroad and student exchanges are beginning to be considered as a form of CLT. For example, a recent study on student exchanges called *Contact and Communication* (Hanna et al., 1980) has looked at exchanges from this perspective.

In a challenging article, significantly entitled "Nurseries, Streets and Classrooms," Macnamara (1973) made the point that in a language class language learning cannot be successful because the natural *faculté de langage* which operates in the nursery or in the street, that is, in an authentic communicative situation, is not engaged. What Macnamara and others are advocating is that a language is learned when the learner becomes involved in real communication so that he is a user of the language rather than a detached observer who analyzes and rehearses the language for later use.

Language teachers have also begun to explore other ways of encouraging communication within the language classroom without going to the more radical solution of "deschooling" language learning altogether. It is in this light that the so-called humanistic techniques, individualization of instruction, and the manipulation of student-teacher relations have contributed to a communicative approach. If the teacher displays genuine interest in the concerns and activities of his students, real communication is likely to occur; equally so if students can talk to each other and share one another's thoughts and feelings. Community Language Learning, the approach developed by Curran (1976), encourages openness to and acceptance of other members of the group as human beings. In such a socially accepting and totally unthreatening group atmosphere, language ignorance can be frankly admitted and gradually overcome by joint group efforts. In this social climate, the relationship between teacher and student can change in a realistic way over a period of weeks and months from dependence to increasing independence as it would if a language learner would find himself in the target language community. The experience of gradual emancipation can establish for both the teacher and student a satisfying personal bond without which communication cannot be genuine.

Within the language class, too, authentic communication can be encouraged by activities, themes and topics, backed-up by materials, which offer substantive content giving meaning to language learning (Mohan, 1979). In our own curriculum development for French as a second language in the OISE Modern Language Centre, for example, we have created "modules" or independent kits in which the main emphasis is on content, *e.g.*, sports, music, or political issues, so that the learner has something of value to communicate (Stern et al., 1980). These topics are not offered as a pleasant sugar-coating for making language points, but the central focus of the material is on subject matter, not language. The general principle of the P approach to CLT in all these examples is: Take care of the substance, then the language will take care of itself.

Certain consequences for learners arise from the use of these techniques. The language input is less controlled, and offered far less in small and predictable sequences. Consequently, it offers an opportunity for language "acquisition," in the terms proposed by Krashen (1978), i.e., the unconscious absorption of language in real use. It also offers the learner a chance of developing coping techniques that the learner needs when he finds himself alone in the new language environment. He experiences his status as a foreigner vis-à-vis a new language, culture and community, and he can gradually develop a relationship to the target community through contact experiences. Techniques of learning to cope with the language on the spot can thus be deliberately cultivated (Stern, 1980).

THE COMBINATION OF L AND P APPROACHES TO CLT

In the foregoing discussion we have tried to distinguish between the two main approaches to CLT that had evolved over the last decade. The distinction between them can be summarized as follows (Table 1):

TABLE 1. Two Approaches to CLT

L Approach (mainly linguistic)	P Approach (mainly psychological and pedagogic)
• Analytical.	• Non-analytical.
• Based on sociolinguistic and semantic research; speech act and discourse analysis; inventories of "notions and functions."	• Based on psychological and pedagogic considerations ("Nurseries, streets, and classrooms"); global/integrated/naturalistic/experiential/participant.
• Has led (a) to language needs analysis, and (b) to new language curricula; notional-functional syllabuses, languages for special purposes and other communicative syllabuses (e.g. Munby).	• Has led to experiments with de-schooled language learning (immersion, residence), real-life simulation in language class, focus on topic (away from language), human relations approaches in language class.
• New classroom materials. New teaching techniques only to limited extent, e.g. Widdowson, 1978.	• New classroom materials.
• Language input controlled.	• Language input less controlled.
• No new assumptions about learner: mainly cognitive approach.	• New assumptions about learner: Emphasis on opportunities for "acquisition" (e.g. Krashen) and coping techniques (communicative strategies, strategic competence, *autonomie de l'apprenant* (e.g. Holec), hence mixed cognitive and non-cognitive approach.
• Expectation of learner motivation by conscious attention to language needs.	• Motivating learners through contact with native speakers and participating in authentic communication.

As we can now see, the P approach to CLT introduces into the language curriculum an experiential element of communicative contact. While the P approach is a participant one, emphasizing the ego involvement of the learner in communicative activities, the L approach to CLT is more objective and analytical. Thus, the L approach involves deliberate *study* and systematic *practice;* it typically occurs in the language class (but it can of course also occur in the field).[7] The P approach involves the *use* of the language in real-life situations in which the learner interacts with target language speakers (but the classroom of course also provides opportunities for "real" communication).[8]

L and P synthesis. How then can these two approaches to CLT be most effectively combined? Allen (1980) has recently advocated a view of the language curriculum which attempts a synthesis. His curriculum scheme consists of three components or levels—structure, function, and experience—as follows:

TABLE 2   Three Levels of Communicative Competence in Second Language Education (adapted from Allen, 1980)

Levels of Communicative Competence

Level 1	Level 2	Level 3
Structural Focus on language (formal features) (a) Structural control (b) Materials simplified structurally (c) Mainly structural practice	*Functional* Focus on language (discourse features) (a) Discourse control (b) Materials simplified functionally (c) Mainly discourse practice	*Experiential* Focus on the use of language (a) Situational or topical control (b) Authentic language (c) Free practice

Allen emphatically maintains that the three components are different aspects operating simultaneously. They are, therefore, not to be thought of as a sequential curriculum, although he believes that in curriculum development a variable focus offers the possibility of greater or lesser emphasis on structure, function or experience at different stages of a language program.

The conceptualization that Allen's three-level curriculum scheme offers is constructive. It builds up on the structural approach of the 1960's and it combines it with a communicative element which clearly identifies both the L and P approaches to communication. Allen's structural and functional components jointly constitute an analytical view of language learning which operates mainly through cognitive study methods and practice, thus extending and diversifying in a semantic and pragmatic direction what the structural approach of the 1960's had initiated. The third element, the experiential approach, introduces a relatively new aspect of authentic participation in language use in a real-life context which had not previously formed an integral part of most FL curricula.

What for the present is not yet quite clear and should therefore be regarded as a subject for experimentation and research is how to relate these different curriculum components to each other. Should language learning move straight into experiential participation, or should it be preceded by a preparatory period of structural-functional study and practice? (Billy, 1980). Should the organizing principle of study and practice be first structural or could it be, as the Council of Europe's scheme suggests, functional from the beginning? Perhaps with a clearer understanding of the relationships between language study, language practice and language use, between classroom and field, between structural, functional and experiential aspects, it should be possible to gain a better understanding and more effective handling of the relative advantages of ordering these different components.

Let us, in conclusion, draw attention to an omission in most of the recent discussions on CLT. Neither the L nor the P approach to CLT has paid sufficient attention to the sociocultural element in language use. In spite of advances in sociolinguistics and cultural anthropology, culture still remains a somewhat unintegrated appendage to language teaching. Yet, language use, whether it is sociolinguistically analyzed or lived as a personal experience, always operates in a sociocultural context. Therefore to incorporate sociocultural awareness seems to the present writer a necessary expansion of current conceptualizations of CLT.

Modifying Allen's three-level scheme of a language curriculum we can visualize the language curriculum of the 1980's (as well as the interpretation of communicative competence) as fourfold:

Structural aspect	Functional aspect	Sociocultural aspect	Experiential aspect
	Language *study* and *practice*		Language *use* in an authentic context

In other words, we are saying that language teaching can and should approach language learning objectively and analytically through the study and practice of structural, functional and socio-cultural aspects and it should offer opportunities to live the language as a personal experience through direct language use in contact with the target language community.

NOTES

1. For example, Canale and Swain (1979; 1980) have traced the linguistic and sociolinguistic bases of communicative teaching and testing; Brumfit and Johnson (1979) have collected and edited key writings which explain or illustrate major trends of thought and practice. Savignon (1977) has pointed out the significance of communicative competence to a renewal of language pedagogy. A three-level curriculum model which recognizes the need to overcome the ambiguities has been proposed by Allen (1980). This model will be referred to below. The present writer, too, has made a previous attempt to clarify some of the issues in a paper presented at the fifth (1978) AILA Congress in Montreal (Stern, forthcoming).

2. *e.g.*, at the University of Edinburgh, Pit Corder (1973), Patrick Allen and Henry Widdowson (1974); at the University of Lancaster, Christopher Candlin (1976; Candlin et al., 1976); and at the University of Reading, David Wilkins (1976); in London, John Trim, the Director of the Centre for Information on Language Teaching, who as chairman of the Council of Europe Language Project can be described as the chief architect of that project (Trim, 1973; 1978).

3. The publications of the Council Cultural Co-operation of the Council of Europe between 1971 and 1980 provide a record of this novel and ambitious scheme. The *Rüschlikon Symposium* (Gorosch, 1971), the proceedings of a meeting at St. Wolfgang (Committee, etc., 1973) and a state-of-the-art report (CCC 1979) given at Ludwigshafen-am-Rhein, illustrate the growth of this project. For useful references see the two articles by Mary Finocchiaro (1978; 1979), and the article by Alexander in this volume. Recently a British publishing house, Pergamon Press, has re-issued some of the writings of the Council of Europe in a more accessible form with introductions by J. L. Trim.

4. Methods of needs identification were developed by a Swiss scholar, René Richterich (Richterich and Chancerel, 1977). The theory and methodology of language needs analysis and curriculum design have been elaborated by a British linguist, John Munby (1978).

5. *e.g.*, in Germany, a small group of applied linguists, Hans-Eberhard Piepho (*e.g.*, 1974), Christoph Edelhoff and Gerhard Neuner, in the context of teacher inservice education in the State of Hessen, have been particularly vigorous in their efforts to translate the concepts of CLT into materials and methods for use in language teaching at school level (*e.g.*, Bundesarbeitsgemeinschaft 1978). A British example of CLT is the *English in Focus* series of textbooks prepared under the editorship of J. P. B. Allen and H. Widdowson. In Canada, in the province of Quebec, a draft curriculum guide, based on the Council of Europe model, was prepared

by the Ministry of Education for teaching English as a second language and French as a second language in the early school grades (Ministère de l'éducation, 1980, a&b). In the U.S.A., independent of the European CLT approaches, Paulston (1979), and others have produced materials and developed teaching techniques from a communicative point of view.

6. French immersion programmes which began experimentally in Montreal in 1965–6 have become well established in several public school systems across Canada as an alternative form of elementary schooling (less so at the secondary stage). This development has been well documented and evaluated by a variety of studies and reports. See, for example, papers by Swain and Stern in the Georgetown University Round Table, 1978 (Alatis, 1978).

7. Both P and L approaches to language learning in the field, i.e., during exchange visits, are discussed by Stern (1980).

8. One idea for using the language class as a place for communication has been developed by Krumm (forthcoming).

REFERENCES

Alatis, J. A. (ed.). *International Dimensions of Bilingual Education.* Georgetown University Round Table on Languages and Linguistics, 1978. Washington, D.C.: Georgetown University Press, 1978.

Allen, J. P. B. "A Three-Level Curriculum Model for Second Language Education." Keynote address given at the Spring Conference of the OMLTA, April, 1980 (mimeo).

———, and Widdowson, H. G. "Teaching the Communicative Use of English." *IRAL, 12,* 1(1974), 1–21.

Austin, J. L. *How to Do Things with Words.* Cambridge: Harvard University Press, 1962.

Billy, L. "Expérimentation d'une Nouvelle Approche en Immersion." *Canadian Modern Language Review, 36,* 3 (March 1980), 422–433.

Brumfit, C. J. "From Defining to Designing: Communicative Specifications versus Communicative Methodology in Foreign Language Teaching." Presented at Communicative Approaches and Second Language Course Design: A European-American Seminar, Oct. 1979 (forthcoming).

———, and Johnson, K. (eds.) *The Communicative Approach to Language Teaching.* Oxford: Oxford University Press, 1979.

Bundesarbeitsgemeinschaft Englisch an Gesamtschulen. *Kommunikativer Englischunterricht: Prinzipien und Übungstypologie.* Munich: Langenscheidt-Longman, 1978.

Canale, M. and Swain, M. *Communicative Approaches to Second Language Teaching and Testing.* Review and Evaluation Bulletins, *1*, 5. Toronto: Ontario Ministry of Education, 1979.

————, and Swain, M. "Theoretical Bases of Communicative Approaches to Second Language Teaching and Testing." *Applied Linguistics, 1*, 1(Spring 1980), 1–47.

Candlin, C. N. "Communicative Language Teaching and the Debt to Pragmatics." in C. Romeh (ed), *Semantics: Theory and Application*, Georgetown University Monograph Series, *Language and Linguistics*. Washington: Georgetown University Press, 1976, 237–256.

————, Burton, L. J. and Leather, J. L. "Doctors in Casualty: Applying Communicative Competence to Components of Specialist Course Design." *IRAL, 14*, 3, 1976, 245–272.

Committee for Out-of-School Education and Cultural Development. *Symposium on a Unit/Credit System for Modern Languages in Adult Education.* Strasbourg: Council of Europe, 1973.

Corder, S. P. *Introducing Applied Linguistics.* Harmondsworth, Middlesex: Penguin Books, 1973.

Coste, Daniel, Courtillon, Janine, Ferenczi, Victor, Martins-Baltar, Michel, and Papo, Eliane. *Un Niveau-Seuil.* Strasbourg: Council of Europe, 1976.

Council for Cultural Co-operation of the Council of Europe. *A European Unit/Credit System for Modern Language Learning by Adults.* Ludwigshafen-am-Rhein, 7–14 September 1977. Strasbourg: Council of Europe, 1979.

Curran, C. A. *Counseling-Learning in Second Languages.* Apple River, Ill.: Apple River Press, 1976.

Dodson, C. J. "The Independent Evaluator's Report." In Schools Council Committee for Wales, *Bilingual Education in Wales.* London: Evans/Methuen, 5–11, 1978.

Finocchiaro, M. "Notional-Functional Syllabuses: 1978 (Part Three)," *On TESOL '78.* Mexico City, April 4–9, 1978. Washington, D.C.: TESOL, 1978.

————. "The Functional-Notional Syllabus: Promise, Problems, Practices." *English Teaching Forum. 17*, 2 (April 1979), 11–20.

Gorosch, M. *Modern Language Learning in Adult Education* (The Rüschlikon Symposium). Strasbourg: Council of Europe, 1971, mimeo (CCC/EES (71)).

Halliday, M. A. K. *Explorations in the Functions of Language*. London: Arnold, 1973.

Hanna, G., Smith, A. H., McLean, L. D., and Stern, H. H. *Contact and Communication: An Evaluation of Bilingual Student Exchanges*. Toronto: OISE Press, 1980.

Holec, H. "Learner-Centred Communicative Language Teaching: Needs Analysis Revisited." Presented at Communicative Approaches and Second Language Course Design: A European-American Seminar. Oct. 1979 (forthcoming).

Hymes, D. "On Communicative Competence." In Gumperz, J. J. and D. Hymes (eds.) *Directions in Sociolinguistics*. New York: Holt Rinehart and Winston, 1970.

Jakobovits, L. "Preface to Savignon S." (1972).

Krashen, S. "The Monitor Model for Second-Language Acquistion." In R. C. Gingras (ed.) *Second-Language Acquisition and Foreign Language Teaching*. Arlington, Va.: Center for Applied Linguistics, 1978.

Krumm, H. J. "Communicative Processes in the Foreign Language Classroom: Preconditions and Strategies." Presented at the European/American Seminar, Communicative Approaches and Second Language Course Design, Oct. 1979 (forthcoming).

Macnamara, J. "Nurseries, Streets and Classrooms: Some Comparisons and Educations." *The Modern Language Journal*, 57, 5-6, Sept.-Oct. 1973, 250-254.

Ministère de l'Education, Gouvernement du Québec. *Programme d'Étude Primaire: Anglais Langue Seconde*. Quebec: MEQ, 1980a.

Ministère de l'Education, Gouvernement du Québec. *Programme d'Étude Primaire: Français Langue Seconde*. Quebec: MEQ, 1980b.

Mohan, B. A. "Relating Language Teaching and Content Teaching." *TESOL Quarterly*, 13, 2, June 1979, 171-182.

Munby, J. *Communicative Syllabus Design*. London: Cambridge University Press, 1978.

Paulston, C. B. "Communicative Competence and Notional/Functional Syllabuses." Presented at Communicative Approaches and Second Language Course Design: A European-American Seminar, October, 1979.

Piepho, H. E. *Kommunikative Kompetenz als Übergeordnetes Lernziel im Englischunterricht*. Limburg: Frankonius-Verlag, 1974.

Richterich, R. and Chancerel, J. L. *Identifying the Needs of Adults Learning a Foreign Language*. Strasbourg: CCC/Council of Europe, 1977.

Rivers, W. M. *Speaking in Many Tongues: Essays in Foreign Language Teaching*. Rowley, Mass.: Newbury House (second edition, 1976).

Savignon, S. J. *Communicative Competence: An Experiment in Foreign Language Teaching*. Philadelphia: Centre for Curriculum Development, 1972.

──────. "Communicative Competence: Theory and Classroom Practice." *SPEAQ Journal, 1*, 3 (Fall, 1977) also in Phillips, M. P. and Arvizu, S. F. (eds.) *Bilingual Education for the Classroom Practitioner*. Rowley, Mass.: Newbury House Publishers (forthcoming).

Searle, J. R. *Speech Acts: an Essay in the Philosophy of Language*. Cambridge: Cambridge University Press, 1969.

Stern, H. H. "The Formal-Functional Distinction in Language Pedagogy: A Conceptual Clarification." Proceedings of the Fifth International Congress of Applied Linguistics, Montreal 1978 (forthcoming).

──────. "Language Learning on the Spot." *Canadian Modern Language Review, 36*, 1980.

──────, et al. *Module Making: A Study in the Development and Evaluation of Learning Materials for French as a Second Language*. Toronto: Ministry of Education of Ontario, 1980.

Trim, J. L. M. *Draft Outline of a European Units/Credits System for Modern Languages Learning by Adults*. Committee for Out-of-School Education and Cultural Development, Strasbourg: Council of Europe, 1973 mimeo (CCC/EES (73) 9).

──────. *Some Possible Lines of Development of an Overall Structure for a European Unit/Credit Scheme for Foreign Language Learning by Adults*. Strasbourg: Council of Europe, 1978.

van Ek, J. A. *The Threshold Level in a European Unit/Credit System for Modern Language Learning by Adults*. Strasbourg: Council of Europe, 1975.

Widdowson, H. G. *Teaching Language as Communication*. Oxford: Oxford University Press, 1978.

Wilkins, D. A. *Notional Syllabuses: A Taxonomy and its Relevance to Foreign Language Curriculum Development*. London: Oxford University Press, 1976.

ABSTRACT

Learning for Communication: Practical Considerations

VIRGINIA FRENCH ALLEN

Seven distinctive features of language learning in the 1980's are discussed: more peer-mediated instruction; more hypothesis-testing; more notional-functional exercises; more content from other fields; more vocabulary learning; more work on listening; more systematic transitions to natural tests from samples in L_2 materials.

Such differences between today's classes and those of earlier times are more evident in ESL programs located in English-speaking communities than in EFL overseas. But the remainder of this decade should witness some practical re-thinking of goals and expectations in EFL and foreign language programs throughout the world. One result may be greater flexibility in defining *communication*. A new view of priorities could conflict with demands which have grown out of the concerns of the 1970's for culturally authentic, socially appropriate usage.

Learning for Communication: Practical Considerations

VIRGINIA FRENCH ALLEN

Throughout the 1970's, professional journals, newsletters and conferences proposed applications of linguistic and psychological theory. How is theory likely to be applied in second language classrooms in the years ahead?

Answers will vary, of course. What the learner does will depend greatly on who and where the teacher is. (A Thai teacher of English in Bangkok? An American teaching ESL in Boston? A Colombian teaching Spanish in Chicago—or English in Bogotá?)

Instructional policies will also depend on who the learners are. (Graduate students? Third graders learning French?) Moreover, in programs that focus on communication, much of what the students do will be conditioned by answers to the question: With whom are they supposed to be learning to communicate? (Is the language going to be used with native speakers, or mainly with others who have learned it as a second language? Will speakers of Language A need Language B mostly for use with speakers of Languages C, D and E?)

How answers to such questions may affect language learning will be considered later in this chapter. But first, some general predictions. Recent contacts with second-language teachers throughout the world suggest we are going to see—

1. more use of peer teaching and small-group activities
2. more language-stretching and hypothesis-testing
3. more notional-functional activities within a prevailing structural framework

4. more content from other subject-matter fields in the second-language class
5. more attention to vocabulary learning
6. more emphasis on listening comprehension
7. more systematic treatment of differences between actual speech and the samples found in L_2 materials

As the years pass, teachers will be finding new and better ways of getting students to help each other learn. Where a foreign language is being learned by Americans, the trend toward peer teaching is speeded by the student demand for involvement and self-direction. Where ESL is taught in schools that also teach English to native speakers, the 1980's will continue to see more designing of instructional tasks that can benefit both partners—the second-language learner and the native speaker whose English still needs work.

In the classrooms of the 1980's, learners have more opportunities to test their own hypotheses about the target language, and to find out how far their growing knowledge can be made to stretch. Reflecting the emphasis on hypothesis-testing that has marked language acquisition research in the 1970's, classroom activities frequently encourage creative use of the language by students.

This happens not only in peer-mediated instruction and role-playing activities, but also in notional-functional exercises like those described by Mary Finocchiaro in ON TESOL '78 (p. 31). Working from a list of real-life uses of language, and phrased in general terms (apologizing, interrupting, praising, complaining . . .), student pairs compose their own dialogs, then consult the teacher before presenting them to the class. In contrast to past decades (especially the 1950's and 1960's, but often the 1970's, too) when "Accuracy Before Fluency" was the slogan in language teaching, the coming years will encourage students to search for ways of expressing their own thoughts. In most programs, however, this will happen only during part of the class period; in other parts there will continue to be systematic development of linguistic competence. Generally, teachers will opt for a syllabus organized on "a syntactic basis, bargaining with a spiralling sequence of notions . . ." (Brumfit, 1979; p. 115).

As we move ahead, vocabulary is likely to receive more attention than in the recent past. It was once quite common in ESL programs of two decades ago, to see a class hour go by with little perceptible expansion of vocabulary. Often the stepchild status of vocabulary teaching was condoned in the belief that words could wait until the grammar had been mastered. But the students themselves have always intuitively felt they needed "more words"; and research (*e.g.*, Johansson, 1978) is beginning to show that their intuition was not far wrong.

In the 1980's, students are being given more responsibility for vocabulary learning. The teacher helps them develop their own individual mnemonic strategies. More time will be spent on context clues and the use of dictionaries.

There may also be a revival of interest in lists designed to show which words are more useful in the widest range of communication situations. In the summer of 1979 (the last year of his life), I. A. Richards was invited to the People's Republic of China to spend several weeks introducing Basic English. Possibly that visit foreshadowed a growing concern for high-mileage vehicles of expression in the 1980's, wherever second languages are taught.

At any rate, more vigorous treatment of vocabulary will be needed in the coming years in programs where students are communicating through peer teaching, role-playing, do-it-yourself dialogs along notional-functional lines, and other forms of language-stretching.

There is a further reason to anticipate more attention to vocabulary: the expectation that content from other fields—one manifestation of English for Special Purposes (ESP)—will play a role. In ESL, particularly, it is already less easy than it once was to find programs virtually devoid of informational content. There are now more classes in which students' general knowledge is growing along with their grasp of the second language. As the students confront those other realms of discourse, vocabulary learning is bound to take place.

As an object of study, pronunciation will receive less emphasis in many programs during the coming years, but there will be more work on listening. During the past twenty years there has been widespread disillusionment over the failure of electronic devices to perform the promised miracles, as Freudenstein illustrates in his chapter in this volume. In reaction against language labs, many teachers overlooked the possibilities offered by a single inexpensive machine, set up in the classroom for what machines do best: helping improve listening comprehension. In the 1980's, there is reason to hope, more teachers will find the cassette player as indispensable as the blackboard.

There will continue to be a greater range of activities that require *attentive* listening—where students are required to show, either verbally or non-verbally, that they understand what they hear. Recordings provide one model for listening. Tapes provide exposure to background sound (corresponding in function to the background music so ubiquitous in American life). Teachers who surround their students with *visual* realia on walls and bulletin boards are beginning to surround them with *aural* realia as well. There are already programs in which recorded songs, commercials and other specially selected samples of language from the world outside the classroom are being played again and again, before and after each class period, simulating the experiences in environmental listening that children have while acquiring their mother tongue.

When actual speech, with its many simultaneous difficulties, is imported into the classroom for listening comprehension, there are problems, of course. As we move into the 1980's, teachers are becoming more skillful in guiding students through natural texts. There is more use of transitional exercises in which dialogs from the textbook, for example, are rendered closer and closer to real-life conversation through a series of progressively more difficult stages. This requires more expertise, more understanding of differences between natural and edited speech, than most teachers have today. Many teachers continue to steer clear of dialogs that have not been tailored to the students' grasp of grammar and vocabulary.

When *natural texts* are discussed (as, for example, by Ruth Crymes in *ON TESOL '78*) it is usually assumed that the texts come out of situations where native speakers are communicating with other native speakers. A related assumption is that the prime goal of any and every communication-based program is ability to engage in face-to-face conversation with native speakers. In the coming years, however, we may see communication redefined. In some programs (especially where English is taught as a Foreign, rather than a Second, Language) it is recognized that communication should mainly involve understanding lectures by visiting experts, and understanding textbooks. In such programs, relatively little work may be done on skills needed for one-to-one interaction with native speakers. True, there have always been courses in which those skills have been given little attention; but wherever programs have been oriented toward *communication*, it has generally been taken for granted that communication means near-native ability to function in conversations.

Broadening definitions of communication are especially predictable in EFL, because it is becoming increasingly clear that English in countless places is serving purposes other than interaction with those for whom it is the mother tongue. One such place is Eastern Europe. In the U.S.S.R., according to Harold Allen, "more than 1,100,000 people . . . were studying English" during a recent year (*ON TESOL '78;* p. 65)—with presumably little expectation of ever meeting a native speaker. How many more millions around the world are learning a second language for use far from its own cultural context? In the 1980's, instructional goals may be more likely to take that question into account.

If stated goals are brought into line with more realistic expectations, the future may witness an interesting conflict, particularly in TESOL. The priorities of programs focusing on English for *international* communication may conflict with demands which have developed in recent years—demands placed upon teachers by the concerns of the 1970's for culturally authentic usage. In the 1970's, teachers were told that their work was far from done when students had achieved "grammatical correctness"; there was still the need to teach "when one of many notionally parallel but structurally different speech forms is [culturally] appropriate. . . ." (Long, 1975; p. 212).

Furthermore, in recent years teachers have been urged to

"learn as much as possible about each student's particular communication style in order to provide the choice of strategies most suited to him or her" and to "provide a range of strategical expressions which the student might not use personally but would have to recognize when they occur in the speech of others." (DiPietro, 1978; p. 151). In many programs during the 1980's, there are and may continue to be practical reasons why teachers cannot accept such responsibilities.

It is common knowledge that English instruction is increasingly widespread, and that people who teach it in most parts of the globe have themselves learned it from non-native speakers. This condition will not improve in the years to come.

It is less commonly known that foreign languages are being taught to increasing numbers of Americans under unprecedented circumstances (*e.g.*, as a required subject in business schools.)

We are likely to see movement away from the traditional view that a little language-learning is worse than none—that anything less than "mastery" is not worth bothering with. In the future, a working knowledge may be considered better than no knowledge at all. Programs now measured in terms of numbers achieving near-native control of the target language may take a more modest view of their goal; they may publicly aim at teaching people enough to permit *entry* into situations where the language is used.

What, then, are we likely to find in classrooms during the rest of the decade? Much will depend—as is always true in communications—on the *who, where, whom* and *why*. Still, as I have suggested above, there is basis for predicting the use of many procedures that teachers would not have tried a decade or two ago—procedures inspired in large part by research done in the 1970's.

REFERENCES

Allen, Harold B. 1978. "The Teaching of English as a Second Language and U.S. Foreign Policy." *On TESOL '78*, 65.

Brumfit, Christopher J. 1979. "Notional Syllabuses—A Reassessment." *System*, 7, 115.

Crymes, Ruth. 1978. "The Developing Art of TESOL: Theory and Practice." *On TESOL '78,* 3–9.

DiPietro, Robert J. 1978. "Verbal Strategies, Script Theory and Conversational Performances in ESL." *On TESOL '78,* 151.

Finocchiaro, Mary 1978. "Notional-Functional Syllabuses." *On TESOL '78,* 24–32.

Johansson, Stig. 1978. *Studies of Error Gravity.* Reviewed by Joel Walz, *TESOL Quarterly* XIV, 1 (March 1980), 98–100.

Long, Michael H. 1975. "Group Work and Communicative Competence in the ESOL Classroom." *On TESOL '75,* 212.

President's Commission on Foreign Languages and International Studies. *TESOL Newsletter XIV,* 2. (April 1980), p. 4.

ABSTRACT

The Evaluation of Second Language Learning

REBECCA M. VALETTE
Boston College

This chapter explores the directions which second language evaluation has taken over the past thirty years in the United States. First, the goals and objectives of language instruction are presented within the framework of the Valette-Disick taxonomy. Then, suggestions are made for evaluating the students' mastery of the elements of language via both discrete-point and integrative test items. Finally, three ways of evaluating communication skills are outlined: tests of the four skills, tests of global language proficiency, and self-assessment techniques. The challenge of the 1980's is to build on the research of the 1970's to develop more efficient and more effective testing instruments for use in the schools.

The Evaluation of Second Language Learning

REBECCA M. VALETTE
Boston College

Over the past twenty years, the theory and practice of second language testing has undergone considerable evolution in the United States. In the pre-Sputnik days, most second language teachers were using global techniques such as translations, résumés, compositions and dictations. Although objective tests in foreign languages had been developed experimentally in the 1920's, it was not until the 1960's that such tests were widely accepted and employed. With the support of public funds, standardized language tests were constructed which provided separate evaluation of the four language skills of listening, speaking, reading and writing, with emphasis on measuring the students' control of specific elements of language, such as phonemes, vocabulary, and grammatical forms. It was thought that by measuring a broad sampling of discrete points, the examiner could determine general language proficiency. The use of multiple-choice items and standardized scoring techniques permitted such tests to attain high levels of reliability and objectivity. In the 1970's, as psycho- and sociolinguists began focusing on the role of language in a communicative context, it became clear that global language tests also had an important role in second language evaluation and that such tests could be scored with a reasonable degree of objectivity.

In recent years, much of the renewed interest in evaluation has come from the areas of bilingual education and English as a Second Language (ESL). Consequently, the direction of language testing has moved beyond the evaluation of elementary and intermediate levels of language acquisition attained by American students of French, Spanish, German and the other commonly-taught foreign languages, and is focusing more heavily on the high intermediate and advanced levels of language skill exhibited by foreign students studying at American universities, and by the students of all ages in bilingual and ESL programs throughout the United States. This broadened range of testing concerns is sure to influence the directions of second language evaluation in the 1980's.

CLASSIFYING LANGUAGE GOALS AND OBJECTIVES

Before one can discuss the evaluation of second language learning, it is necessary to clarify precisely what is to be tested. The Valette-Disick taxonomy in Figure 1, provides one way of showing the interrelationships between the simplest language goals (Stage 1) and the most complex (Stage 5).

The term "stage" is used rather than "level," for within each stage exist various levels of proficiency. It should also be recognized that second language learning is not a simple sequential progression from one stage to the next on the taxonomy. In fact, it is a highly complex activity which varies from individual to individual and in which there is a constant interplay among the five taxonomic stages, or at least among the first four.

In the traditional classroom environment, students first learn the sounds and spelling system (Stage 1) and the vocabulary and forms (Stage 2) of the target language, and then practice using these elements in guided drills and exercises (Stage 3). Activities of these types can be equated with what Krashen calls "language learning" (Krashen, 1978) and what Rivers refers to as "skill-getting" (Rivers, 1975).

In an immersion environment, learners from the outset are forced to use the target language for communication (Stage 4). As their comprehension increases, their speech also progresses from monosyllabic utterances at the outset to more complex and fluent output. This form of language learning corresponds to Krashen's "language acquisition" and Rivers' "skill-using."

Many second language learners begin their study at the lower

FIGURE 1   Valette-Disick Taxonomy of Second-Language Learning

Stage	Internal Behavior	External Behavior
1. *Mechanical Skills:* The student performs via rote memory, rather than by understanding.	*Perception:* The student perceives differences between two or more sounds or letters or gestures and makes distinctions between them.	*Reproduction:* The student imitates foreign language speech, writing, gestures, songs, and proverbs.
2. *Knowledge:* The student demonstrates knowledge of facts, rules, and data related to foreign language learning.	*Recognition:* The student shows he recognizes facts he has learned by answering true-false and multiple-choice questions.	*Recall:* The student demonstrates he remembers the information taught by answering fill-in or short-answer questions.
3. *Transfer:* The student uses his knowledge in new situations.	*Reception:* The student understands recombined oral or written passages or quotations not encountered previously.	*Application:* The student speaks or writes in a guided drill situation or participates in cultural simulations.
4. *Communication:* The student uses the foreign language and culture as natural vehicles for communication.	*Comprehension:* The student understands a foreign language message or a cultural signal containing unfamiliar material in an unfamiliar situation.	*Self-Expression:* The student uses the foreign language to express his personal thoughts orally or in writing. He uses gestures as part of his expression.
5. *Criticism:* The student analyzes or evaluates the foreign language or carries out original research.	*Analysis:* The student breaks down language or a literary passage to its essential elements of style, tone, theme, and so forth. *Evaluation:* The student evaluates and judges the appropriateness and effectiveness of a language sample or literary passage.	*Synthesis:* The student carries out original research or individual study or creates a plan for such a project.

(Valette and Disick, 12: p. 41)

stages of the taxonomy and then progress to the stage of communication (Stage 4). On the other hand, students in an immersion environment often find it most helpful to receive more formal instruction about the elements of language: pronunciation practice (Stage 1), study of vocabulary and grammatical patterns (Stage 2), and guided language practice through carefully sequenced exercises and activities (Stage 3).

In preparing second language tests, the test writer must decide which stages of the taxonomy are to be covered. If the emphasis of a course is on pronunciation, spelling, knowledge of specific lexicon, or manipulation of grammatical structures, the corresponding tests will most likely be made up of "discrete-point items" which test one element at a time and which lend themselves to objective scoring. It is also possible, however, to test the mastery of elements of language in natural contexts and to require the students to use full sentences, and perhaps even more than one language skill (*e.g.*, written answers to oral questions). Test items of this latter type are called "integrative items" for they bring together several discrete points in one question. Integrative items at Stages 1, 2 and 3 elicit specific answers from the students and lend themselves to objective scoring.

Where the focus of a course is on communication ability, the corresponding test items will be integrative in nature and will also require realistic language use. Oller has written widely about "pragmatic tests" which he defines as "any procedure or task that causes the learner to process sequences of elements in a language that conform to the normal contextual constraints of that language and which requires the learner to relate sequences of linguistic elements via pragmatic mappings to extralinguistic context" (Oller, 1979).

In advanced language courses, where the emphasis is on stylistics, linguistic analysis, creative writing, free composition or public speaking, the corresponding tests will require the cognitive skills of analysis, synthesis and evaluation. In tests of this sort, there should be little difference between students for whom the target language is a first or second language: it is assumed that students can communicate readily in the language under study.

EVALUATING MASTERY OF THE ELEMENTS OF LANGUAGE

Although it is now clear to second language educators that a mastery of the elements of a language does not of itself imply or lead to the ability to use that language for communication, there are nonetheless times when the language teacher needs to determine which sounds, words or syntactic patterns are still causing the students problems.

A. Discrete-Point Items

There is a substantial literature available on the construction of discrete-point items for second language tests. Interested readers will want to consult the handbooks by Clark (1972), Harris (1969), Heaton (1975), Lado (1961), and Valette (1977).

In the 1960's, the challenge to test writers was to develop items which would use correct language in natural sentence contexts. Here are several examples of how discrete items were improved:

POOR item: wrong forms presented to students
Je m' _____ Jeanne.   a. appelle   b. appeles
c. apelle
(My name is Jeanne.)
ACCEPTABLE item: all forms are "real French" but only one is appropriate
Je m' _____ Jeanne.   a. appelle   b. appelles   c. appeler

POOR item: no context
present: I go   past: I _____   (went)
ACCEPTABLE item: natural sentence context
Every day I *go* shopping. Yesterday I _____ shopping with Tom.

POOR item: unnatural mix of languages
Quiero que Pablo _____ (to come) conmigo.   (venga)

ACCEPTABLE item: languages kept separate
I want Pablo to come with me.
Quiero que Pablo —————— conmigo.   (venga)

POOR item: artificial introduction of cue word
Monday night Anne —————— (come) home late.   (came)
ACCEPTABLE item: cue word introduced naturally
When did Anne come home?
She —————— home at one.   (came)

The research of the 1970's has shown that students learn a language more effectively and remember it longer if it is presented in a meaningful manner. Although the teaching materials of the past twenty years have for the most part practiced new forms of grammar and vocabulary in whole sentences, the context of the drill or exercise as a whole was more often than not a meaningless jumble of unrelated statements. In fact many published drills read like excerpts from the Theater of the Absurd or examples of surrealist poetry. It is not surprising that the test items of this period have often reflected this same absence of meaningful context. Student performance on tests was usually reduced to mere manipulation of forms and identification of words and structures.

The challenge of the 1980's will be to construct sets of discrete items which retain the reliability of their predecessors and which correspond more closely to actual language usage. Meaningful contexts can be created through imaginary situations or by means of pictures.

GOOD item: all sentences are contextually meaningful
Susan is leaving for Australia tomorrow. Say that she did all the following things:

1. Did she pack her suit-   (She packed her suitcase to-
   case today?   day.)
2. Did she buy her ticket?   (She bought her ticket.)
3. Did she get her pass-   (She got her passport.)
   port?

BETTER item: Student response depends on the context
Susan is leaving for Australia tomorrow. Look at the picture and say whether or not she did the following things today.

1. Did she pack her suit-case yet?	(She did not pack her suit-case yet.)
2. Did she find her pass-port?	(She found her passport.)
3. Did she pick up her ticket?	(She picked up her ticket.)

Although the two above items test only the students' control of past tense forms, they are much more valid items than those presented earlier because they correspond to a meaningful, though somewhat contrived, use of the second language.

B. Integrative Test Items

Integrative test items involve more than one vocabulary point or structure and may call on two different language skills. In the 1960's, such items were characterized as "hybrid" and contrasted with the "pure" discrete-point items which were then the focus of the test writers. By the mid 1970's, however, integrative items were frequently used to test mastery of elements of language, especially in classroom quizzes. As in the case of discrete-point items, such tests had only one set of correct responses and could be scored reliably and rapidly.

One widely-used integrative item type is that in which the teacher reads the cues or questions while the students write out the responses. Most of the drills and exercises in current teaching materials can thus be easily transformed into classroom quizzes. Since the teacher reads the items aloud and then pauses as the students write the responses, the entire class finishes the quiz at the same time. As with discrete-point items, test questions of this sort are most valid when they incorporate the target language into a meaningful context.

Integrative item types may also be based on pictures. Students hear or read a series of statements and match each one with an appropriate picture. Here is an example of such a set of items taken from a new secondary school textbook series (Valette and Valette, 1976):

FIGURE 2

2. Situations *(24 points)*

Look at the four pictures, A, B, C, and D. Each one depicts a different situation. You will hear 12 sentences, each one read twice. After you have heard each sentence the second time, decide which picture is most appropriate. Next to the item number, write the letter – A, B, C, or D – of the picture you have chosen.

Modèle: Cette voiture ne marche pas.

Modèle: ___c___
1. _____
2. _____
3. _____
4. _____
5. _____
6. _____
7. _____
8. _____
9. _____
10. _____
11. _____
12. _____

1. Mon frère est mécanicien.
2. Je veux être médecin.
3. Je suis content d'aller en Afrique.
4. Monsieur Moreau est commerçant.
5. Je suis triste que mes amis partent.
6. Il faut que j'aille dans ce magasin.
7. Il est possible que Michèle soit malade.
8. Il faut que vous restiez une semaine au lit.
9. Qu'est-ce que vous voulez que nous achetions ici?
10. Je souhaite qu'ils passent de bonnes vacances.
11. Si j'étais toi, je vendrais cette voiture.
12. Voyageriez-vous si vous aviez de l'argent?

(Valette and Valette, 10:19,23)

Simple contrived translation tasks also function as integrative items. In translating short sentences to or from their native language, students demonstrate their control over several language features within a single sentence. ("Real" translation tasks, based on authentic samples of language, would be considered tests of communicative skills.)

EVALUATING COMMUNICATION SKILLS

At Stage 4 of the taxonomy, the second language is used for communication, either to express one's own ideas in speech or writing, or to understand what others have said or written. The vehicles for communication are the four skills of listening, speaking, reading and writing, but underlying these skills is the individual's "global language proficiency."

A. Tests of the Four Skills

In the 1960's, teams of test writers developed separate tests for each of the four skills.[1] However, in so doing they often failed to differentiate between items testing elements of language and items testing communication ability. Thus a "reading test" would contain discrete-point items of grammar and vocabulary as well as "reading comprehension" items based on selections of one or more paragraphs in length. But even the "reading comprehension" questions did not always require a general understanding of the text; some were simply vocabulary or grammar items tied to words or structures in the passage. The "speaking tests" would likewise contain a combination of item types, some of which (like the repetition of sounds or phrases) tested only the control of specific elements of language.

The types of single-skill tests that do in fact evaluate communication skills include the following:

Listening to recorded passages and indicating whether corresponding statements are true or false. (Note: Recorded multi-

1. For instance, the *MLA Cooperative Foreign Language Tests* (1963) and the *Pimsleur Modern Foreign Language Proficiency Tests* (1967), now available from the Psychological Corporation, 757 Third Avenue, New York, NY 10017.

ple choice items are highly unnatural and require retention as well as comprehension.)

Talking about a picture or a series of pictures.

Reading a passage and answering content and interpretation questions.

Writing a letter or short essay according to a set of general instructions or guidelines.

The challenge of the 1980's will be to prepare better tests of the four skills. For the comprehension tests of listening and reading, it is necessary to select passages with natural contexts and with a vocabulary level appropriate to that of the class. In the past, many comprehension items had a strong vocabulary bias; in order to answer correctly, the student had to know the meaning of a specific word and could not deduce the answer to a corresponding item through inference or word association techniques. Hence, the students who had memorized long lists of words often did better than students with more reading practice. In the future, it should be possible to increase the difficulty of a comprehension test by the introduction of a speed element. Listening passages of equal lexical and syntactic difficulty could be recorded at different rates from slow, formal to rapid conversational speech. If desired, different types of pronunciation could be used, *e.g.*, Standard American English, British Received Pronunciation, Georgia-style Southern speech, highly nasalized variants, etc. Reading speed could be controlled by projecting texts line by line on a screen (as for speed-reading) or simply by allowing students only a specific amount of time to read each passage.

In speaking and writing tests, the challenge is to create stimuli which will elicit the desired samples, and then to develop reliable scoring systems which are easy for teachers to apply. One direction will probably lie in the area of sequential pictorial cues, such as cartoons without words.

Finally, the 1980's should see a continued research interest in communication tests which combine both comprehension and self-expression. The oral interview as a testing technique has received considerable attention in recent years and one hopes that more and more classroom teachers will learn how to administer such real-life tests to their students. Writing tests where students answer a letter or write a résumé of a film or an article should also receive renewed attention. The closer a test comes to natural language use, the greater its validity. The challenge is to arrive at acceptable levels of scorer reliability and practical procedures which do not prove to be too time-consuming.

B. Tests of Global Language Proficiency

Tests of global language proficiency require the student to process natural samples of language within certain time constraints. Moreover, such tests must assume a format that lends itself to relatively quick and reliable scoring. Typically, more than one language skill is involved, but this is not an essential feature of global proficiency testing. The most commonly used global proficiency tests are the dictation (Oller, 1979), the noise test (Gradman and Spolsky, 1975), and the cloze test (Oller; Brièce and Hinofotis, 1979).

The dictation may be considered a test of global language proficiency when the selection is read at natural speed with pauses only at the end of each sentence or clause. When an easy dictation is read slowly word for word it tends to become a spelling test. The students are required to remember longer segments of the target language and to demonstrate their comprehension by writing down what they have heard. Spelling mistakes are usually not counted if they do not interfere with comprehension, but this decision rests with the teacher.

The noise test is a variant of the dictation. The text is recorded at normal speed and then redundancy is reduced by the addition of extraneous noise or static. The sentences themselves would be relatively easy for the students to understand if the recording had not been artificially distorted. Here again spelling mistakes are often not counted as long as the scorer feels that the student understood what was said.

In the cloze test, the students are presented with a reading passage of average difficulty in which every *nth* (usually fifth, sixth or seventh) word has been deleted and replaced by a blank. Normally, the opening sentence of the passage is given in its entirety

FIGURE 3 Self-Assessment Form: Speaking

☐ I speak the language as well as a well-educated native.	5
☐	4.5
☐ I speak the language fluently and for the most part correctly. I have a large vocabulary so I seldom have to hesitate or search for words. On the other hand I am not completely fluent in situations in which I have had no practice with the language.	4
☐	3.5
☐ I can make myself understood in most everyday situations, but my language is not without mistakes and sometimes I cannot find the words for what I want to say. It is difficult for me to express myself in situations in which I have had no opportunity to practice the language. I can give a short summary of general information that I have received in my native language.	3
☐	2.5
☐ I can make myself understood in simple everyday situations, for example asking and giving simple directions, asking and telling the time, asking and talking about simpler aspects of work and interests. My vocabulary is rather limited, so it is only by a great deal of effort that I can use the language in new and unexpected situations.	2
☐	1.5
☐ I can just about express very simple things concerning my own situation and my nearest surroundings, for example asking and answering very simple questions about the time, food, housing and directions. I only have a command of very simple words and phrases.	1
☐	0.5
☐ I do not speak the language at all.	0

(Oskarsson, 10: p. 42)

to help establish the context. Students are scored according to how many blanks they have filled in with either the exact word of the original or an acceptable synonym.

These tests of global language proficiency are all quick to administer and easy to score. They are particularly effective as placement instruments for they can be administered to large groups of students and the results can be quickly obtained. Given the standard error factor, some students may be placed in the wrong class—but this occurs even with much longer achievement batteries. In fact, researchers have developed multiple-choice, machine-scorable variants of the above tests to make their administration even more economical.

C. Self-Assessment

In recent years, the Council of Europe has begun to explore the advantages and difficulties of student self-assessment (Oskarsson, 1978). It is clear that learners should be able to judge the effectiveness of their efforts at communication, for in so doing they will participate more actively in the learning process. Self-assessment is also a very inexpensive and practical alternative to formal placement testing. Figure 3 shows one of the forms which has been used experimentally in Europe to evaluate proficiency in the four skills.

CONCLUSION

As society enters the 1980's with a renewed awareness of the importance of possessing a second or third language, so language teachers will require new and more efficient testing instruments and evaluation techniques. Much basic research has been carried out during the 1970's. Now the challenge is to put what we know into practice.

REFERENCES

Brière, Eugène J. and Hinofotis, Frances Butler, eds. *Concepts in Language Testing: Some Recent Studies*. Washington: TESOL, 1979.

Clark, John L. D. *Foreign Language Testing: Theory and Practice*. Philadelphia: Center for Curriculum Development, 1972.

Gradman, Harry L. and Spolsky, Bernard. "Reduced Redundancy Testing: A Progress Report." In Randall L. Jones and Bernard Spolsky, eds., *Testing Language Proficiency*. Arlington, VA: Center for Applied Linguistics, 1975.

Harris, David P. *Testing English as a Second Language*. New York: McGraw-Hill, 1969.

Heaton, J. B. *Writing English Language Tests: A Practical Guide for Teachers of English as a Second or Foreign Language*. London: Longman, 1975.

Krashen, Stephen D. "The Monitor Model for Second Language Acquisition." In Rosario C. Gingras, ed., *Second Language Acquisition and Foreign Language Teaching*. Arlington, VA: Center for Applied Linguistics, 1978, pp. 1–26.

Lado, Robert. *Language Testing: The Construction and Use of Foreign Language Tests*. London: Longman, 1961; New York: McGraw-Hill, 1964.

Oller, John W., Jr. *Language Tests at School*. London: Longman, 1979.

Oskarsson, Mats. *Approaches to Self-Assessment in Foreign Language Learning*. Oxford: Pergamon Press, 1980.

Rivers, Wilga M. *A Practical Guide to the Teaching of French*. New York: Oxford University Press, 1975.

Valette, Jean-Paul and Valette, Rebecca M. *Test Guide to Accompany the Testing Program, French for Mastery 2*. Lexington, MA: D.C. Heath, 1976.

Valette, Rebecca M. *Modern Language Testing*, second edition. New York: Harcourt Brace Jovanovich, 1977.

————, and Disick, Renée S. *Modern Language Performance Objectives and Individualization: a Handbook*. New York: Harcourt Brace Jovanovich, 1972.

ABSTRACT

Optimal Language Learning Environments

MARINA BURT and HEIDI DULAY

Bloomsbury West, San Francisco

This chapter summarizes the results of our efforts to answer the question: What features of students' language environments enhance second language acquisition? A body of empirical evidence points to four features: (1) natural communication, (2) communicative interactions that match the learner's level of language development, (3) comprehensibility of the language input, and (4) availability of target language models with whom the learner will identify. These features seem to allow learners' internal language learning processors to function at optimal capacity. They facilitate learners' "creative construction" of the second language.

We are grateful to Stephen D. Krashen who collaborated with us on a first draft of this paper and who gathered many of the research studies cited here.

Optimal Language
Learning Environments

MARINA BURT and HEIDI DULAY
Bloomsbury West, San Francisco

Language learning is a two-way street. Learners, and all the mental and physical machinery they come with, comprise one dimension. The environment, including the teacher, the classroom and the surrounding community, is the other. During the last ten years of second language research, the focus was mostly on the learner: on learning strategies and styles, on attitudes and motivation, on cognitive and neurological mechanisms. In the last few years, the research pendulum has begun to swing in the other direction; researchers are paying attention to the environment surrounding the learner. Describing the kind of speech learners hear—"motherese," "teacher talk," and "foreigner talk," for example—is a favorite topic.

We have put the learner and the environment together in this effort to present facts about language learning that will be maximally applicable to teaching. We begin with the assumption that learners do not pay equal attention to, nor do they try to process, everything they hear or read. In other words, not everything available in the environment—even language directed at the learner—will trigger learning. Crucial to a description of language learning, therefore, are answers to the question: *What features of the environment enhance second language acquisition?* This chapter summarizes the results of our efforts to answer that question.

We have scoured the research literature and have accumulated a cache of relevant studies, enough to draw four major conclusions. In this paper we present these conclusions together with supporting data, and we offer suggestions for their application. Finally, we locate the environment within the broader context of the entire language acquisition process.

MAJOR FINDINGS

A Natural Language Environment Is Necessary for Optimal Language Acquisition

A natural language environment exists whenever the focus of the speakers is on the content of the communication rather than on language itself. An ordinary conversation between two people is natural, and so are natural verbal exchanges at a store, a bank or a party. The participants in these exchanges care about giving and receiving information or opinions, and although they use language structures, they do so with virtually no conscious awareness of the structures used. Likewise, reading for information or entertainment, or film or television viewing are also natural uses of language. All these activities provide the participants with *natural exposure* to the language.

Observed effects of natural exposure. John Carroll's (1967) much publicized survey of nearly 3000 college foreign language majors was one of the first to demonstrate the beneficial effects of natural language exposure for second language acquisition. Carroll found that most of the French, German, Russian, and Spanish majors in American colleges and universities did not demonstrate very good foreign language skills. Their average scores on the Modern Language Association *Foreign Language Proficiency Test* corresponded to a Foreign Service Institute rating of two-plus (out of five): between "limited working proficiency" and "minimum professional proficiency."

Naturally, some students did better than others, and this is where Carroll demonstrates the benefits of natural exposure. He found that students who reported a year's study abroad performed best; those who reported a summer or a tour abroad performed next best; and both of these groups outperformed those who had never studied in a host country, but only in a formal foreign language learning environment (such as learning French in the United States).

The host language environment (such as French in France or English in the United States) is one which permits learners to talk with native target language speaking peers about issues relating to their lives in the new environment. It provides maximum opportunities for natural language exposure.

With careful planning, natural language exposure can also be made available within a foreign language environment. When it is, language learning results improve noticeably. For example, one group of researchers (Scott, Saegert and Tucker, 1974) studying students learning English in Egypt and Lebanon found that all students studying English did not automatically improve over time. Only some did. Students who had experienced learning academic subjects in English improved steadily over time, while those who only studied English in a formal language classroom situation did not improve as steadily.

Using a content subject such as biology to expose students to a new language is a way of providing natural exposure to the language. The focus of the participants is on the content—biology—and this is the necessary ingredient for a natural language environment.

The much discussed "immersion programs," such as those in Canada (Lambert and Tucker, 1972), also show the value of natural language environments for language acquisition. Immersion programs were designed for students who speak a majority language (such as English in the United States or Canada) as their first language and who wish to learn the minority language (such as Spanish in the United States) as a second language. In these programs, the language the students are learning is used as the medium of subject matter instruction.

French immersion programs have existed for English-speaking children in Canada for over a decade, and a Spanish immersion program for English-speaking children has been operating for several years in Culver City, California. In evaluating the programs, it has been demonstrated that the children developed a level of language competence in their second language "that even the most optimistic second language teacher would not set for a student following the traditional FLES (Foreign Language in the Elementary School) program" (Bruck, Lambert and Tucker, 1974:203).

In immersion programs, the language is used as a vehicle to focus on subject matter content. Since content is the focus of the participants, immersion programs provide a natural language environment.

Communicative Interactions Must Match the Learner's Level of Language Development

When learning a new language, learners appear to pass through at least three kinds of communication phases: *one-way, partial two-way,* and *full two-way.*

In *one-way communication,* the learner listens to or reads the target language, but does not communicate back. The communication is one-way, towards the learner, not from the learner. Listening to speeches and radio programs, watching films and most television programs, and reading books and magazines are examples of one-way communication.

In *partial two-way communication,* the learner may respond orally to someone, but the communication is not in the target language. The response may be in the learner's first language or may be nonverbal, such as a nod or other physical response.

In *full two-way communication* the learner speaks the target language, acting as both recipient and sender of verbal messages in the target language.

Learners appear to tend toward these types of communication at different times during the learning process.

Observations of natural language learning. When left to their own devices, learners have been shown to rely on one-way and partial two-way communication during the early stages of language learning, waiting until much later to participate in full two-way communication. This tendency is exemplified by the Vaupes River Indians in South America (Sorenson, 1967) who may well be the world's leading experts in practical language learning. Almost two dozen mutually unintelligible languages are spoken in a small area populated by a group of about 10,000 people. It is the custom in this Indian culture to marry outside one's language group—people must find mates who do not speak their language! As a consequence, children must learn at least three languages from the start: their mother's, their father's and the lingua franca of the area (Tukano). More languages are typically acquired as the individual grows up, and this extraordinary language learning continues throughout adolescence, adulthood, and even into the later years.

What do these extraordinary people do to help them learn a new language? Sorenson writes that "the Indians do not practice speaking a language they do not know well yet. Instead, they passively learn lists of words, forms, and phrases in it and familiarize themselves with the sound of its pronunciation . . . They make an occasional attempt to speak a new language in an appropriate situation, but, *if it does not come easily, they will not force it*" (Sorenson, 1967:680, *emphasis ours*).

Sorenson's description documents learners' reliance on one-way and partial two-way communication in the early learning stages. Not until learners feel ready to speak the new language do they even attempt to do so.

Children learning their *first* language have almost always been observed to understand language before being able to produce it. Researchers and observant parents have all noticed that children begin by listening to language from one to three years before beginning to speak it (Brown, 1973; Bloom, 1970). All the while, of course, they are developing comprehension skills, demonstrating their understanding by doing the things asked of them, such as drinking their milk (partial two-way communication).

Researchers studying children learning a *second* language have also observed the gradual transition from one-way to two-way communication. Unless adults (teachers or others) force children to speak in the new language, they typically exhibit a *silent period* from one to five months. During this period, the young second language learners concentrate on comprehension and opt for one-way or partial two-way communication.

For example, one otherwise outgoing immigrant boy learning English at a school in southern California said nothing at all for the first two weeks and spoke only a few words during the next two weeks, mostly memorized phrases to communicate essential needs

(Huang and Hatch, 1978). English-speaking children aged four to nine, enrolled in Swiss schools where French was the language of instruction, did not volunteer anything in the new language for a prolonged period; some said nothing for several months (Ervin-Tripp, 1974). Similarly, Hakuta (1974) reports that he could not begin his study until some five months after his subject had been exposed to English because she produced almost no speech before that time. Instead, the little girl demonstrated only comprehension of the language.

It appears that second language learners naturally begin by listening, then they respond nonverbally or in their own language, and finally they start producing the new language.

Classroom research on the effects of a silent period. Two studies on the effects of a *silent period* for the first one to three months of language instruction provide support for incorporating the natural tendencies of language learners into a curriculum. Postovsky (1974; 1977) experimented with American adult students studying Russian in an intensive six-hour-per-day course at the Defense Language Institute in Monterey, California. Students were instructed not to respond orally, but to write their answers to classroom exercises (partial two-way communication). Students who experienced the silent period during the first month of the intensive course outperformed those who were made to speak from the beginning in both pronunciation and control of grammar (Postovsky, 1977:18).

Fifty English-speaking children learning Spanish in a southern California school were studied during the first five months of instruction (Gary, 1975). Half of the children received a regular Spanish course in which oral responses in Spanish were required (full two-way communication). The other students experienced a silent period first. They did not practice any oral Spanish for the first fourteen weeks of the course (they indicated comprehension nonverbally) and responded orally only for the first half of the lesson during the remaining eight weeks. At the end of the twenty-two weeks, both groups of children were tested for production and comprehension skills in Spanish. In listening comprehension, the partial two-way group outperformed the full two-way group, as might be expected. The partial two-way group, however, also did as well on the *speaking* tests as the group which had been practicing speaking since the first day.

Apparently, matching the type of communicative interaction with the learners' level of language development maximizes the students' likelihood for success.

Target Language Input Must Be Comprehensible to the Learner

Students' ability to organize the new language system depends largely on how well they can understand what they hear or read. When students are at the early stages of learning how to speak a new language, they know few words in the language and therefore need to *see* the meaning of much of what they hear. *Concrete referents* for verbal input comprise, therefore, an important ingredient of a learner's early language environment.

Concrete referents refer to extra-linguistic items that can help the learner grasp the meaning of the sounds of the new language. They include things and activities that can be seen, heard, or felt while the language is being used. Experienced teachers usually provide concrete referents in the form of visual aids, motor activities and other "here-and-now" kinds of extra-linguistic support.

Examples of the here-and-now principle abound in the literature on children's learning of a first language. Parents or others describe what children are doing, or what they have just done: *That's a nice sandcastle! Oh, you spilled your milk!* Or they tell children what to do: *Drink your juice! Stop that!* Or they ask questions about the children's ongoing activities: *Is that a doggie? Where is your sock?*

These native speakers do not generally talk to children about activities displaced in time and space, such as what will happen next week, what is going on down the block, not to mention next year or events in another country.

Language environments for young second language learners are also often concrete. Questions such as *Is this your ball? What color is your car?* follow the here-and-now principle and give the learner the extra-linguistic support necessary to understand the new language (Wagner-Gough, 1975). Native speaking peers who play with the newcomers in school appear to realize the importance of concrete referents for comprehension. Fillmore (1976) notes that when an English-speaking child she studied wanted to tell a fairly new immigrant child about an upcoming television program, the first child asked a bilingual adult to tell the second one about it in Spanish, because "he won't know what I'm saying." The English-speaking child realized he could not provide any concrete referents for a future television program, so he asked a bilingual to say it in his playmate's native language.

While concrete referents are often provided in second language classrooms for younger children, they are often forgotten for older learners, who need them just as much. For example, one re-searcher documented the following questions being asked of a newly arrived immigrant who was thirteen years old: *What are you gonna do tonight? What do you do at home? What do we mean by 'question mark'?* (Wagner-Gough, 1975). Although these questions may not seem difficult to a native English speaker, the absence of a single concrete referent makes it impossible for the learner to figure out what the meaning is without knowing the meaning of the words already.

Older learners, like younger ones, benefit from adherence to the here-and-now principle, especially in the early stages of in-struction. Rather than talking about doggie or toys with older stu-dents, one would select more appropriate objects and activities, such as money or food. But whatever the choice, the objects and activities chosen should have concrete referents so that learners can figure out the meaning of the language used.

Language Learners Attend to, and Acquire, the Language and Dialect Spoken by People with Whom They Identify

The source of the language the learner hears is the fourth signifi-cant environmental factor that researchers have found influences a language learner's performance. Several speaker models may be available (anyone who speaks the target language is a potential model), but learners do not draw on them equally. To date, evidence has been presented which demonstrates speaker model preferences of three sorts: peers over teachers, peers over parents, and one's own ethnic group members over non-members.

When both a teacher and peers speak the target language, learners have been observed to prefer their peers as models. For example, a seven-year-old Japanese speaking child who had immigrated to Hawaii acquired the Hawaiian Creole English of his agemates, rather than the Standard English of his teachers during his first school year. When the boy moved to a middle class neighborhood the following year, he quickly picked up the Standard English that his new friends spoke (Milon, 1975).

In immersion programs where the teacher is typically the only native speaker of the target language to whom the children are exposed during the school day, children show unexpected gaps in their control of the target language, even after four to seven years in the program (see Bruck, Lambert and Tucker, 1975 for the St. Lambert French immersion program; Plann, 1977 for the Culver City Spanish immersion program).

The development of such "immersion varieties" of target languages does not appear to be attributable to any learning problems of the children, nor to the quality of the target language spoken by the teachers during the school day. Instead, the outcome seems to be directly attributable to the preference these children have for their peers as speech models. In the immersion programs, it happens that all the preferred models are themselves struggling with the new language.

Peers are also preferred over parents as language models, whether they speak standard or nonstandard varieties of the target language. In first language learning, it has been found that when the speech characteristics of peers and parents differ, the children will tend to acquire the speech characteristics of their peers (Stewart, 1964; Labov, 1972).

Finally, some children have been observed to tend towards the dialect or language spoken by members of their own ethnic group. For example, Benton (1964; cited in Richards, 1974) reports that Maori children learn the English dialect of their own ethnic group rather than the standard New Zealand English spoken by other children.

These examples indicate the language learners attend *selectively* to different target language speakers. They learn from some but not from others.

INSTRUCTIONAL APPLICATIONS

The environments we have discussed here that make a difference in language learning seem to be those that enhance the students' "creative construction" of the new language. They provide learners with rich exposure to natural language used by people with whom the learner identifies, at a level of comprehension and learner participation that is attuned to the learner's stage of second language development. [1]

Optimal language learning environments can be (and have been) created by teachers in classrooms. One just has to be willing to subordinate linguistic form to subject content for a major part of the curriculum. One also has to be willing to explore materials that may not have been designed for language teaching purposes but can be adapted to meet those needs. Conversely, adapting existing language teaching materials so that they more readily conform to the requisite characteristics is often necessary.

Among the activities that are most frequently suggested as effective second language lessons are science experiments. They usually involve doing things and giving and receiving instructions that have concrete referents. Although science experiments may illustrate an abstract physical law, the experiment itself involves activities firmly rooted in the here-and-now. Science in general is a good choice for the content of a second language course. Science lessons lend themselves to natural, concrete communicative interactions which may be one-way, partial two-way, or full two-way, depending on the learner's readiness to use the new language. The nature of the interactions can be planned in advance by the teacher in response to the students' states of readiness to use the language. Science projects also provide opportunities to pair or group together students of various proficiency levels, so that the

---

1. See Dulay, Burt, and Krashen (1981) for a more detailed presentation of optimal language learning environments than is possible in this short chapter.

less, proficient have peer language models while the more proficient have opportunities to use the new language without feeling linguistically inferior.

Not all language teachers take readily to science, however. Arts and crafts, some business and finance topics, cooking, or health, nutrition and safety provide equally effective topics for language lessons. Since the ultimate objective of a language class is to teach language, a teacher need not feel obligated to teach any particular content, unless, of course, the program is one designed for special purposes (such as scientific German or business English). Otherwise, areas in which the teacher is most at ease and the students most interested will probably be the best choice.

Other effective activities that traditionally have been part of second language classes are nonlinguistic games (such as indoor baseball), communication games, and role play. For these and the other activities described above to be successful, the focus of both teacher and students should be on the activity rather than on the language forms they are using. Correction of student errors should, therefore, be kept at a minimum, while communication should be maximized. Teachers should accept students' use of their native languages in the second language classroom while they themselves use only the target language.

During the silent period at the beginning of language learning, the teacher has to work extra hard, since she or he does most if not all of the talking. Films, film strips, cassettes and records, however, may provide some respite to the teacher, while getting students used to the sounds and rhythms of the new language. Reading activities are also useful, as long as students are not asked to read aloud. The "total physical response" method developed by Asher (1965; 1969; and Asher, Kusudo, and de la Torre, 1974) has been integrated into a text which provides many ideas and lessons for the silent phase of an English curriculum (Romijn and Seely, 1979).

In a *host* language environment, where the target language is that used by the community at large, teachers may draw on the rich language resources outside the classroom. Taking students on field trips or arranging events in which native speakers of the target language who are peers of the second language students participate are a few such out-of-classroom activities which provide good language learning opportunities, if organized well. In a host language environment, a language teacher who can incorporate outside resources into the curriculum will be helping students make optimum use of a rich natural second language environment.

Foreign language teaching is more difficult. The teacher has virtually no outside help, since the target language is not spoken outside the classroom. Thus the teacher, along with films, film strips, records and tapes, becomes the sole source of a learner's target language environment. In such situations, it is probably realistic *not* to expect great accomplishments from students but to be satisfied if a student reaches what Virginia French Allen calls "entry level" skill in the new language. (See V. F. Allen's chapter in this volume.) Encouraging students to visit the countries in which the target language is spoken, and giving them cultural information to ease their initial adjustment, comprise, therefore, an important part of a foreign language course. Further, if subject matter classes in the foreign language are offered at the same institution (*e.g.*, biology in English taught at the American University in Beirut, or physics in English taught at the University of Puerto Rico), students of English should be encouraged to attend, if only to acquire better English (rather than learn a lot of physics or biology).

Finally, in applying research findings on language learning, it is best to use Mary Finocchiaro's framework for program development as a checklist to ensure comprehensive and cohesive application. Dr. Finocchiaro suggests the acronym "COMET" to remember all the program components into which instructional changes should be incorporated (Finocchiaro & Ekstrand, 1977:217):

> **C**-urriculum
> **O**-bjectives
> **M**-ethods and materials
> **E**-valuation
> **T**-eachers (preparation and skills)

INTERNAL CONTEXT
FOR ENVIRONMENTAL INPUT

Lest we have given the impression that all that matters in language learning is the environment, we conclude with a picture of the entire language acquisition process, of which environmental input is a part (Figure 1).

FIGURE 1   Working Model for Creative Construction in L_2 Acquisition*

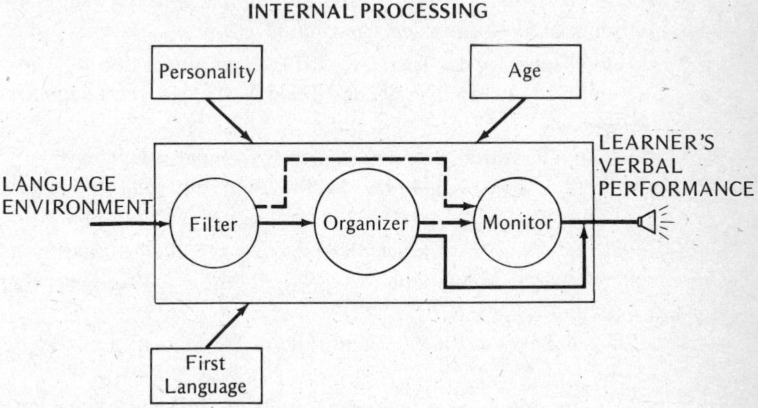

INTERNAL PROCESSING

*This is an updated version of the model presented in Dulay and Burt, 1977.

Elsewhere we have described in detail each aspect of the process (Dulay, Burt and Krashen, forthcoming; Dulay and Burt, 1977). Suffice it here to say that the environment provides the raw language material which the learner filters, organizes and monitors according to principles applicable to most human beings. These principles are responsible for similarities in errors, acquisition orders and transitional rules that have been observed in the performance of second language learners the world over. Differences in environment, age, personality, and first language background of learners also affect language processing and result in variations in verbal performance. These variations, however, do not obscure the regularities which attest to the universal internal mechanisms at work in language learning.

Teaching a second language means creating for students a part or all of their target language environment. It means working with their natural language learning capacities and tendencies in a process which is a two-way street.

REFERENCES

Asher, J. 1965. "The Strategy of the Total Physical Response: An Application to Learning Russian." *International Journal of Applied Linguistics 3.* 291–300.

———. 1969. "The Total Physical Response Approach to Second Language Learning. *Modern Language Journal 53* 1.3–7.

———, Kusudo, J. and De La Torre, R. 1974. "Learning a Second Language Through Commands: The Second Field Test." *Modern Language Journal 58.* 24–32.

Benton, R. 1964. "Research into the English Language Difficulties of Maori School Children, 1963–1964." Wellington, New Zealand: Maori Education Foundation.

Bloom, L. 1970. *Language Development: Form and Function in Emerging Grammars.* (Research Monograph No. 59) Cambridge, MA: The MIT Press.

Brown, R. 1973. *A First Language.* Cambridge, MA: Harvard University Press.

Bruck, M., Lambert, W. E. and Tucker, G. R. 1974. "Bilingual Schooling Through the Elementary Grades: The St. Lambert Project at Grade Seven." *Language Learning 24.* 183–204.

———, Lambert, W. E. and Tucker, G. R. 1975. "Assessing Functional Bilingualism Within a Bilingual Program: The St. Lambert Project at Grade Eight." Paper presented at the TESOL Convention, Los Angeles, California.

Carroll, J. 1967. "Foreign Language Proficiency Levels Attained by Language Majors Near Graduation from College." *Foreign Language Annals 1.* 131–151.

Dulay, H. and Burt, M. 1977. "Remarks on Creativity in Second Language Acquisition." In M. Burt, H. Dulay and M. Finocchiaro (eds.) *Viewpoints on English as a Second Language.* New York: Regents.

———, Burt, M. and Krashen, S. (forthcoming). *The Second Language.* New York: Oxford University Press.

Ervin-Tripp, S. 1974. "Is Second Language Learning Like the First?" *TESOL Quarterly 8.* 111–127.

Fillmore, L. 1976. *The Second Time Around: Cognitive and Social Strategies in Second Language Acquisition.* Ph.D. Dissertation, Stanford University.

Finocchiaro, M. and Ekstrand, L. 1977. "Migration Today: Some Social and Educational Problems." In M. Burt, H. Dulay and M. Finocchiaro (eds.) *Viewpoints on English as a Second Language.* New York: Regents.

Gary, J. O. 1975. "Delayed Oral Practice in Initial Stages of Second Language Learning." In M. Burt and H. Dulay (eds.) *New Directions in Second Language Learning, Teaching, and Bilingual Education.* Washington, D.C.: TESOL.

Hakuta, K. 1974. "Prefabricated Patterns and the Emergence of Structure in Second Language Acquisition." *Language Learning 14.*287–298.

Huang, J. and Hatch, E. 1978. "A Chinese Child's Acquisition of English." In E. Hatch (ed.) *Second Language Acquisition: A Book of Readings.* Rowley, MA: Newbury House Publishers.

Labov, M. 1972. *Sociolinguistic Patterns.* Philadelphia, PA: University of Pennsylvania Press.

Lambert, W. and Tucker, G. R. 1972. *Bilingual Education of Children.* Rowley, MA: Newbury House Publishers.

Milon, J. P. 1975. "Dialect in the TESOL Program: If You Never You Better." In M. Burt, and H. Dulay (eds.) *New Directions in Second Language Learning, Teaching and Bilingual Education.* Washington, D.C.: TESOL.

Plann, S. 1977. "Acquiring a Second Language in an Immersion Classroom." In H. D. Brown, C. A. Yorio and R. H. Crymes (eds.) *Teaching and Learning English as a Second Language: Trends in Research and Practice.* Washington, D.C.: TESOL.

Postovsky, V. 1974. "Effects of Delay in Oral Practice at the Beginning of Second Language Learning." *Modern Language Journal 58.*5–6.

———. 1977. "Why Not Start Speaking Later?" In M. Burt, H. Dulay and M. Finocchiaro (eds.) *Viewpoints on English as a Second Language.* New York: Regents.

Richards, J. 1974. *Error Analysis: Perspectives on Second Language Learning.* London: Longman.

Romijn, E. and Seely, C. 1979. *Live Action English for Foreign Students.* San Francisco: The Alemany Press.

Scott, M., Saegert, J. and Tucker, G. R. 1974. "Error Analysis and English Language Strategies of Arab Students." *Language Learning 24.*69–98.

Sorenson, A. 1967. "Multilingualism in the Northwest Amazon." *American Anthropologist 69.*674–684.

Stewart, W. A. 1964. "Nonstandard Speech and the Teaching Methods in

Quasi-Foreign Situations." In W. A. Stewart (ed.) *Nonstandard Speech and the Teaching of English*. Washington, D.C.: Center for Applied Linguistics.

Wagner-Gough, J. 1975. *Comparative Studies in Second Language Learning*. M.A. Thesis, University of California at Los Angeles.

SECTION III

FOCUS ON SECOND LANGUAGE TEACHING MATERIALS

INTRODUCTION

As the pendulum in second language education has continued to swing in the direction of the learner as the major subject for in-depth research since the early 1970's, it has become clear that the "learner-centered classrooms" of today and tomorrow require learning *materials* for today and tomorrow. The nature of the second language curriculum or syllabus has changed over the decades, often as a reaction to changes in teaching procedures or teacher demands. Not infrequently, however, by analogy to placing the cart before the horse, our teaching practices have been determined by the available materials, rather than vice versa.

In the 1980's, better understanding of learner needs and interests result in the posing of such questions as:

How should specialized learning content be selected and organized?

How can learning content be matched to learner needs and interests?

How should content be structured in learning materials?

What roles can "hardware" play in meeting learner needs and interests?

The five papers in this section focus on second language materials in the 1980's. Widdowson and Brumfit explore issues in the design of language teaching syllabuses. Jenks considers criteria for matching materials to learner needs and interests. Lado and Alexander view the issues in materials design from American and European perspectives respectively. Finally, Freudenstein considers both the history of media use in second language teaching and the prospects for the effective use of "hardware" in the 1980's.

ABSTRACT

Issues in Second Language Syllabus Design

HENRY G. WIDDOWSON   CHRISTOPHER J. BRUMFIT
University of London

Structural syllabuses are based on formal linguistic categories. Criteria for moving from simple to complex are undefined. Possible alternatives include types of communicative syllabuses discussed in this chapter. But do such "communicative syllabuses" facilitate use any better than structural ones, which are economical and involve no break with tradition? Neither type seems ideal. Possible improvements may be found by examining: (1) traditional pedagogic practices from a communicative perspective, (2) the value of fluency activities (a methodological solution), (3) attempts to "marry" functional and formal requirements, and (most important), (4) the role of content. True communicative teaching may depend on our stressing language as a means to acquire knowledge, rather than as an end in itself.

Issues in Second Language Syllabus Design

HENRY G. WIDDOWSON
CHRISTOPHER J. BRUMFIT
University of London

This paper exploits a tension between principles and practice. On the one hand, syllabus design must be subject to careful discussion and investigation; on the other, particular syllabuses are designed to cope with real contingencies which impose practical constraints and call for immediate solutions. On the one hand, advance will only be possible if we are prepared to speculate, to think divergently, to question tradition; on the other, syllabuses must relate to real people, students and teachers, who cannot be subjected to controlled experimentation, and who cannot be treated as the passive recipients of speculation from above. As theorists we may need to withdraw from involvement to achieve a perspective from a detached vantage point, but as educators we cannot avoid responsibility to the world of practical pedagogic affairs to which we must ultimately be accountable. In this chapter we hope both to speculate and to support our speculations, but we also hope to relate these speculations to the world of real teachers and real classrooms.

A language syllabus (like any other) is a device for helping learners to arrive at their objective in the most economical way. It is a rational contrivance which is necessary because natural learning is inefficient or impracticable. It is sometimes said that the best way to learn a foreign language is to live with the people who speak it as intimately as possible, most effectively by means of marriage. It would be hard to demonstrate by empirical evidence that this is always the case and in any event it would involve a course of action

which many learners would be reluctant to take. So we need syllabuses.

Since a language syllabus represents a planned route to an objective, we obviously have to be clear what this objective is. At the
most general level, there is very little controversy about this: the
objective is to develop the ability to use the foreign language as a
practical means of communication. There will, of course, be differences in the way more specific objectives are defined, but at this
general policy level there seems to be agreement that what is to
be learned is a mode of activity, knowing how to use language and
not knowing about it as an abstract system. The definition of the
objective of language teaching in communicative terms has been
with us for some time and it is not a matter of dispute. What *is* a
matter of dispute is the route that has to be taken to achieve that
objective.

A syllabus represents a developmental sequence of elements
which is to be transferred into progressive learning over time. Two
questions arise. How should such elements be defined? On what
principle should they be sequentially ordered?

Proponents of the structural syllabus assumed that these elements should be defined by reference to certain formal items of
linguistic description, and adopted the sentence as the basic teaching unit. These items were organized along a dimension of increasing complexity. It was supposed that if the learner could be led in
this way to accumulate a knowledge of the underlying system of
the language, acquired through active participation and so linked
to performance, then he would have sufficient directions to use the
language communicatively when occasion arose.

There are a number of difficulties here. To begin with, sentences are units of linguistic analysis and not of natural language
use. They may be made manifest through structures, and performed in the sense that they are given a physical embodiment in
the classroom, but they remain projections of abstract categories.
They are not utterances. How then, one must ask, can this learning of sentences prepare the learner for his encounter with the
communicative use of language which will require him to cope
with utterances? For the coping with utterances requires him to
reverse the direction of dependency from language-situation to sit-

uation-language. By this we mean that in the teaching of sentences, the situation is devised to duplicate information so that the meaning of the sentence can be understood in self-contained isolation. In natural language, on the other hand, language is needed to extend situational information: the meaning of the utterance has to be inferred by reference to situational factors which complement the information it expresses. The meaning of sentences, their signification, is invariant and can be established by internal reference to other sentences in a paradigm. The meaning of an utterance, its value, will vary according to the context or situation which extends it.

Thus the signification of the *sentence:*

The dog is chasing the cat

is a function of its relationship with other sentences that can be structurally associated with it. Such associations are conventionally displayed in the familiar substitution table:

The		is		the	
	dog	was	chasing		cat
A		has been		a	

The meaning of any one combination of items reading from left to right is established by contrasting it with any other combination of items:

cf. The dog is chasing the cat.
cf. The dog *was* chasing the cat.
cf. A dog was chasing the cat.
cf. A dog *is* chasing the cat.

Each sentence is a complete unit of meaning which functions as a term in a system. The meaning of the *utterance:*

The dog is chasing the cat

is, on the other hand, incomplete. If seriously uttered it would prompt questions like "Which dog?" "Which cat?" "Where?"

which call for information to extend the proposition only partially expressed. It would also prompt questions like: "Why are you telling me this?", "So what?" which call for information to extend the utterance so that its communicative or illocutionary function is clear. Sentences signal their own meaning because they are units of analysis; utterances do not because they are units of behaviour and so depend on human agency to derive meaning from them. And it is precisely this ability to derive meaning by extension that constitutes the communicative use of language.

So what the structural syllabus deals with are elements which do not figure in the objective that it is designed to achieve, and the learning of these elements provides no model for their use. Classroom performance of formal items may contribute to the more effective learning of the system as such, but it does not in itself prepare for performance in the communicative sense. The learner is left with the problem of reversing dependency, of developing procedures for utterance extension in discourse. Matters are further complicated because, while most commentators agree that classrooms have not generally solved the problem of developing communicative ability, there is disagreement over whether this has been because of deficient methodology, with too little provision made for the exercise of communicative skills in classrooms concentrating too heavily on the controlled presentations and practice of linguistic forms, or because of a fundamental flaw in the design of the syllabus itself, being based on structural rather than communicative principles. This disagreement has practical implications, as we shall see later, for a methodological change will only come about through a direct approach to teachers, while a change in syllabus design may result from approaches to administrators or examining bodies, but will have subsequent implications for teaching. In either case, though, we need to be clear that the traditional, structural syllabus cannot provide a neat model as a basis for learning.

Another difficulty has to do with the way the items are ordered. Appeal is usually made to the notion of complexity. How is this to be defined? Where there are dependency relations between structures, then there is an internal measure of complexity within the system. Thus it seems reasonable to say that a structure which contains an embedded sentence is more complex than one that does not, since the embedding is dependent on a prior matrix. By the same token, a noun phrase containing an adjective is more complex than one that does not since there has to be a prior noun phrase established beforehand. But there are, of course, many syntactic structures which are not dependent in this way, and which cannot be so obviously ordered. One might propose that kernel sentences should appear before their transforms, but how would one order the kernels or indeed the different transforms? And even if we arranged structures according to the sequence required for transformational operations, we would be committing ourselves to one way of doing grammar which, as the work on the derivational theory of complexity makes clear, has no necessary psychological validity. A commitment to TG would, for example, require us to introduce relative clauses before attributive adjectives.

It does not seem that linguistic description can provide us with straightforward criteria for complexity. This is really not very surprizing since such a description records a synchronic state and makes no claim to account for development. This is presumably the difference between a descriptive and a pedagogic grammar; the latter must in some way be designed to key in with learning processes and so must have a built-in dynamic. But if models of linguistic description cannot serve as a source of reference to establish degrees of complexity which might determine sequence of presentation, what other insight is available? Two possibilities suggest themselves.

The first emerges from interlanguage studies, and research into second language acquisition. It is the notion of a "built-in" syllabus, corresponding to universal acquisition principles, which is discernible in patterns of error, in the appearance of morpheme sequences, and so on. If we could discover underlying patterns of acquisition which characterize all language learning, this would obviously provide us with a principled way of ordering items in a syllabus. The difficulty here is that very little reliable evidence has emerged, and there is anyway the suggestion that universal psychological principles are less likely to provide an explanation than constraints imposed by the communicative use of language in social situations.

This brings us to the second possibility. This is best approached by considering the kind of order which designers of structural syllabuses adopted, particularly for the early units. If linguistic descriptions provide no sure guide, where did the designers get their order from? Probably from an intuitive sense of the discourse function of the formal items they dealt with. Why should, for example, *This is. . . .* or *I am/you are. . . .* appear in the first units, and structures like *The pen is on the table* afterwards? There is no obvious measure which could assess the former as less difficult or complex than the latter. It seems likely that there is a criterion of functional value operating here. If you are going to say anything, you have first to identify the topic, then locate it for the hearer, and next make some comment about it. Hence the sequence *This is a pen. The pen is on the table. The pen is red.*

But the problem here is that, having arranged language items by reference to their utterance functions as part of discourse, they are presented as sentences, and the discourse function is left unrealized. Instead of getting learners to infer extensions from one utterance to another, they are directed to the paradigmatic relations between these items as sentences. The question now is: how far can one make these intuitions more definite so that language items can be presented to build up to larger discourse units? How far can discourse analysis provide us with a guide to utterance sequences?

We have shifted from the sentence to the utterance as the basic element in the syllabus. At this point we touch on proposals for organizing a syllabus along notional lines. The view that syllabuses should be based on categories more appropriate for learners than for linguists appeared very attractive in the early 1970's. Essentially, it was argued that learners needed to use the foreign language, as native speakers do, to express meanings and perform social activities, so the syllabus should reflect not a classification of the system of the language, but a classification of language meanings, or notions, and language uses, or functions. Hence there has been a search for generalisations about such notions and functions.

There is, however, one basic flaw in this procedure. Any syllabus must necessarily reflect generalisations about language, and whether these generalisations are based on the organization of the language structurally, functionally or notionally, it will be a generalised and idealised description when set against any instance of actual use. Description of use is not the same thing as use. Any justification for a functional or notional syllabus must rest on the claim that such an organization will necessarily facilitate language use in students better than a structural syllabus can. As we have already seen, there are problems about the way the content of a structural syllabus is conventionally defined and about the way this content is sequentially ordered. However, there are two advantages of the structural syllabus which are worth considering, one theoretical and the other practical.

The theoretical advantage is that a structural syllabus is, to some extent at least, economical. That is, a limited set of rules can lead to a very large amount of operational skill. It is skill, as we have already indicated, which is not immediately exploitable, for exploitation requires what we have called a reversal of dependency, whereby the learner moves from the composition of sentences to the ability to make utterances meaningful by extension. Nonetheless, a relatively limited set of rules does, in practice (and in combination with a progressively extending vocabulary), enable learners to move a long way in a short time. However appropriate notional or functional categories may appear to be, they will need to demonstrate that they do not have to be learnt one by one as separate and unsystematisable items before they can compete with the rules of a generative grammar in economy, and therefore possibly in ease of learning. This is not to say necessarily that economy outweighs relevance as a criterion, but, as was suggested above, the idealised functions and notions may not be quite as relevant as originally appeared, and there are strong arguments from learning theory to support economy as an important criterion.

The practical advantage is that linguists and teachers have many years of experience with grammatical syllabuses to call upon. There are many analyses of errors and languages in contrast, many reports of successes and failures in teaching, many textbooks and syllabuses from which we can draw valuable understanding. The existence of a tradition to exploit is not a strong reason for rejecting change, but we need to be very sure of our grounds for dissatisfaction with the tradition before advocating revolution rather than evolution.

One of the problems with a non-generative basis for syllabus design is that it is difficult to determine criteria for content. In practice, functional syllabuses have tended to turn to needs analyses, of greater or lesser sophistication. However, needs analyses pose their own problems. The major problem is the simplistic view of the learning process which they encourage, as if the learner has to be filled up with items like marbles in a tin. Difficulties we face in providing an order for grammatical items are small when compared with the problems of categorising and ordering the needs of learners, whether expressed functionally or notionally, in any but the most severely restricted settings. And of course it is in severely restricted settings that language use (because of its high predictability) is least like normal, natural language. The point is that we are not trying to learn how to fulfil each of our linguistic needs; we are trying to learn a linguistic system which enables us to fulfil an enormous range of needs, which are by definition unpredictable. A system is not the same as the output of that system, we must aim to teach a *capacity* to behave, not a particular piece of behaviour.

There are shortcomings, then, in both structural and communicative proposals, so where do we go from there? It is important to note, first of all, that the shortcomings arise from different causes in each case. Structural syllabuses have been around for a long time, and provide us with a great deal of data to examine. It may be sensible to accept the force, if not the letter, of the scepticism with "expertise" shown by many teachers, and to start looking more scientifically at "unscientific" activities. We can afford to examine, in the light of our greater understanding of language functions, many of the procedures used in the past in language teaching. In spite of—or perhaps in unconscious opposition to—the strong pragmatic tradition of teachers, language teaching theory has tended to detach itself from historical context and to attempt more often than not to reject rather than understand the past. But it may well be sensible, at this stage, to re-examine traditional pedagogic practices such as the use of translation and literary texts,

the association of language and "culture" and the techniques for
contextualising and practising language, and to consider how they
look from a communicative point of view. Certainly, we would do
well to examine more carefully the practise of successful teachers,
from the past and the present, in order to interpret their behaviour
in terms of present attitudes. Such a study should give us some
idea of how teachers transcend the limitations of their syllabus design, of how they modify the general linguistic paradigm to the
needs of specific situations, of how the structural mould has been
broken in practice. For sensitive teachers have, of course, always
been "functional" and "notional" insofar as they have related
their work directly to the learning needs of their students, and the
use of structural syllabuses has *not* been one unmitigated record of
failure.

Fuller understanding of what has happened, and is happening
in classrooms using structural syllabuses will help us to recognise
defects in the principle of the structural syllabus and will possibly
help us to see how—pragmatically—communicative teaching may
develop. Problems with communicative proposals require further
theoretical investigation, however, for so far they have scarcely developed beyond speculation. To some extent, we are dependent
on developments in theoretical disciplines beyond our immediate
concern—speech act theory, pragmatics, interlanguage studies will
all have a role to play. But syllabus design, as an applied activity,
will always be in this position. There must still be discussion of the
possibilities, given our current level of understanding.

One possibility is to reject the syllabus model altogether, but to
retain the communicative objective. It could be argued that most
of the problems that communicative syllabuses address themselves
to can be solved methodologically by a greater emphasis on fluency
rather than accuracy activities. The assumption underlying this argument is that as human beings we are naturally programmed to
interact, and that—once we have been provided with the system,
and with opportunities for making use of our natural abilities—we
do not need to be "taught" how to reverse from sentence to utterance. This is not to say that there needs to be no assistance with
items of cultural information relevant to interaction, but only that
all language users will naturally produce a language-using com-

munity given appropriate motivation, and that experience of the kind of adaptation and negotiation needed will equip learners to be able to adapt, adjust and negotiate appropriately in a new culture. Such a methodological solution will require a syllabus for input (quite possibly organized on very traditional lines, but not necessarily so), and extensive opportunities for native-like linguistic behaviour in group activities, role-play exercises, simulations, projects, communication games, and so on. It will not require new organization for syllabus input, only new procedures for integrative work to draw out from students, naturally and unconsciously, what has been put in, however deficient at first that may be. An advantage of this approach is that it centres innovation on the teacher, so that the risk of a lack of fit between administrative or theoretical ambitions and classroom practice is minimised. There is, however, no reason why it should not prepare the ground for a subsequent revision of syllabus design. It is probably preferable (as we have implied) for innovation to evolve from methodology and to then affect syllabus design rather than to have it imposed as a revolutionary edict from above.

A similarly cautious procedure in syllabus design is to start with the structural core, which is the least unsatisfactory way of organizing the syllabus in light of present knowledge and experience. To this core, one adds items derived from a traditional structural syllabus as well as others from notional, functional or indeed any other appropriate taxonomies. This procedure for textbook or syllabus organization is represented in the spiral diagram below. It has the merit of recognising that some parts of the syllabus can be systematised, while others cannot be, so that important but essentially nonce items (items of appropriate cultural information, perhaps related to external organizational criteria, school visits abroad or unexpected visits by native speakers to the school, for example) will appear in the spiral in accord with external considerations; other elements, also in the spiral because they are unsystematisable, will be selected as needed. The spiral thus operates as a check-list which feeds in to the core. The core has an internal structure while the spiral has none. Thus, it is possible to sequence the content of the core but not of the spiral.

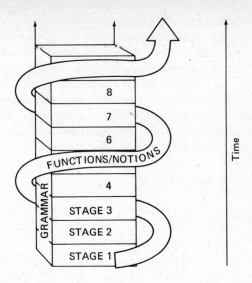

It should be noted that in the teaching of other subjects in the curriculum, the core/spiral dependency is altered. In language teaching, the syllabus core contains the linguistic structures for expressing the varied curricular content found in the spiral; in other disciplines, just the opposite seems to be true. The core is the curricular content and the spiral consists of the language-related ways of dealing with that content. It might be beneficial, therefore, to investigate how language course design could parallel the core/syllabus relationship found elsewhere in education.

Many of the difficulties we have discussed here seem to arise directly out of the inherent limitations of foreign language teaching in classrooms. As teachers we have concentrated so much on teaching language as a system for future use that (outside second language situations, which have their own, mainly socio-political, difficulties to contend with) we have neglected the role of genuine meaning altogether. Plenty of pseudomeanings can be created, through classroom games or role-play, but these happen at odd intervals without there being any real conceptual development associated with language work. In real language use there is no separation between concept and expression. Our normal language typically engages external knowledge to make sense. A truly communicative course could not transcend the limitations of the classroom, but it could make this weakness a strength. If the teaching of a subject were to be carried on through the medium of the foreign language, many problems associated with communication would disappear. But without a serious concern for the syllabus development of *content* it is difficult to see how any significant notional development could be possible.

ABSTRACT

Learners' Needs
and the Selection
of Compatible Materials

FREDERICK L. JENKS
Florida State University

In any learner-centered approach to instruction, materials must be selected according to the needs of the student. Needs assessment leads to the establishing of goals, outcomes, and instruction. The language content of the instruction is a factor of materials employed and strategies selected, both of which are determined by the learner's goals. Recent research in applied and theoretical linguistics is mentioned as it relates to possible materials development during the forthcoming decade. Also, technological breakthroughs which may have a significant impact on the production and transmission of future language instruction are discussed. The core of the chapter is a chart of the learner-centered approach to instruction with emphases on needs assessment and materials selection.

Learners' Needs
and the Selection
of Compatible Materials

FREDERICK L. JENKS
Florida State University

The explosion of curricular options in second language teaching
provokes in many teachers a feeling of optimism offset by frustration. Picture the ESL teacher who has just read through a professional journal during a free period in the class day and, gazing out
a window, searches for a key to instructional synthesis . . .

> How am I to deal with the
> flood of information
>   that swirls around my desk
> and causes endless consternation?

> There's grammar of expectancy
>   and period of latency,
> and notional/functional syllabi;
> it makes me want to sit and cry.

> There are speech acts and new facts,
> monitor models, discourse analysis.
>   And here sit I before a class,
> stricken by instructional paralysis.

> Egads! now it's dyads . . .
> Gee! Here's ESP.
> Oh well, there's always C/LL.
> You don't say! The Silent Way?

> Now I read where learners' needs
> are just waiting to be filled.
>   Oh heck, I think I'll shut the
> door and
>   get these patterns drilled.

The motivating force behind any change is that things should be better as a result. However, attitudes towards change differ; some educators interpret change as progress, others as tinkering. The purpose of this chapter is to present a bridging position between these two groups in the selection of instructional materials to meet learners' needs.

Two areas receive the bulk of attention: assessing needs and matching materials to those needs. However, this chapter's parameters are the following:

1. ESL instruction receives more attention than does either foreign language learning or bilingual education;
2. No reviews or analyses of specific books or materials are included;
3. No deliberate restatement of information found in other chapters in this volume is attempted.

The definitions of terms used in this chapter are short; thus, many of them require that the reader explore the broader meanings of the terms in other sources, some of which are listed in the bibliography. A *need* is a want, a requirement, a gap, and a request. An *objective* is a goal, an aspiration, a point to reach. An *assessment* is a weighing or a measuring; an *evaluation* is a measuring plus a judging. *Materials* include books, workbooks, films, audio tapes, and all other items through which the course's content is displayed. *Equipment* refers to "hardware." Although every teacher can cite cases where a learner's *interests* may be completely divorced from a learner's *needs*, both terms are used interchangeably herein.

Examining the Needs

Even though our primary focus is on the student's specific needs, other sources of influence upon the classroom affect the instructional environment. The chart below (Fig. 1) illustrates where these influencing agents enter into the *learner-centered* approach. Indeed, a truly learner-centered approach would be a totally individualized one; that it could exist in a formal school is very doubtful. However, strong elements of this approach can serve to shape a language learning program if similar needs of several learners are

FIGURE 1   Learner-Centered Approach to Instruction Via Needs Assessment and Materials Selection

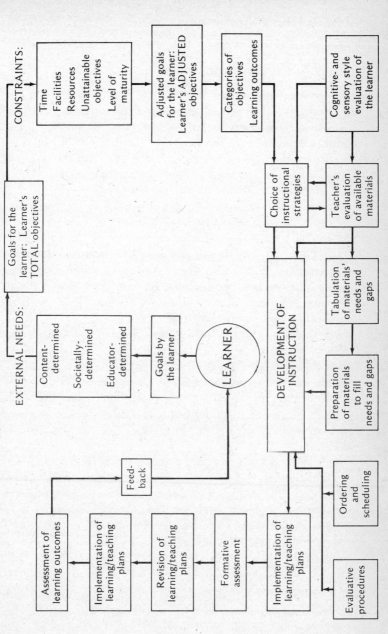

With thanks to my colleague, Dr. Robert Gagné, for his advice and time.

given a due measure of importance in the developing of the curriculum.

The Teacher-Centered Approach

Teacher-centered approaches to ESL are frequently the same as *materials-centered* approaches; a given set of materials is sequentially followed by learners under the direction and guidance of an instructor. Certainly, each teacher makes adjustments in the manner of presentation, the scheduling of activities, and the depth of investigation. Often, these adjustments are made to aid the instructor in reaching objectives of the teacher-tailored program. These approaches presume that the teacher knows precisely what students must learn, how they must learn it, in what order the language must be taught, and what the outcomes must be. Also, absolute faith in the insights and abilities of the materials designers must be exercised. Since all of these presumptions are either frail or false, the approaches are usually accompanied by learner dissatisfaction and, subsequently, teacher frustration. The usual response?—order a new textbook series.

What I choose to call the *institutional-centered* approach is that through which a societal organization (i.e., the government, professional societies, schools and universities) exercises its authority over the content of instruction. For example, the State Department of Education in Florida requires that all recipients of a teaching certificate in foreign languages have completed a course in the teaching of reading in English; no rationale for the requirement exists!

None of these approaches long endures the myriad variables of formal education. Each tends to incorporate aspects of the others; each is subject to constant erosion caused by the rubbing of inevitable constraints. Let us, therefore, turn to what has come to be called the *learner-centered* approach in order to examine the way(s) in which materials may be chosen.

THE LEARNER-CENTERED APPROACH

It is from the learner that the needs are derived, these needs being later formulated into objectives. Although it is possible that a person may be capable of clearly stating all of his needs and properly generate all the concomitant objectives, the chances are extremely slim that this ever occurs. Guidance from external parties serves to expand occasionally the listing of needs and to translate the needs into learning objectives. Thus, the learner's self-expressed need to, for example, speak English exactly like a Bostonian *may* appear in the *total* objectives as, "the learner will speak exactly like a Bostonian." However, when eroded and/or refined by the influences of time, facilities, resources, achievability, etc., the *adjusted* objective might read, "the learner will demonstrate orally the ability to correctly pronounce the *ar* (in p*ar*k) as it is pronounced by many native-born Bostonians (p*ah*k), etc."

Needs assessment, then, is a process highlighted by cooperation, redefinition, and perception clarification which leads to the formulation of educational objectives prior to the determination of instructional content or format (Richterich and Chancerel, 1978). Thus, in the chart, *total* objectives are not necessarily "achievable" objectives; *adjusted* objectives may be more capable of being reached by the learner, but they may not bring him or her anywhere close to either attaining the *TOTAL* objective or meeting the self-expressed need (see English and Kaufman, 1975; Medley, 1979).

Next, by categorizing adjusted objectives (shown in Figure 1 as "Categories of objectives; Learning outcomes"), the teacher and pupil group specific goals according to numerous similarities such as function, content, or task. This, then, proceeds to a careful consideration of the instructional strategies to be applied when development of instruction transpires. It is at this planning point that a learner's styles and sensory preference, and the teacher's sensitivity to the learner's characteristics and personality enter as factors in the instructional process. Hereafter, these features affect all subsequent stages of instruction, including materials selection. Space, however, prohibits the constant reiteration of this factor at all following steps of the illustration.

To satisfy this chapter's intent, one need proceed no further than the development of instruction since it is at this stage where what began as the learner's needs is now paired with instructional materials. Numerous other factors from equally important areas merge in the instructional developmental stage, among which are evaluative procedures and ordering/sequencing/scheduling.

Materials selection in a learner-centered approach must remain dormant until the learning outcomes have been categorized and instructional strategies have been considered. To make selections prior to this point in planning would indicate that the learner's goals are dependent upon the categorization of outcomes. One fits the materials to the learner's needs; to act in a contrary manner is to shift to a *teacher/book-centered* approach.

Selecting the Materials

A major role in the determination of applicable materials is played by the teacher(s). It is a responsibility for which the professional educator should be trained; it requires experience and patience. The teacher must maintain a constant vigil for new and recently revised materials that might relate more accurately to an individual learner's specific objectives. Perhaps no other teacher-task is as unrewarding as the reviewing of textbooks seems to be. Rare is the educator who reads textbooks for the derivation of pleasure or cerebral stimulation. It's work, fatigue-producing work. Relief is often delivered in the form of book reviews in professional periodicals, scrutinization of new materials at exhibits, and participation in conference sessions devoted to current retail releases in the field and presentations concerning the learner's specific objectives. Of equal importance is the teacher's regular participation in workshops or courses dealing with teaching techniques and instructional materials. Any instructional approach which prevents the teacher from spending a major portion of work time on the selection of materials automatically precludes focusing instruction on learner's needs.

The mechanics of materials selection entail much "cutting and pasting"—dovetailing certain portions of a workbook with specific exercises in a textbook and the listening to an audio tape from another instructional series. It is conceivable that a learner's entire instructional program can be organized from existing materials. Conceivable, but unlikely. It is possible that many learners will be able to satisfy their major needs by pursuing the same instructional program, as in an English for specialized or specific purposes. Possible, but not probable. It is this matching of individuals, their needs, strategies and materials that makes formalized instruction a humanistic venture (Logan, 1973).

There are bound to be gaps between what the learner wants to learn and what is contained in available materials. Since the categorization of objectives acts as an outline of a learner's goals, these deficits are noticeable as one aligns useable materials with each specific objective. The gaps, then, are visible on the teacher's "pairing worksheet" for each student. When continued searching yields no results, the teacher must either prepare relevant materials or request that the learner change his or her goals. The former is much more desirable for the learner and much more laborious for the teacher.

Looking Ahead Ten Years

In a book released five years ago, trends in instructional materials for second language curricula were projected (Jenks, 1975). That all sixteen trends noted therein have continued into the 1980's is not coincidental. Rather, it is indicative of the sequential nature of instructional change in this communication-dependent field of study. The "content" of language shifts slowly, whereas an emphasis on learning a particular slice of the "content" may crest or fall rapidly. Many vital findings of linguistic research completed ten years ago have yet to make even a modest impact on major commercial publications (even where the findings were applicable to learning and teaching). By the time that existing hardware which is capable of enhancing the delivery of instruction becomes cost-effective to apply to the formal school setting, it will be hopelessly outdated. Even if a massive effort were launched to educate today's teachers of ESL in the essentials of "methods," materials selection, assessment of learning, and communication-based instruction with a goal of delivering the equivalent of ten semester hours of instruction to seventy-five percent of these educators, that objective would have little chance of being reached within the next ten years. The general conclusion is that changes in education occur slowly, much more slowly than the needs of learners.

This conclusion need not be viewed as negative; it should be seen as a description of pedagogical reality. A few bright lights illuminate today's language curriculum and signaling beacons are on the horizon. Changes are before us! To be examined further are English for specialized/specific purpose (ESP) materials, print-machine materials, and advances in telecommunications.

Furthermore, one can only hypothesize what particular areas of contemporary research and investigation may have a major impact on yet-to-be-written ESL materials. Potential, although limited, application of findings from second language acquisition and development research may be expected (Dulay and Burt, 1974; Fathman, 1975; Fuller, 1978). In some specific learning situations, materials and instructional procedures may be influenced by their findings. Likewise, work in discourse analysis (Sinclair and Coulthard, 1975), speech acts (Searle, 1969) and notional syllabuses (Wilkins, 1976) may permit educators to translate new and deeper insights concerning the nature of human communication into learning activities.

The remaining years of this century provide the seeds for the "era of communication" (Kendig, 1979). The forthcoming years will be marked by numerous areas of growth within second language instruction; experiencing unparalleled growth will be materials and programs for learning English for specialized and/or specific purposes. Although initial entries in this area were oriented toward vocational pursuits for adult learners with some communicative proficiency in English, the scope of the ESP movement is rapidly expanding to include learners at the lowest levels of English proficiency who have been selected to work in industrial settings, as well as children in ESL classes at the elementary school level who require English for academic purposes (EAP) prior to being "mainstreamed" into an English-only curriculum. It is only a matter of a few years before we see the development of specialized programs and books which focus on, for example, "English for Raising One's Socialization Expertise" (EROS), through which an English learner may feel prepared to ask a native speaker of English for a date! As such materials relate more closely to widely accepted aspects and functions of communication, the carry-over from one ESP experience to others will provide even greater benefits to the learner.

ESP Materials

One of the major tasks facing developers of ESP materials is performing thorough task analyses of the specialized topic prior to making any decisions regarding instruction. Assume that some pupils require career-oriented ESL in restaurant services, specifically in the jobs of waiters and waitresses. The materials designer will invariably seek people with prior experience in these jobs and supervisors/employers in order to gather information regarding the tasks performed in the labor. It is common strategy for the materials writer to act as a customer in places where native speakers as well as non-native speakers of English work as food service employees. Given these analyses of tasks derived from contact with employers and workers on the job at tableside, will the designer be prepared to organize good career-oriented materials? Not completely.

In order to better perceive the gaps, the developer should take note of prior task analysis projects whose objectives were to improve instruction. The New Office Business Education Learnings System (NOBELS) project (Lanham and Cook, 1969) was a major educational effort to determine the precise tasks required of secretarial workers *and* the amount of time plus effort required by each task. To complete this assessment, analysts spent thousands of hours with employees in several hundred corporations in a major American urban area. Time and motion studies were completed, samples of all business forms that the workers were required to complete were collected, specific typewriting tasks were noted, unique office procedures were documented, and inter-staff communications were explored. By scrutinizing the tasks as performed by the laborers on a continuing basis, the designers created instructional programs which were custom-tailored to the needs of broad categories of employing agencies.

The importance of this type of project can best be understood when the enormous disparity between the supervisors' or employers' perception of tasks performed and the laborers' actual performance is examined. For example, employers may have stated that secretaries must be capable of taking shorthand at the rate of seventy-five words per minute for up to thirty minutes when, in actual practice, this skill was rarely called upon by employers. When required, the taking of dictation via shorthand never consumed more than about eight minutes. Instead, several hours per day were spent by secretaries listening to and typing from recorded dictation.

In the designing of ESL career-oriented materials, communication acts must undergo a similarly intense investigation since the learner's needs are derived from interfacing communicative incidents with requisite job skills. Returning to the role of waiter as an example: although current career ESL materials may emphasize listening comprehension development (i.e., to be able to write down an orally-delivered food order), future materials must prepare the learner to react appropriately to different kinds of complaints as they are made by a variety of individuals (i.e., customers, co-workers, employers).

One of the exemplary curricular efforts in this field is the Adult Performance Level Study (APL) project (Northcutt, 1975; Lyle, 1977). This endeavor has taken the designers through most of the activities mentioned above; the successful effort is expected to grow in the coming years as additional career need areas are indicated by ESL learners.

Technological Breakthroughs

A second feature of the "communications era" is the boom in word processing systems. The merging of the separate technologies of computers, data processing, lasers, and printing has resulted in the formation of efficient equipment for storing, editing, and producing printed words. Applying this technology, in combination with print-out equipment and relatively inexpensive trunk terminals, to the educational setting opens many ways for the personalization of instruction at great speed. This educational assistance must not, however, be confused with computer-assisted instruction. Word processing systems are capable of supplying the teacher and the student with relevant printed materials including textbooks, workbooks, specialized products, and teachers' lesson plans. In short, the entire instructional program can be produced in print form. The technology exists presently, and is being applied in thousands of industrial settings. Unfortunately, little impact has been made on education in general and on language learning in particular.

The absence of software—instructional lessons and other related information—in computer storage as it relates to learning ESL serves as the major hurdle. If one major project were funded internationally for collecting, editing, coding, and storing ESL instructional materials at all levels and for all currently perceived purposes, the result would be a *corpus* with ability to grow, shrink, or establish internal linkages. From this computer-based corpus, a publisher or an individual may extract an entire instructional program that is custom-selected for a learner by entering into the equipment the proper "descriptors" as related to the learner's objectives. Word processing technology then prints the information in a high quality manner onto paper and/or a visual screen. The sequentialized "book" is instantaneously bound and delivered to the learner, its content being related to all facets of instructional pre-planning (as portrayed in the chart above).

Telecommunications advances are only partially comprehended by most educators. Not only have schools shied away from technology because of apparent cost factors but also because initial attempts to "replace the teacher" with technological equipment failed. As individuals learn to use technology as an aid "enhancer" to learning, steps forward are made. Perhaps no better example of this exists than that of instructional television, a system tried in hundreds of schools to teach languages, among other subjects. Gross failure was experienced due to the then-prevalent absence of two-way visual and audio communication between the televised teacher and the students. The conclusion was that television was not well-suited to the learning of a language in a formal school setting. Today, that conclusion is being proved false.

Less than ten years ago, Texas Instruments Corporation installed an instructional television system which encompasses the vast area of urban Dallas, Texas. The system links no less than ten universities and dozens of public schools to each other. A project of the Texas Association of Graduate Education and Research (TAGER), the network broadcasts up to sixteen live classes simultaneously on a similar number of channels. For example, an ESL lesson being broadcast from one school can be relayed to another school forty miles away. Since the two sites are linked by direct two-way audio communication (via telephones with external speakers), the teacher can listen to learners in distant locations and is able to respond to them instantly. TAGER personnel believe that their system is one of the answers to delivering inexpensive instruction to a large number of sites, thereby eliminating the need for individual learners to commute great distances (spending time as well as money in order to appear at one instructional site). Furthermore, the system does not eliminate teachers; their role is altered insofar as they become instructional advisors, designers, and evaluators who work in a learner-centered mode.

As one ponders the implications of TAGER's network, it is important to realize that communications satellites are already hovering above earth, each prepared to broadcast thousands of television programs immediately to any set in the world on thousands of television channels! The logical extension of this existing phenomenon is that anyone may receive audio-active language instruction from any other person situated anywhere in the world instantaneously, and in full color. So much for today's simulation activities within the classroom walls!

All too often, mankind has awakened to find that yesterday's dreams are today's realities. The programmable pocket calculator which costs less than thirty dollars today is the direct technological offspring of a bulkier item which cost over seven hundred dollars ten years ago. The age of communications brings with it manageable expenses and viable routes for instruction.

Conclusion

The path of language instruction in the near future will not be followed blindly. Teachers and learners, armed with new goals, strategies, and materials, always advance while performing a pedagogical "two-step." For every two strides forward, one is made to the rear for the purpose of looking ahead to where we have just been, where we were before beginning, and how we must move in order to progress further. The result is a steady movement toward linguistic and communicative expertise with

constant redefining of needs and subsequent matching of supportive learning tools.

REFERENCES

Dulay, Heidi and Burt, Marina. "Natural Sequence in Second Language
Acquisition." *Language Learning,* 1974, *24,* 37–53.

English, F. and Kaufman, Roger. *Needs Assessment: A Focus for Curriculum Development.* Washington, D.C.: Association for Supervision and
Curriculum Development, 1975.

Fathman, Anne. "Language Background, Age and the Order of Acquisition of English Structures." In M. K. Burt and H. C. Dulay (eds.), *New
Directions in Second Language Learning, Teaching, and Bilingual Education: On TESOL '75.* Washington, D.C.: TESOL, 1975.

Fuller, Janet Kayfetz. *An Investigation of Natural and Monitored Morpheme Difficulty Orders by non-Native Adult Speakers of English.* Unpublished doctoral dissertation, Florida State University, 1978.

Jenks, Frederick L. "Foreign Language Materials: A Status Report and
Trends Analysis." In G. Jarvis (ed.), *Perspective: A New Freedom.* Skokie, Illinois: National Textbook Company, 1975, 93–128.

Kendig, Frank. *Language and Communication in the Year 2000.* Keynote
address delivered at the American Council on the Teaching of Foreign
Languages (ACTFL) Conference, Atlanta, 1979.

Lanham, Frank and Cook, Fred. *Development of Performance Goals for
a New Office and Business Education Learnings System (NOBELS).* Research performed pursuant to a grant with the Office of Education, U.S.
Department of Health, Education, and Welfare. USOE proposal No. 8-
0414, 1968 and 1969.

Logan, Gerald E. *Individualized Foreign Language Instruction: An Or-
ganic Process.* Rowley, Massachusetts: Newbury House, 1973.

Lyle, Buel. *Adult Performance Level Project (APL).* Austin: University of
Texas. Division of Continuing Education, 1977.

Medley, Frank. "Identifying Needs and Setting Goals." In J. Phillips
(ed.), *Building an Experience—Building for Success.* Skokie, Illinois:
National Textbook Company, 1979, 41–65.

Munby, John. *Communicative Syllabus Design.* Cambridge: Cambridge
University Press, 1978.

Northcutt, Norvell. *Adult Performance Level Research Project (APL).* Austin: University of Texas. Division of Extension, 1975.

Richterich, René and Chancerel, Jean-Louis. *Identifying the Needs of Adults Learning a Foreign Language*. Strasbourg: Council of Europe, 1977.

Searle, John. *Speech Acts: An Essay in the Philosophy of Language*. Cambridge: Cambridge University Press, 1969.

Sinclair, J. M. and Coulthard, R. M. *Towards an Analysis of Discourse*. London: Oxford University Press, 1975.

ABSTRACT

Materials Design:
Issues for the 1980's
An American Point of View

ROBERT LADO
Georgetown University

The challenge of the applied linguistics model of the 1940's and 50's by the Chomskian revolution in linguistics left a theoretical void which produced the plethora of methodological proposals of the 1970's. A brief overview of the proposals shows contradictory claims that cannot be reconciled in any cumulative way. In order to discuss the issues from a broader perspective, four universal learning stages are outlined. The issues for the 1980's include: communicative use of utterances in context; diversification of materials for different students; functional study of grammar; reading skill as a distinct objective; listening skill as a distinct objective; writing skills for academically-oriented students; going beyond language; ESP for limited objectives; teachers' manuals as supplementary references; variety of techniques rather than arbitrary restriction to any single technique; creativity as expression of individual interests; and a professional attitude of responsible inquiry toward potential learning capacities of students.

227

Materials Design:
Issues for the 1980's
An American Point of View

ROBERT LADO
Georgetown University

BACKGROUND

We cannot discuss materials design for the 1980's without considering the forces that shape it. The structural linguistics movement of the 1940's and 1950's, the transformational grammar revolution of the 1960's, the methodological proposals of the 1970's are present in current materials and will influence those of the future. To ignore them would severely limit our vision of current trends and future developments.

The structural linguistics movement has been well-summarized by Moulton (1961) in "Linguistics and Language Teaching in the United States 1940–1960." In that view, "language is speech, not writing"; "a language is a set of habits"; we "teach the language, not about the language"; "a language is what its native speakers say, not what someone thinks they ought to say"; and "languages are different." Fries (1945) and associates at the University of Michigan also incorporated the concepts of patterns of English sentences, pattern practice, graded structures, phonemics, intonation, and contrastive linguistics which influenced practically all subsequent materials. There is no reason to expect that such basic contributions will all vanish suddenly at the turn of the decade.

With the passage of the NDEA (National Defense Education Act) in 1958, foreign language study and teaching in the U.S. went into high gear. The audiolingual linguistics model was adopted for the design of materials, and audiolingualism in various forms became the mainstream practice in foreign language teaching in the U.S. in the late 1950's and the 1960's.

In the 1960's Chomsky (1957; 1965) challenged structural linguistics, denied the relevance of linguistics for language teaching, and attacked the idea that habit was part of language competence. His theoretical postulation of surface structure derived from deep structure by means of transformational rules, and his focus on competence rather than performance had a profound influence in linguistics. Theoretical linguistics switched almost universally to Chomsky's model. But Chomsky's theory was designed to explain the competence of an idealized native speaker, not that of a learner of a second language. Consequently, the materials used to teach English and other languages to those who did not possess native competence continued to be basically audiolingual with cosmetic adaptations to the new terminology.

METHODOLOGICAL PROPOSALS OF THE 1970's

With the challenge of the theoretical basis of audiolingualism and the vacuum created by the absence of a generalized model in applied linguistics came the plethora of methodological proposals of the 1970's. In retrospect, it seems almost predictable that such a variety of proposals from the most diverse sources should have occurred.

The proposals were usually advanced as absolute solutions to the "poor performance" of our students, to the "boring pattern practice drills," to the "lock step" syllabus, etc. It was claimed that our students were not performing like native speakers and that they were not creating language but merely overlearning it. Our problems would be completely solved if only we adopted cognitive grammar and cognitive psychology, and repudiated behavioristic psychology and structural linguistics. But cognitive grammar easily became memorization of rules rather than functional use of the language. And cognitive psychology left out attitudes, emotions, and performance. As the proposals failed to produce easy miracles, new proposals appeared:

1. Based on psycholinguistic research on language acquisition by young children (McNeill, 1970; Brown, 1973), it was proposed that language could not be taught, it could only be acquired. If

only we adopted language acquisition in second language teaching our problems would be solved. Psycholinguistic research on first language acquisition is of great interest, but its application to second language teaching is a very different matter. Should we immerse students in an informal all-day L_2 environment as the child is immersed, or should we begin teaching all school subjects in L_2 as in the St. Lambert School project in Canada (Lambert and Tucker, 1972)? The first alternative was inapplicable with school-age students, and the second applied only when a number of special conditions obtained (Tucker, 1979).

2. Another proposal of the 1970's was communicative competence. Since the function of language is to communicate, it is postulated that all teaching must involve communication. Communicative competence has become widely accepted today, but problems arise when it is presented as a total method. Piaget (1959:36–39, 49, 126) observed that approximately forty-five percent of children's use of language at the language acquisition age up to 6½ was ego-centric rather than communicative. Furthermore, communicative competence presupposes linguistic competence, or we end up with utterances like, "*Me no espeak English. *You wrong." Such creations are clear in their communicative denotation but detrimental to the speaker or explosive in their connotation because of secondary reactions to their non-standard linguistic features. Sociolinguistic considerations are to be added to linguistic competence in L_2 teaching and learning; they are not to replace it.

3. Discourse analysis of conversations shows rules that go beyond the sentence and beyond language. For example, we do not always answer questions directly but use non-linguistic strategies to obtain additional information before answering. These and other characteristics of extended utterances should be made clear to students, but to expect that a beginning student will use subtle strategies which even native speakers may be at a loss to manipulate effectively is asking for the moon without a supporting earth. Discourse analysis will prove most useful, but not as a total solution to L_2 teaching in the 1980's.

4. The immersion model of the St. Lambert School type proceeds basically as if the students were native speakers of the sec-

ond language, which they are not, and teaches all subjects in that language. When all the students are English speakers studying through the medium of French, good teachers will inevitably take that fact into account and adjust the work accordingly. But when only half of the students are English speakers while the other half are native speakers of French, the teachers cannot easily adjust to the learning styles of both groups at the same time.

Moreover, when the students come from culturally advantaged homes, the development of their native language does not suffer, but when they come from culturally deprived homes, or when their native language is under pressure of extinction in the community, total immersion in the target language will result in lack of development of the native language, possible extinction of it in the individual student, and an educationally impoverishing language switch rather than the acquisition of a second language.

5. A better proposal for the latter situation is the bilingual education model which consists essentially in the study of both languages as language and the study of content subjects through both (Andersson and Boyer, 1978). The bilingual model provides for the uninterrupted and balanced development of the first language as well as the second. The aim is to develop balanced bilingual biliterate and bicultural persons for our times.

6. As a reaction against purely grammatical syllabuses comes the proposal of notional/functional syllabuses (Wilkins, 1976). The notional part refers to semantic grammar, grammatical notions based on categories of meaning rather than on form, and the functional part refers to "the function of the sentence (utterance) as a whole in the larger context in which it occurs" (p. 22). A functional syllabus arranges the learning material according to selected functions regardless of the grammatical constructions that may be necessary to fulfill those functions. There is no question that merely teaching grammar to construct sentences for the sake of showing that one can construct them is incomplete language teaching, and students so taught cannot be expected to use language for communication in context. But to begin the teaching of language in its full functional use without regard to the difficulty of the grammatical complexities involved will result in overloading the acquisition capacity of students and produce unnecessary frustration. A systematic

presentation of functions may easily result in a grammar of functions rather than a pedagogically graded assimilation of the language and its functions.

7. The increasingly active development of materials in ESP (English for Special Purposes) is conceptually related to functional syllabuses. This idea results in pedagogical materials for specific limited uses based on the fact that many users of English cannot devote the time and effort needed for an extended study of the language in all its aspects, yet will be motivated to study some limited corpus for occupational or other specialized objectives. There is no question of the validity of such a view, provided the specialized use is sufficiently restricted to permit a useful selection of a special corpus, and provided also that the users know what their specialized interest is. General courses, however, must still remain the basic fare for students who are learning English as part of their education.

8. Other methodological proposals focus more on the manner of presentation of the lessons and the responses of the students, attempting to tap hidden learning capacities that human beings supposedly have and which are not being reached by present methods. Total Physical Response proposed by Asher et al. (1974) introduces the language in the form of commands that are executed first by the teacher and then by the students. The commands are simple at first, "Run! Stand up! Walk! Stop! Turn! Sit down!" and gradually become more complex, "Walk to the door! When Luke walks to the window, Marie will write Luke's name on the blackboard!" (pp. 26–27). It is claimed that practically the entire language can be introduced in the form of commands and that the deep memory of the students is reached more effectively ths way.

9. In partial conflict with the proposal is Curran's Community Language Learning (Curran, 1972) based on experience with group therapy in clinical psychology. The students form a group and ask the teacher in the native language how to say things they wish to address in the second language to other students. This results in a completely spontaneous sequencing of the learning material rather than the teacher-selected sequence in Total Physical Response. Although both techniques have something to offer in a language

course, one wonders why it is necessary to restrict a class for an entire semester or year to only one such activity. Students obviously learn through active participation in both types of linguistic performance, but they also learn by other techniques, and if for no other reason than for variety, a standard class should probably not be restricted to any one technique.

10–11. Two other proposals that are in partial conflict with each other are "The Silent Way," developed by Gattegno (1972), and "Delayed Oral Response," proposed by Postovsky (1970). Gattegno attempts to tap hidden learning powers by presenting new utterances only once. The students have to exert a great effort to learn the new material, because they know that the teacher will not repeat it. The students, however, speak at will as they attempt to learn it. This is in direct oposition to Postovsky's Delayed Oral Response in which the teacher presents new utterances orally as many times as needed while the students remain totally silent and transcribe the material instead. Postovsky claims that after six weeks of intensive silent listening, students soon outpace those who have been required to speak from the beginning. Without attempting to resolve the conflict, it is evident that both proposals cannot be right at the same time, and teachers cannot follow both simultaneously.

12. Finally, Lozanov, a psychiatrist from Sophia, Bulgaria, proposes the use of relaxation techniques, including music, while listening to the new language material in order to overcome the defense mechanisms that normally keep us from freely using our untapped learning potential. Early exaggerated claims did not help the credibility of the proposal, but more moderate recent findings indicate significant enhancement of learning from the techniques (Lozanov, 1978; Bancroft, 1978; Racle, 1975). Nevertheless, the closed nature of the system makes it difficult to explore its innovative features without surrendering whatever progress we have made in teaching languages professionally. The selection of utterances and functions to be taught and the necessary adaptations we must make to meet the needs of different age groups, educational levels, and linguistic and cultural backgrounds, among other matters, require a broader professional base than can be supplied by any one source.

ISSUES FOR THE 1980'S

We could not adopt all the methodological proposals of the 1970's because they are in conflict with each other, and we cannot adopt any one *in toto* because each is incomplete in some vital aspect or is unduly restricted to special situations or students. The generalized audiolingual model was challenged on theoretical grounds, but we have not developed adequate substitutes.

In order to find some broader overall frame of reference to discuss the issues we face, let us focus on universal learning stages (Lado, 1980) that seem to be valid in language learning regardless of teaching method. Such a frame of reference should help in evaluating materials design and the methodological proposals now before us and others still to appear. The stages are: (1) listening with understanding, (2) assimilating the language system, (3) developing skills in listening, speaking, reading and writing, and (4) going beyond language into various functional uses.

These are not levels of proficiency such as those we label "beginning," "intermediate," and "advanced." They are qualitatively different phases of learning that may go on simultaneously until full learning is achieved. And the stages apply not only at the beginning of a language course but at all levels when new material is introduced to the students or when they come in contact with it outside of class.

Stage 1, listening with understanding, is observed when we come in contact with a new utterance in a language we do not know. The first urge and need is to perceive and understand the utterance, i.e. to answer the implicit questions, "What did he/she say?" and "What does it mean?" Perceiving and understanding the utterance completes the communications cycle. Without completing this basic cycle, very little learning will take place.

Stage 2, assimilating the language system, requires that the student understand and retain its functional rules and units in deep memory for future use in understanding and producing new utterances. This assimilation of the system does not require that all the rules be made explicit, since many are acquired without conscious realization, but it does require that the system be assimilated for functional use regardless of method.

Stage 3 is the development of the basic skills. Skill means facility to use the language for communication with speed and ease so that the user can carry on the linguistic functions simultaneously with intentional thinking. The learner must perform at the skill stage before we can say that the language has been mastered.

Stage 4 involves using the language for some systematic purpose other than merely learning language. The typical use of language involves socializing, studying, buying and selling, obtaining and giving information, special knowledge such as required in ESP, special rules that go beyond language, and adaptations of the language to new experiences, ideas, and attitudes to achieve the intended goals. We must therefore recognize a fourth universal stage in language learning, i.e., going beyond language into selected functional uses. This fourth stage has to be reached for full mastery.

If these stages are universal as claimed, the methodological proposals can be evaluated by asking what provision they make to facilitate their attainment and how effective those provisions are. For example, we can ask how Community Language Learning provides for completing the communication cycle, and the answer is, "through the native language." In The Silent Way, on the other hand, we get a complete rejection of the native language as also in Total Physical Response, but we find full use of the native language in Suggestopedia.

How do the various proposals provide for assimilating the language system? Are the provisions adequate? Do the proposals contain any help to develop reading skill, one of the most valued objectives for almost every purpose (Lado, 1977)? As a matter of fact, most of the proposals of the 1970's say nothing about reading as an aid to mastering the language or about developing reading skill as a major objective in its own right.

Do the proposals make any provision for stage 4, using the language for some purpose beyond language? Except for ESP, little if anything is done about that stage. Functional syllabuses seem to be restricted to the stage of assimilating the functional system in necessarily contrived situations rather than using the language for some systematic purpose other than learning it.

DESIGNS FOR THE 1980'S

In view of the problems we face and the knowledge and experience at hand, what are the essentials for improved designs in this decade? Again, attempting to look beyond specific methods, it would seem desirable, perhaps imperative that:

1. any new design provide for maximum participation of the students in communicative use of utterances in context. Arbitrary exclusion of or arbitrary restriction to the native language, pictures, actions, role playing, context, etc. based on some unproved limiting hypothesis must yield to the need to facilitate the completion of the communicative cycle by the most effective means for the particular students and the particular problem at hand.

2. In order to provide for full communicative participation by the students, it is imperative that the teaching and the materials be diversified. Total diversification is uneconomical and probably impossible because no two classes are exactly alike, but we can easily identify a number of major differences among students and settings that make some diversification imperative. The foreign student attending or preparing to attend a college or university in the U.S. will enroll in an intensive course which should include advanced reading and writing skills. This differs from the needs of the thousands of refugees who must learn survival English first. And even among the refugees there are major differences represented by the Vietnamese, Cambodian, Cuban, and Russian groups, to mention only a few.

Quite distinct are the needs of bilingual children attending school, and among these there are further differences resulting from their differing language and cultural backgrounds. There are also the millions of children studying English as a foreign language in their native countries as part of their school work. And there is increasing recognition of the need for ESP materials for technical training of various types.

When the students are of a uniform linguistic and cultural background, the materials can easily be adapted to the learning needs of those students, but when classes are of mixed language and cultural backgrounds, adaptation is more difficult. Nevertheless, supplementary glossaries and cultural notes can be provided at least for major subgroups. Local informant resources can be tapped for individual students for whom special glossaries are not available. The communication cycle must be completed somehow before proceeding further into assimilating the language system.

3. The ambivalence of the profession toward the formal study of grammar will remain with us during the 1980's; that is, there will continue to be disagreement between those who, regardless of theoretical discussions, believe that the study and teaching of a second language is fundamentally the study of grammar, on one hand, and those who abhor the formal study and teaching of grammar in any form, on the other. It is probably necessary and perhaps imperative that those who believe in the teaching of grammar take into account meaning or semantic grammar as well as usage, and that the materials they favor provide adequately for contextualized use of the language. The study of grammar as an isolated subject for the sake of grammar is the domain of the grammarian and linguist, but it is incomplete and inadequate as a method of teaching English for functional use.

At the same time, those who abhor the study and teaching of grammar will have to provide for assimilation of the language system in some way that permits the student to use all of his or her learning powers, not just the subconscious acquisition capacity for discovering hit or miss rules as they are experienced in haphazardly organized learning materials. Some sort of formalization or confirmation of rules seems hard to ignore or dismiss.

4. The development of reading skill as a legitimate objective in its own right seems imperative in the designs of the 1980's. Probably the greatest weakness of the audiolingual approach was the erroneous assumption that if the students learned to speak and understand speech, reading would take care of itself. It did not, and as a result, performance in tests, which depended heavily on reading, suffered. And linguistic competence itself was not strengthened, as shown in subsequent research comparing listen-

ing alone versus listening and reading simultaneously (Lado, 1972; 1977).

Reading skill is understood as silent reading for meaning at normal language processing speed without translating. Surface translation (Lado, 1979) is not a substitute for reading skill and actually interferes with the full use of the linguistic competence of the students. True reading skill makes possible a more effective development of ESP in those cases that depend on reading to provide the necessary specialized knowledge.

Cloze exercises, though requiring some degree of reading skill, do not represent true reading performance since they require that the student supply arbitrarily deleted words rather than understand the meaning of what is read when all the words are supplied. Reading comprehension does not require recall of specific words; it requires thinking in terms of ideas that are stimulated by the text. Cloze exercises may actually interfere with good reading habits.

5. The recognition that listening can be enhanced as a distinct skill by means of specific listening exercises has become generally accepted. The materials of the 1980's should provide adequate practice in listening to difficult short utterances and to fully contextualized extending utterances, especially for those students going into adacemic pursuits or other listening-dependent activities.

6. Writing skill, in the sense of ability to produce written texts at an acceptable speed without engaging in surface translation, should also be dealt with in materials for advanced students going into academic work in English. Various techniques of controlled composition provide a gradual transition to free composition.

7. Using the language for purposes that go beyond language and require knowledge of etiquette, formality-informality choices, communicative strategies, and special formulas for the multiple functions of language need to be given specific attention in materials design. Wilkins' lists of functions (1976), and the results of discourse analysis research must be considered in providing for stage 4, going beyond language. But we cannot teach Wilkins' hundreds of functions, and all the strategies that research identifies, without considering also the complexities of the linguistic

competence required. A complete switch to functions and strategies without regard for grading of the vocabulary and structures will overload the acquisition capacity of the students and destroy motivation in the process. Functions need to be added to graded materials in appropriately graded doses or they will result in frustration and failure rather than enhancing learning and motivation.

8. ESP must be considered on at least two different planes: stage 4, going beyond language, in connection with a full curriculum, and in courses with very limited objectives when a restricted corpus can be identified and overlearned without a major commitment to a full course of English. As part of a full curriculum in English, ESP can be combined with developing reading skill in individualized reading outside of class.

9. In order to facilitate the professional work of the teacher, which is very complex, the materials should supply a teacher's manual, not to prescribe every step of the teaching, but to explain the lexical, grammatical, pronunciation, and cultural problems that are likely to be encountered by the students, to provide supplementary material that the teacher might use as needed, to suggest successful techniques for particular problems, and to describe games and other activities that will enhance motivation and contribute to good classroom management. This in addition to a listing of the new material introduced in each unit and notes as to their sociolinguistic appropriateness and functional uses.

10. The designs of the 1980's should move away from single restrictive techniques to make use of a variety of things that will permit teachers to better meet the needs of the students and the learning tasks at hand. Variety is essential for good motivation, and in addition some features of different methodological proposals can be made part of the teacher's arsenal in any method. For example, grading is essential to orderly progression, but there is good reason to allow students to ask how to say specific things that are of interest to them at a particular time even if the linguistic complexity puts these beyond their competence at the time. The motivation to learn a particular utterance will help them overlearn it willingly.

11. Creativity has become a prestige word in teaching and learning, but it is ambiguous. Creativity in one sense (Dulay and Burt, 1977) means the ability to construct new utterances accord-

ing to the rules of the language. But that means surrendering of creativity in another sense to rule-governed behavior. It refers to the human capacity to behave according to a complex system of rules. Creativity in a deeper sense is the ability to perceive and express new relations and metaphors which capture new concepts, feelings, realities, or fantasies on canvas or in poetry, in music or in stone. Creativity in poetry may even violate linguistic rules.

Multiple response exercises give more alternatives than single track transformation drills, but they do not really represent creativity in the deeper sense. It would be naïve to attempt to produce literary geniuses or successful entertainers who can enrich our lives with literary masterpieces on assignment or entertain us with their social wit, but we can respond to the students' interests by letting them use the language to learn more about them and express their views, i.e., to use the language as an instrument for what motivates them in life.

12. And still the designs will have to wait until we can learn through research and experience whether classical music, art, and other forces unlock hidden learning powers, as some have suggested. We must keep an open mind to new research on learning and we must welcome the results of research on discourse and communicative strategies.

But we must resist attempts to oversimplify language learning by overstating potentially useful insights and suggestions. Teaching English to speakers of other languages is a highly complex matter that requires professional knowledge and a professional attitude. Patent medicine solutions will not do. We must be able to analyze the needs of different groups of learners and provide linguistic experience appropriate to their needs, abilities, and background knowledge and experience.

REFERENCES

Andersson, Theodore, and Boyer, Mildred. Second edition revised by Theodore Andersson. 1978. *Bilingual Schooling in the United States*. Austin, Texas: National Educational Laboratory Publishers, Inc.

Asher, James J., Kusudo, JoAnne, and de la Torre, Rita. 1974. "Learning a Second Language Through Commands: The Second Field Test." *Modern Language Journal* 58: 24–32.

Bancroft, W. Jane. 1978. "The Lozanov Method and its American Adaptations." *Modern Language Journal* 62, No. 4: 167–175.

Brown, Roger. 1973. *A First Language, The Early Stages.* Cambridge, Massachusetts: Harvard University Press.

Chomsky, Noam. 1957. *Syntactic Structures.* The Hague: Mouton.

———. 1965. *Aspects of the Theory of Syntax.* Cambridge, Massachusetts: MIT Press.

Curran, Charles A. 1972. *Counseling-Learning: A Whole-Person Model for Education.* New York: Grune and Stratton.

Dulay, Heidi, and Burt, Marina. 1977. "Remarks on Creativity in Language Acquisition." In: *Viewpoints on English as a Second Language.* Edited by Marina Burt, Heidi Dulay, and Mary Finocchiaro. New York,: Regents Publishing Co., Inc.

Fries, Charles C. 1945. *Teaching and Learning English as a Foreign Language.* Ann Arbor, Michigan: University of Michigan Press.

Gattegno, Caleb. 1972. *Teaching Foreign Languages in Schools: The Silent Way.* New York: Educational Solutions, Inc.

Lado, Robert. 1972. "Evidence for an Expanded Role for Reading in Foreign Language Learning." *Foreign Language Annals* 5: 187–192.

———. 1977. "Why Not Start Reading Earlier?" In: *Viewpoints on English as a Second Language.* Edited by Marina Burt, Heidi Dulay, and Mary Finocchiaro. New York: Regents Publishing Co., Inc.

———. 1979. "Language and Thought: Effect of Translation vs Interpretation. *TESOL Quarterly* 13, No. 4: 565–571.

———. 1980. "Universal Learning Stages Regardless of Teaching Method." Paper presented at the TESOL '80 Convention, March, 1980.

Lambert, Wallace E., and Tucker, G. Richard. 1972. *Bilingual Education of Children: The St. Lambert Experiment.* Rowley, Mass.: Newbury House.

Lozanov, Georgi. 1978. *Suggestology and Outline of Suggestopedy.* New York and London: Gordon and Breach.

McNeill, David. 1970. *The Acquisition of Language: The Study of Psycholinguistics.* New York: Harper & Row.

Moulton, William G. 1961. "Linguistics and Language Teaching in the United States 1940–1960." In: *Trends in European and American Linguistics 1930–1960.* Edited by Christine Mohrmann, Alf Sommerfelt, and Joshua Whatmough. Utrecht, The Netherlands and Antwerp, Belgium: Spectrum Publishers.

Piaget, Jean. 1959. *The Language and Thought of the Child.* Third edition. London: Routledge & Kegan Paul Ltd.

Postovsky, Valerian A. 1970. "Effects of Delay in Oral Practice at the Beginning of Second Language Learning." *Modern Language Journal* 58: 5–6.

————. 1977. "Why Not Start Speaking Later?" In: *Viewpoints on English as a Second Language.* Edited by Marina Burt, Heidi Dulay, and Mary Finocchiaro. New York: Regents Publishing Co., Inc.

Racle, Gabriel. 1975. "Experimentation with Suggestopaedia in Canada." *A Teaching Experience with the Suggestopaedic Method.* Ottawa, Canada: Publication Service of Canada. 225–232.

Tucker, G. Richard. 1979. "Implications of Canadian Research for U.S. Bilingual Education: Setting the Record Straight." *NABE News,* National Association for Bilingual Education 3, No. 2: 1, 4–5, 7.

Wilkins, D. A. 1976. *Notional Syllabuses.* Oxford, England: Oxford University Press.

ABSTRACT

Materials Design:
Issues for the 1980's
A European Point of View

L. G. ALEXANDER

This chapter begins by describing the immediate historical background in Europe: the theoretical and analytical foundations developed in the 1970's under the sponsorship of the Council of Europe. This account is followed by a comparison between structural and functional approaches to course design (the traditional syllabus vs. the functional/notational syllabus) and remarks on some of the limitations of conventional designs and methods. Four possible course designs based on functional/notional syllabuses are then examined in detail and their suitability for different kinds of materials is considered. The chapter concludes with a brief survey of some of the implications of functional/notional syllabuses for practical methodology.

Materials Design:
Issues for the 1980's
A European Point of View

L. G. ALEXANDER

THE IMMEDIATE HISTORICAL BACKGROUND

From a materials design point of view perhaps the 1970's will come to be seen as a preparation for what language course designers will be doing in the 1980's. For it was in the 70's that in Europe, at any rate, it dawned on us that we ought to be investing at least as much time and energy considering what it is we have to teach and learn as we spend on creating materials which are based on nothing more than changing fashions, arbitrary examination syllabuses and market forces. This awakening of our collective consciousness was far from accidental. It began with a symposium sponsored by the Council for Cultural Co-operation (CCC) of the Council of Europe at Rüschlikon in 1971, the expressed aim of which was "to examine the possibility of organizing modern language teaching/ learning in the form of a unit/credit system in order to allow an approach based on the individual motivation and capacities of the adult learner." (*Rüschlikon Symposium Report,* p. 1, 1971).

From this modest beginning, the Council of Europe Modern Languages Project, under the direction of John Trim, was launched. This led to the setting-up of working parties and the publication of thought-provoking and influential papers on many aspects of foreign language acquisition, first published separately, then collected in a single volume entitled *Systems Development in Adult Language Learning* (CCC, 1973). These papers were followed by the development and publication of sets of specifications, which can only be described as "proto-syllabuses" for the teaching of the major European languages: *The Threshold Level* (van Ek, 1975) and *Waystage* (van Ek et al. 1977) for the teaching of English as a foreign language; *Un Niveau Seuil* (Coste et al., 1976) for the teaching of French; with specifications for the teaching of German (*Kontakt Schwelle*), Italian (*Livello Soglia*) and Spanish (*Nivel Umbral*) due in the early 1980's.

At the ideas level, the theoretical foundations for work in the 1980's have already been laid: the emphasis is on language as an instrument for communication moving firmly away from the unfortunate tendency in the 1960's to reduce language (from a teaching/learning point of view) merely to a collection of kernel sentences, transformations and substitutions. The theoretical foundations have been significantly implemented by the publication of proto-syllabuses which have, in turn, provided the analytical foundations for the work of materials designers in the 1980's.

PROTO-SYLLABUSES AND THEIR USES

The production and development of specifications constitute a major move towards greater efficiency in the classroom, for they oblige us to question and re-appraise everything we have done and are doing. From such proto-syllabuses we can derive practical working documents to meet our precise needs when designing courses, planning curricula, devising tests and examinations and so on. All these specifications have a common aim: they attempt to define objectives in terms of the presumed communication needs of the adult learner. Their starting point is what the learner wants to *do* through language. "The basic characteristic of the model is that it tries to specify foreign language ability as a *skill* rather than *knowledge*. It analyses what the learner will have to be able to *do* in the foreign language and determines only in the second place what language-forms (words, structures, etc.) the learner will have to be able to handle in order to *do* all that has been specified" (van Ek, 1976). The specifications therefore provide the basis for "functional/notional" syllabuses rather than structural syllabuses.

A common objection that is sometimes raised against such attempts to specify student needs is that these assessments are subjective, which is true. But at least they are usually *collectively* subjective, reflecting, as they do, the input of many experienced practitioners. The dilemma is expressed succinctly by van Ek: ". . . it is *normal* for educational innovation projects to be carried out on a ridiculously tight budget by people who cannot really spare the time. It is also normal, if practical results are the aim, to set aside most of one's theoretical scruples and academic reservations. . . . Society just cannot afford to wait for the experts to solve their problems to their own satisfaction before it introduces innovations into its structure. For the experts this entails the obligation to recommend courses of action even *without* having solved most of their problems, in other words to stick their necks out even if they would much prefer not to do so" (*St. Wolfgang Symposium Report*, 1973, p. 32).

A COMPARISON BETWEEN STRUCTURAL AND FUNCTIONAL/NOTIONAL APPROACHES TO COURSE DESIGN

There are important differences between a structural syllabus and a functional/notional syllabus which need to be established. A structural syllabus generally consists of two inventories, one of structures (often in a presumed order of difficulty) and one of vocabulary, both of which the course designer is required to bring together when writing a course. The main objective (for both course designer and learner) in such a course is to cover a grammatical syllabus and to build up a command of high-frequency vocabulary. A detailed example of such a syllabus can be found in *English Grammatical Structure* (Alexander et al., 1975) which lists structures and exponents in a six-stage progression. Communication skills are often regarded as the by-product of this undertaking. By comparison, a course based on functional/notional specifications does exactly the opposite. It consciously sets out to teach communication skills. Structure and vocabulary, though carefully selected and graded, are the by-product of this objective. Whereas most structural courses deal primarily with two factors, structure and vocabulary, a course setting out to teach communication skills must take into account at least the following, to encompass the principal factors involved when we communicate:

1. **Functions:** These are "language acts": i.e., what we want to use the language to do: *e.g.*, agreeing, refusing, offering, apologizing, expressing hope, fear, etc.
2. **General notions:** These are abstract time-and-space relations which connect with functions: *e.g.*, existence/non-existence; presence/absence; mobility/immobility, etc.
3. **Specific notions:** These are items which are directly determined by the topic. The three factors can be exemplified as follows: Inquiring about (*function*) the existence (*general notion*) of a bank (*specific notion*): *e.g.*, "Is there a bank near here?"
4. **Settings:** That is, where people are when the transaction or interaction takes place and how (if at all) the setting influences what is said.
5. **Social, sexual and psychological roles:** That is, who is talking to whom, what their relationship is and how they feel; how these factors influence the language the speakers use.
6. **Style/Register:** That is, the way we express ourselves to reflect our attitudes which can range between extremes: *e.g.*, formal-informal; serious-jocular; courteous-rude; positive-tentative, etc.
7. **Stress and intonation:** Attitude and emotion are conveyed not only by what we say but by the rise and fall of the voice. For example, a speaker may use polite expressions, yet his intonation may convey rudeness, irony, indifference, etc.
8. **Grammar:** i.e., the means we use to express ourselves, which is the product of the factors listed above. (General notions often have a grammatical content.)
9. **Vocabulary:** i.e., the lexical items we need, which are a product of the factors listed above. (These are often the same as the "specific notions.")
10. **Paralinguistic features:** Such as gesture, facial expression, etc., none of which has, as yet, been satisfactorily coded for language learning purposes.

It will be clear that a functional/notional approach to course design is concerned as much with the rules which are part of the system of social behaviour as with grammar rules; it requires the student to produce the language which is not only grammatically acceptable, but socially appropriate in any given situation. This is particularly vital for the adult learner who is acutely aware of the social rules, but in a foreign language cannot cope with situations which cause him little or no trouble in his mother tongue. When using his mother tongue, "the mature adult has learnt a complex body of social and linguistic rules which have made him a fully integrated member of a number of interlocking social groups. He knows how to behave with them, what to do and what to say, when, where, how and to whom." When this same adult becomes a foreign language learner, he suddenly "finds himself confronted with a range of situations, which, despite all the knowledge and skill he has built up in his previous experience, he is incompetent to handle," whether at a public or a private level (Trim, 1977).

A broad comparison of the two approaches to course design, logico-grammatical progression vs. functional/notional and the kind of organization and practical methodology they lead to can be made as follows:

TRADITIONAL SYLLABUS = Structure list + Vocabulary	*FUNCTIONAL/NOTIONAL* *SYLLABUS =* Functions/General & Specific Notions Settings Social/Sexual/Psychological Roles Style and Register Stress and Intonation Grammar + vocabulary
↓	↓
POSSIBLE COURSE DESIGN BASED *ON:* Structural grading (linear and/or cyclical sequencing) + "Situationalised structure."	*POSSIBLE COURSE DESIGN BASED* *ON:* Purely functional organization OR Structural/functional organization OR Functional/structural organization OR "Thematic area" organization
↓	↓
PRACTICAL METHODOLOGY Generally A/V and/or A/L: text-based repetitive routines in lesson formats.	*PRACTICAL METHODOLOGY* Highly varied methods to suit highly varied language activities and learner needs.

Increasingly (and the trend is already firmly established) we must see a marked move away from the traditional simplistic syllabus and the kind of methodology it has given rise to. But exactly how far we can manage to disentangle ourselves from the comfortable assumptions of our own making is going to be one of the major issues of the 1980's.

SOME LIMITATIONS IN CONVENTIONAL DESIGNS AND METHODS

For all their much-publicised (and often well-justified) virtues, audio-visual and audio-lingual course designs and methods have severe shortcomings. For example, grading in terms of presumed difficulty is arbitrary, often making a student wait several years before he is allowed to say something as socially vital as "May I have . . . ?" on the grounds that, e.g., the use of modals is "difficult" and must be delayed. The situations presented are, in turn, equally arbitrary, serving simply as contexts for the structure(s) to be taught. The compartmentalization of language into "four skills," while convenient for the purposes of A/V presentation ("Nothing should be written before it has been read; nothing should be read before it has been spoken; nothing should be spoken before it has been heard") is highly misleading and has fossilized into a kind of dogma that makes a mockery of what we actually *do* with language. (The listening skill, for example, must be re-defined as "Listen and . . .": Listen and respond/assimilate/take notes/interpret/report/recall, etc.) The method of presenting situations and then exploiting them in fixed lesson formats has become formalised and has led to repetitive routines in the classroom. Much of the practice provided involves the language of reporting: e.g., question-and-answer based on the text, e.g., "What did John do then?" etc. The situations invariably involve L_1-to-L_1 interlocutors in L_1 settings and take little account of the needs of non-native-to-native or non-native often in alien settings (e.g., a German and Japanese using English as a lingua franca in Mexico City). The drilling is habit-forming behaviouristic (= concerned with conditioning), rather than behavioural (= concerned with the way we behave as human beings). While such drilling might be effective in training

students to produce acceptable utterances, it often over-values the
need for grammatical correctness and is rarely concerned with situational appropriateness. The content of courses is generally intended to be actively acquired *in toto*, so authentic language and
therefore training in receptive areas such as gist-listening and
gist-reading is usually ignored. Until recent times, transfer/impro-
visation work, requiring personal creativity from the student, was
generally absent. Testing has been (and still largely is) psychometric "discrete point," designed for objective marking and based on
Lado's dictum, "Testing control of the problems is testing control
of the language." The washback effect of such testing on materials and methods *where the techniques used to test a language are
conflated with the methods necessary to teach one* can only be described as pernicious.

POSSIBLE COURSE DESIGNS BASED ON
FUNCTIONAL/NOTIONAL SYLLABUSES

The logico-grammatical progression, co-ordinated with "situation-
alised structure," has three things in its favour: it is easy to understand, easy to apply, and easy to teach. But because communication is generally left to chance, and objectives (other than purely
grammatical ones) are ill-defined, it can be highly inefficient and
frequently ineffective. By comparison, a functional/notional syllabus is much harder to understand, much harder to process, and
less predictable in its application, therefore making far greater demands on course designer, teacher and learner. But because it defines communication objectives precisely and seeks to achieve
them through the shortest possible route, it is highly effective in
bringing the learner rapidly up to the limit of his individual potential. It is hardly surprising that the idea has found such a ready
response among thinking language teachers for the simple reason
that it makes such immediate sense. However, learning how to
handle this more complex approach to course design is going to be
one of the major tasks of the 1980's.

The four designs models listed in the comparative table above
are tentative definitions. They are all based on the proto-syllabuses
Waystage and *The Threshold Level* and should be seen not as al-

ternatives, but as variables, each of them is valid for different kinds of materials and each must be considered in turn for its suitability in particular applications:

1. Purely Functional Organization

A form of organization based purely on functions ("Today I'm going to teach you to commiserate and tomorrow I'm going to teach you to rejoice") would be unthinkable in a course design intended for classroom use. Teachers would rightly reject the idea of presenting language through slot-and-filler functional utterances in a way which undervalues grammatical content so that the learner is ultimately not capable of operating the grammatical system.

However, not all learners want to operate the grammatical system. A purely functional course design might be admirable at a level which we could define as "survival." This level does not pretend to be concerned with communication in the ordinary sense. It is not language we are dealing with, but (to adopt a phrase by Spolsky) "language-like activity," enabling the learner to obtain food and shelter, ask for and give directions, and so on. At this level it is not necessary (or even desirable) for the learner to operate the grammatical system beyond the limitations of simple slot-and-filler utterances. A carefully-designed syllabus could take the user through a modest number of essential communicative areas, first teaching him fixed expressions (e.g., "Please," "Thank you," "That's all right," etc.) which he would have to learn by heart and then through functional/notional categories like the following:

Availability/non-availability:	e.g. I've got/haven't got/a reserved seat/.
Requests:	e.g. I'd like /a ticket/ please.
Existence/non-existence:	e.g. Is there /a train/ to /Madrid/ today?
	There's /a train/ to /Madrid/ today.
	There isn't /a train/ to /Madrid/ today.
Location:	e.g. Where's the nearest /bank/ please?

The relevance of such a purely functional course design at this most humble level of language acquisition (at present often ludicrously catered for by conventional phrase books) will be immediately apparent. Such a design, based entirely on slot-and-filler utterances and linked to a lexical retrieval system in which all the items listed were carefully selected to go into slots, would enable the user (assuming he has learnt the key sentences by heart) to find what he wants to say at the time he needs it simply by looking up the word in a bilingual lexicon and slotting it into the space in the pattern. Five to twenty hours' learning of key patterns (depending how many the learner wants to acquire) would be adequate preparation for such a system. A method of this kind has already been applied in the *Survive in . . .* series (Longman, 1980) for the acquisition of minimal French, German, Italian and Spanish and can certainly be extended to embrace less accessible languages like Arabic, Japanese, Serbo-Croat, etc. Thus phrasebooks, virtually unchanged in their mode of compilation since their inception in the nineteenth century, and so long the province of the travel industry (perhaps because they have been considered unworthy of serious attention by practising linguists) can be totally re-defined and the mass-market of travellers (tourist and business) can be adequately catered for.

2. Structural/Functional Organization

This is the most obvious and immediately attractive way of attempting a course design which will simultaneously meet the need for some kind of orderly progression and grading in terms of difficulty and the broader requirements of a functional/notional syllabus. To this extent, such a form of ordering might be applicable at the beginners' level where concurrent mastery of structure and function is essential.

In such a design, the conventional linear sequencing of structures would be re-applied, but given a functional rather than a purely structural connotation. For example, many conventional courses begin with the structure "This is . . ." and then take students through a series of purely empirical utterances ("This is the window," "This is the door," "This is my head," "This is my nose," etc.). In place of these pen-of-my-aunt utterances (always absurd and uncommunicative!) we could teach *e.g.*, *introducing people:* "This is Mr X and this is Mrs. Y."; or *naming of parts:* "This is the ON/OFF switch." When teaching "What's this . . . ? It's a . . ." (another well-tried favourite in Book 1, Lesson 1), a great variety of functional interpretations is possible: *e.g.*, *identifying the names of things in L₂:* "What's this in English?—It's an envelope/It's paper"; *identifying objects/substances you can't recognise:* "What's that? (in, *e.g.*, a self-service restaurant)—It's fish (believe it or not!)"; *identifying something you can't recall:* "What's that? It's Beethoven's Fifth"; *identifying technical terms:* "What's this?—It's the ON/OFF switch." In these examples, the student is coping with simple structures but being made aware of their communicative value in a social context.

This kind of organization has an immediate appeal, but is actually very difficult to apply successfully because the structural sequencing (inevitably) tends to predominate so that the end product is little more than a structural-course-by-another-name and functional connotations are forced to fit that particular mould. In the light of present knowledge (until proved otherwise) the approach can only be described as pseudo-functional (or, if you prefer, crypto-structuralist!). However, a work like *A Communicative Grammar of English* (Leech et al., 1975) contains innumerable insights into the communicative application of structure. Perhaps the most useful awareness to be gained from this approach is retrospective. Teachers working from traditional materials (and they are the majority) can adapt them on a day-to-day basis, illuminating the structures they are presenting by examining their communicative ramifications.

3. Functional/Structural Organization

In this approach functional objectives would predominate and the structural implications would be subsequently taught. Thus, for example, if we were teaching *advising* we might do so by presenting exponents like "Have you thought of . . . ?" "Why don't you . . . ?" "You should/ought to . . ." etc. (all in proper contexts) and then go on to examine the grammatical implications of these exponents. It will be apparent at once that such an approach would be difficult (if not impossible) to apply in a beginners' course. It is inconceivable to compile a hierarchy of functions and to superimpose any kind of systematic ordering in the way we can readily conceive of a hierarchy of structures. Questions like "Do I teach *requesting* before or after *recommending*?" are self-defeating and lack any kind of credibility. Other problems abound. No two functions can have the same value in any presumed syllabus. *Proposing a toast* (exponent: "Cheers!") is easily mastered; *asking* is a total system of exponents which many students never manage to master in a lifetime of study. Furthermore, we have to confront questions like "How many ways of saying the same thing may (must?) I teach?" and so on.

In such an approach the acquisition of grammar would be far too unsystematic for any beginner to make useful connexions. However, at intermediate and advanced levels (where more than a modicum of grammar has already been acquired) the approach is attractive. There is less need for rigid systematization at these levels; students *do* need to be taught different ways of expressing the same thing and the stylistic value of varying exponents. So, for (say) *agreeing*, we may teach *positive agreement* ("I agree!" "Fine!" etc.); *doubtful agreement* ("Do you really think so?" "I'm not so sure," etc.); *positive disagreement* ("I can't agree," etc.) and special context utterances like "Nonsense!" "Rubbish!" and so on. We may also teach implied functions: *e.g.*, "It's cold in here" (implying—depending on intonation—"Shut that window!" or "Would you mind shutting that window?" etc.) There are already examples of intermediate materials which make use of this form of organization, such as *Advanced Speaking Skills* (Arnold & Harmer, 1978).

4. "Thematic Area" Organization

This is by far the most radical of the four models. It attempts to take account of the fact that when one element in a course design is carefully organized, other elements are inevitably disorganized. A systematic ordering of structures, for example, pre-supposes a random presentation of functions; a purely functional syllabus, by comparison, presupposes a random presentation of structure. This is a critical problem when we are designing materials for beginners in particular and is barely solved by the second model (structural/ functional organization). As we have seen, it is not just necessary to teach students to do things through language. They also need to master the grammatical structure necessary for this purpose— otherwise they will progress no further than slot-and-filler substitution. By operating the grammatical system they learn to say not only *e.g.*, "Can I have a glass of water?", but also "Can my mother have a glass of water?". The need to control grammatical paradigms is intensified rather than diminished in a properly organized functionally-based course.

The thematic area approach takes as its starting point a number of broader themes, some purely functional, some notional and some topical. These themes are very basic aspects of everyday life and social communication. Examples of such themes are: the identification of self and others; requests, offers and suggestions; finding the way; location; time; information about things, substances and conditions; likes, dislikes and preferences, etc. The term "thematic area" must not be confused with "centres of interest" (*e.g.*, shopping, the garage, the bank, etc.). They are altogether broader in their application. For example, when you have covered an area like "information about things, substances and conditions" learning in the meantime how to handle notions of size, colour, weight, price, etc. you are equipped to deal with most common shopping situations (*e.g.*, specifying what you want if you are buying a suit of clothes).

In a course based on this approach, each thematic area is regarded as a major objective and is broken down into smaller objectives. Thus to master the major objective "finding the way" you would have to cover the following small-scale objectives:

Distinguishing between left and right.

Ordinal numbers 1st–5th.

Direction (location/existence): out of doors, short distances: Where's the nearest /bank/ please? It's /first/ left. etc.

Imperatives: out of doors, short distances: Go /straight on/, then turn /left/. etc.

Landmarks: /Go/ . . . and you see/come to a /cinema/. Then
. . . etc.

Location/existence:indoors: It's on the /third/ floor. etc.

Imperatives and landmarks: indoors: Go down this passage
and you'll come to . . . etc.

Out of doors: longer distances: /Drive/ two miles along this
road . . . etc.

Mode of transport: How can I get to . . . By . . . etc.

Distance: It's two miles away/five minutes' walk. etc.

Essentially, what we are saying to the student is: this is what
you have to do to cope with finding the way. At the end of the
process we can test how well you can do it (not how much you
know). The components of the task are analysed and sequenced
while, at the same time, the grammatical structure necessary to
perform the task is carefully graded. If we look at this example
from a purely structural point of view, the student is presented
with the following sequence: Where is . . . ? It's . . . ; Is there
. . . ?, There's a . . . /There's one . . . + static prepositions indicating location; How can I get to . . . ?/Can you tell me the way
to . . . ? + imperatives, negative and affirmative, and so on. This
sequencing would conform with accepted ideas about easy-to-dif-
ficult structural progression which might apply in a structure-based
course. The point is, however, that the structures are not taught
for their own sake, but for their communicative validity and relevance in this particular thematic area.

Mastery of such a thematic area would involve not only gaining
grammatical control of the structures necessary for asking for and
giving directions but the great variety of skills involved: *e.g.,* decoding complicated verbal instructions (listening for gist) so you
learn to discard redundant information and listen for global meaning; note-taking (*e.g.,* instructions given on the telephone); coping
with maps (street maps, road maps, sketch maps); coping with grid
references; interpreting hand-written notes; coping with public
signs (indoor and outdoor); decoding intonation patterns to understand, *e.g.,* when someone has finished giving instructions and so

on. Each thematic area is tackled in a comprehensive way so that the student can clearly see that he is being trained to accomplish a particular skill and he can usually tell for himself how he is getting on. The techniques ultimately used to test him would have to be similar to those used to teach him or they would have little relevance as a true indicator of attainment and in turn proficiency.

In conventional courses, "grading" is taken to refer wholly to the sequencing of structures. In functionally-based courses the whole idea takes on a completely new meaning. It is not just structures which are graded, but total situations. The same situations can recur in a course, increasing in complexity every time they make their appearance. For example, you can learn to check into a hotel as soon as you have learnt to say "My name's. . . ." At a later stage, you can add "I'd like a room." At a still later stage, you can specify: "I'd like a /twin bedded/ room with/without bath." At a much later stage you should be able to make complex utterances like: "I wrote to you two weeks ago booking accommodation for my wife and myself for three nights" etc.

This type of course design has so far been applied in *Mainline Beginners A & B* (Alexander, 1978/79) and has provided the basis for the multi-media series *Follow me*, first broadcast in Germany 1979–80. Only time will tell whether the approach is valid and how much further refinement is needed.

A FEW IMPLICATIONS
FOR PRACTICAL METHODOLOGY

A brief survey of just a few of the practical implications of this new approach to course design is worth attempting in areas where our present views are likely to be modified. For example:

The Four Skills

The skills of understanding, speaking, reading and writing do not exist in isolation. As we have already seen, the skills must be redefined as "Listen and . . . ," "Read and . . . ," "Write and. . . ." It will be more helpful if we think of the skills as "language activities." "Listen and interpret simultaneously" or "Read in detail and take notes" are examples of such activities.

Varying Methods

If we accept the principle of "language activities," it follows that each activity requires its own methodology. The method for presenting and exploiting a dialogue must differ from the one for (say) responding to a photograph or looking up a telephone directory. Language courses must therefore use methods which are appropriate to the materials they present rather than attempt to process all materials through some kind of "universal method," in the way that audio-visual and audio-lingual course designs involved us in unvarying routines.

The Nature of Conversation

Much sharper definitions are required when we teach "conversation" (often based on nothing more than hit-or-miss methods like questions round the class). We need to distinguish between *transactions* (*e.g.*, broadly predictable sequences) like ordering a meal at a restaurant where the setting influences the choice of language, and *interactions* (the non-contentious exchange of information or discussion and argument) where the setting barely influences the discourse. A growing understanding of the nature of discourse will inevitably affect the methods for teaching and learning it.

Receptive and Productive Skills

Training students to discard redundant information (aural and written) is a major undertaking involving the use of authentic materials even when we are teaching zero-level beginners. We are already moving away from the idea that the student must productively acquire everything that is in a course.

Improvisation

The core of any course based on functional/notional specifications must be *improvisation* or *transfer* in which students are invited to cope with real-life situations (transaction and interaction) where they are required to recombine the language learnt in one context to meet the exigencies of another.

Relevant Situations

Situations practised in adult courses in particular must be ones which the student may actually encounter, not L_1-to-L_1: e.g., you are seeing your bank manager about a loan to buy a car. We also need to distinguish between "English for foreigners" where students visit the U.S.A. or Britain (usually for short periods) to learn English (invariably in multi-lingual classes) and "English as a foreign language" where English is acquired over very long periods at home (invariably in monolingual classes). Furthermore, we need to develop the idea of student-as-protagonist in situations which are highly motivating precisely because they can be seen to meet actual communication needs.

Grammar

The teaching of grammar in functionally-based courses is intense but selective since we choose and drill only those items which have an immediate application in communicative contexts. Students may be referred to grammatical paradigms to study for themselves those elements we have not had time to drill. Grammatically difficult utterances must be introduced and learnt like vocabulary items long before they are formally introduced if they are indispensable for communication at early stages of learning.

Sign-posting

We can expect some kind of sign-posting to be a feature of new course materials; students need to be made aware of what they are learning and why so that they can actively participate in the learning process in order to reach defined objectives.

Pacing

We have to decide whether we want courses arranged in "lessons" on facing page layouts and so on, or in frames. A book arranged in "lessons" (however artificial the arrangement) tends to pace the teacher. Because of the great variety of language activities, functionally-based courses can sometimes best be organized in frames, so the teacher can pace the course.

Testing

After years of developing highly sophisticated psychometric tests, we are now, paradoxically, in the position where we have to begin afresh to develop new kinds of techniques which reflect the new content of courses. Ideally, the methods used to test performance should not be far removed from those used to teach it.

Correctness

We are not trying to create native speakers. While we must draw the line at wholly unacceptable utterances, the degree of error we are prepared to tolerate is bound to vary in accordance with the abilities of individual learners. "Defective but effective communication" is a worthy aim.

CONCLUSIONS

Misconceptions about a functional/notional approach already abound and our first task in the 1980's is to clarify potential misunderstanding. It will already be clear that this is not a "utilitarian" approach to language acquisition (interpreting the word "functional" in its lay sense to imply, *e.g.*, "how to change money at a bank"). It is *not* a "method" (a viable alternative to, *e.g.*, "the audio-visual method"). It does not imply a "phrase-book" approach to methodology. It does *not* devalue grammar or indeed any of the factors we have come to associate with sound course construction and traditional methodology. It is first and foremost an approach to syllabus design and therefore, in turn, to course design.

There are innumerable difficulties in coming to terms with these new ideas, not least of which (from the point of view of practical methodology) is the problem of metalanguage. We have long been conditioned by A/V and A/L methodology that language teaching should never involve use of the mother tongue, but there are many instances where it now seems desirable—particularly when teaching beginners—when we wish to explain what we are doing and why, and when we wish to set up improvisation/transfer situations for students to take part in. Against difficulties of this kind we can look forward with a sense of excitement and anticipation to increasing our understanding of the endlessly fascinating problems posed by second and foreign language acquisition.

REFERENCES

Council of Europe Documents
(CCC = Council for Cultural Co-operation, Council of Europe, Strasbourg, France.)

Systems Development in Adult Language Learning, CCC, 1973, containing:

van Ek, J. A. *Analysis of the Problems Involved in Defining in Operational Terms a Basic Competence Level (or Threshold Level) in Foreign Language Learning by Adults*. 1972.

———. *Proposal for the Definition of a Threshold Level in Foreign Language Learning by Adults*. 1972.

Richterich, R. *Analytical Classification of the Categories of Adults Needing to Learn Foreign Languages*. 1971.

———. *A Model for the Definition of Language Needs of Adults Learning a Modern Language*. 1972.

Trim, J. L. M. *Draft Outline of a European Unit/Credit System for Modern Language Learning by Adults*. 1973.

Wilkins, D. A. *An Investigation into the Linguistic and Situational Content of the Common Core in a Unit/Credit System*. 1972.

van Ek, J. A. *The Threshold Level*. CCC, 1972.

———. *The Threshold Level for Schools*. Longman, 1976, with L. G. Alexander and M. A. Fitzpatrick: *Waystage: An Intermediary Objective Below Threshold Level*. CCC, 1977.

Trim, J. L. M. *Report on Some Possible Lines of Development of an Overall Structure for a European Unit/Credit Scheme for Foreign Language Learning by Adults*. CCC, 1977.

Coste, D. (et al). *Un Niveau-Seuil*. CCC, 1976.

Roulet, E. *Un Niveau-Seuil: Présentation et Guide d'Emploi*. CCC, 1977.

The reports of three major symposia:

The Rüschlikon Symposium. CCC, 1971.

The St. Wolfgang Symposium. CCC, 1973.

The Ludwigshaven Symposium. CCC, 1977.

Other References:

Alexander, L. G. *Mainline Beginners A & B*. Longman, 1978, 1979. (et al.): *Survive in . . . ,* Longman, 1980.

————, Allen, W. Stannard, Close, R. A., O'Neill, R. J. *English Grammatical Structure*. Longman, 1975.

Arnold, J., and Harmer, J. *Advanced Speaking Skills*. Longman, 1978.

Leech, G., and Svartvik, J. *A Communicative Grammar of English*. Longman, 1975.

Munby, J. *Communicative Syllabus Design*. Cambridge University Press, 1978.

Rundfunk, Bayerische, et al. *Follow Me*, 1979, 1980.

Wilkins, D. A. *Notional Syllabuses*. Oxford University Press, 1976.

ABSTRACT

Media in the Second Language Program: Forms and Uses for the Eighties

REINHOLD FREUDENSTEIN
Marburg University (Federal Republic of Germany)

In the past, research concentrated mainly on the effectiveness of media in the context of specific teaching methods. This attitude has changed; the learning process of the individual student has become a major factor in foreign and second language programs. This does not affect media forms, but media uses. The application of media is not alone prescribed by functions which they can fulfill anymore, but by individual decisions which always have to be made anew for each instructional environment. Success or failure of media use in the eighties will mainly depend on the question of whether or not teachers are both willing and able to make these decisions.

Media in the Second Language Program: Forms and Uses for the Eighties

REINHOLD FREUDENSTEIN
Marburg University (Federal Republic of Germany)

MEDIA USE: TWO OPPOSING VIEWS

In one of the leading professional journals in Germany, a media specialist recently commented on terms which have been applied to foreign language teachers who use technical media in the teaching and learning process (Pürschel, 1980; p. 12). "Look, there's our 'mediot' again," can be heard when one of the teachers carries a tape-recorder through the school building. "Good morning, Don Folio," is a common greeting formula for teachers who are known for frequently using the overhead-projector (in German, transparencies for the overhead-projector are known as "Folien"). Are these terms an expression of admiration, or are they being used to ridicule the persons involved? Whatever the case, Pürschel concluded he would not stop encouraging his student-teachers to get to know and to use audio-visual media in the foreign or second language classroom.

Those who felt sympathetic to Pürschel's attitude did not have to wait too long for a reaction. It appeared in the next issue of the same journal and expressed the view of a great number of foreign language teachers in Germany, and in other parts of Europe as well. A teacher of English in secondary education and a language laboratory director of his school summarized his view on the basis of everyday experience in the following way (Kunze, 1980; p. 123):

1. According to empirical research, the level of learning resulting from the use of audio-visual media is either the same as or less

than that which results from traditional ("chalk and black-board") methods.

2. The support for media use in language teaching is nothing but a pedagogic ideology.
3. Young teachers prefer ready-to-use materials.
4. Diagrams, tables, etc. do not allow one to gain insight into the complexity of many (teaching) problems.
5. Looking at pictures and watching films support the entertainment effect, obstruct creative thinking, and lead to the neglect of verbal expression.

Although both views of media use in language programs are extreme examples, they are nevertheless realistic and viable. The use of even the most sophisticated hardware does not automatically guarantee good learning results; the "chalk-and-blackboard" method can very well be the basis for interesting and successful teaching. It all depends on the most important "medium" in any instructional process: the teacher. Success and failure of media use in the foreign or second language program are directly related to the way in which teachers have learned to handle "machines," have experienced their use in the classroom, and are—or are not—willing to accept and work with them. If teachers can decide which functions can be fulfilled by media in a better way than by themselves alone, they will most probably be more satisfied when using audio-visual equipment, and thus more successful. Teachers who are uninformed, emotionally opposed or unwilling—for any reasons whatsoever—to enrich their teaching with audio-visual material most certainly feel more comfortable in a media-free environment. There is no empirical proof of the fact that media use *per se* accounts for more motivation, interesting teaching, or better learning results, nor will there ever be. Machines can always be only as good and helpful as the individual teacher thinks they are.

MEDIA USE IN THE PAST

This position is the result of some twenty or more years of practical experience with modern technological aids. Around 1960, it was common thinking to believe in revolutionary changes brought about by new audio-visual techniques on the basis of programmed learning. The attention of the profession was focused on the refinement of *methods;* better teaching methods were expected to make language learning easier, more interesting, and automatically successful regardless of the individual factors of the learner. Thousands of language laboratories were installed all around the world. Audio-visual courses with integrated sound, picture, and film material were devised (first in France and Yugoslavia) and used in most industrialized countries that could afford to buy and introduce them into their educational systems. There were even times when teachers were allowed to work with certain audio-visual courses only after they had obtained a special diploma. *Teaching* was regarded as the sole key to success.

About ten years later, an important book on media use in language instruction came out, and its title indicated the change of approach that had taken place in the interim: It was the *learning* process which had become more important than anything else. This shift in emphasis was the result of a process of experimentation and classroom experience. This had led to the conclusion that the more one tries to incorporate media use into teaching methods, the more one is inclined to neglect the human factors in teaching. In order to better understand why the scene has changed one has to look more closely into media use of the past. The decade between 1960 and 1970 was the most important and most crucial time in the development and use of modern media. It was the time when language laboratories, tape- and cassette-recorders, overhead-projectors, teaching machines, slides, films, and television courses—to name just a few of the most widespread—were advertised, applied and empirically researched. Hundreds of studies were conducted in order to prove that using media in the teaching of foreign or second languages could bring about superior results as compared with traditional, media-free instruction. None of these studies, however, could offer figures or data which showed an overall significant difference in learning results. If one tries to analyze and to summarize all of the research findings from this time, one comes to the conclusion that:

1. the use of media in language programs can *sometimes* support the teaching objectives;
2. in *many* cases, media use does not harm the learning process;
3. results obtained under controlled conditions can *sometimes* be repeated in the normal, everyday classroom situation.

These conclusions parallel perfectly individual teachers' beliefs and attitudes. Some of them are enthusiastic media supporters, a large group simply does not care, and others are opposed in principle to the use of modern media. (Incidentally, a fourth group should not be forgotten: teachers who would like to, but are not in a position to work with media. I still remember when I read a paper in a remote area of Nigeria; I wanted to show slides but I couldn't because there was neither electricity nor the possibility of darkening the lecture hall. So I *had* to do without media, and I got my message across anyway.)

RESEARCH AND THE TEACHING-LEARNING PROCESS

There are three major reasons which account for the instability of different research results. First, most of the studies with positive results were conducted under carefully controlled conditions by persons who favored the media they researched. Their research plans were outlined in such a way that favorable results were likely to be achieved. Each (controlled or uncontrolled) pedagogic situation is unique because it involves human beings who are different. Even the most sophisticated statistical methods cannot do away with these differences. This is why two or more studies on the same topic can bring about very different results, and the teacher's role in these studies is often of utmost importance. The same, of course, holds true for the uncontrolled everyday teaching situation.

A second reason why research in the media field was unreliable in the past is that many studies were carried out under conditions which neglected the setting of foreign or second language teaching. A good example for illustrating this point is the Pennsylvania Project (Smith, 1970). Thousands of students and hundreds of teachers were mathematically subdivided into learning groups which had to follow pre-established instructional patterns devised according to purely theoretical premises. At a time when communicative skills were demanded and practiced, what could one expect of experimental classes that were taught on the basis of the grammar-translation-method with and without the help of media? It is not astonishing that improper research planning must necessarily result in negative findings. But even in this case there were students who learned anyway. Obviously they were ready and prepared to accept the instructional offering regardless of method and media.

Interestingly enough, Schumann arrives at similar conclusions, although in a different research context. He says: "It is my opinion that whether we use the audio-lingual method, the cognitive code method . . . or an individualized method, we will achieve equally unsatisfactory results in the long run because language learning is not a matter of method, but it is a matter of acculturation, and where acculturation cannot take place . . . we cannot expect to achieve much more than we are now in our foreign language programs" (Schumann, 1978; p. 47). If acculturation is the process of getting to know and appreciate new value systems, we again encounter the importance of the human element on both the teacher's and the student's part.

MEDIA MISUSE

Finally, one of the factors which made a well-balanced use of media impossible in the past is undoubtedly the misuse of media perpetrated by some "mediots." It is common thinking that not everything which is theoretically possible in the field of media use must or should be practiced. And yet, "specialists" tried over and over again to devise gadgets which became important sales arguments but were never really needed or used in everyday classroom teaching. I do not want to argue the case of different modes of language laboratory use, although I believe that working with simpler technology in the beginning would have served the cause of media instruction more and better than experimenting with highly complex systems.

To exemplify the misuse of media I would like to refer to the "multi-media instruction room" which was installed in Berlin (Mackiewicz and Mindt, 1974). The idea was to build a classroom in which all media relevant to language instruction were available all the time. The following instructional possibilities were provided for: (1) All kinds of classroom instruction (including partner and group work) without any obstacles that might result from permanently installed furniture or technical devices; (2) audio presentation; (3) video presentation; (4) simultaneous audio and video presentation; (5) language laboratory work; (6) video-supported language laboratory instruction; (7) transition from one form of interaction to another at any time. In this room there were no traditional language laboratory student booths; the technical equipment was put in specially constructed student chairs which could be moved freely in the room and—whenever necessary—connected to one of fifty-three electric outlets in the floor of the room. Whichever outlet the student used, his chair could always be monitored from the teacher's desk. Also available were: one overhead-projector on a movable table, one 16-mm film projector, one super-8-cassette projector, three slide projectors, four projection screens (two at the front, and one at each side of the room), two mobile video-recorders and two monitors. The room could be automatically darkened, and most of the technical equipment worked on remote control. One can easily imagine the manifold activities that could go on at the same time in this room: one group of students is watching a television program, in another corner of the room six or eight students are working on structural drills, there is also a film presentation (screen three on the left wall), the teacher is working with slow learners by using the overhead-projector, and in the middle of the room a group is practicing drama techniques in order to improve the communicative competence of its members.

Fortunately, this concept has not become common practice. If it had, it would have been a perfect example of the dehumanizing effect of media use without consideration for actual instructional needs. About five years before the Berlin multi-media room was installed, Grittner had stated about programmed learning: "Experience has shown that the 'hardware' (i.e., the machine) tends to be developed to a high level of sophistication before the 'software' (i.e., the educational program). Yet the program is the most basic aspect" (Grittner, 1969; p. 177). The same holds true for other media as well. It is not the availability of hardware that counts, but the right use of a particular medium for specific purposes at the right time. In order to be able to make the right decisions, teachers must be informed about the functions which media can fulfill in the teaching and learning of foreign and second languages.

MEDIA FUNCTIONS
IN THE LANGUAGE CLASSROOM

In former times, long before the advance of instructional technology, media used to be called "teaching aids." It is the teaching aspect which is still the most important one today. Forms and kinds of aids have changed; however, their functions in the language program have basically remained the same. From the teacher's point of view, they can generally serve four general purposes (Gutschow, 1973; p. 139):

1. Media can help to simplify the teaching process, and they can help to perfect it.
2. Machines allow the teacher to practice the principle of object teaching and illustration.
3. With the help of media the use of the mother tongue of the students can be avoided.
4. Media are instruments of motivation if they are used in such a way as to stimulate learning.

Since media use is not restricted to teacher-directed classroom instruction, this list can be supplemented by adding functions media can fulfill when used by individual learners outside the school situation:

1. Media can help to simplify the learning process, and can help to perfect it.
2. Machines allow the student to better understand the content of what is being taught.

3. Media can help to shape the learning process.
4. Media can stimulate interest in the language program and thus provide for a motivational impulse.

The objectives behind these functions are necessary elements of any foreign and second language program regardless of whether or not media are used. Therefore it is the user's task to decide if, when, and why specific media should be employed.

If one wants to arrive at the right decision, one must ask: "What can a particular medium contribute to specific teaching and learning goals, and can it really do it in a better than any other way—including the teacher's performance?" This seems to be a very simple question, but it has not been asked too often in the past.

NEW TECHNOLOGIES FOR THE CLASSROOM IN THE EIGHTIES?

There is a danger in assuming that whatever is new is good. The latest example is the case of the microprocessor. In an international newsletter, it was commented on in the following way: "We are witnessing the beginnings of another technological revolution which is bound to affect modern foreign-language teaching in one way or another" (Jung, 1980; p. 7). The author refers to a tiny electronic device which could be called a highly sophisticated calculator. It can process an enormous number of linguistic units in a fraction of a second, and can translate them from one language into another. If it is equipped with a speech synthesizer it can even "speak" the message one wants to express. One enters, for example, the digits $7 + 209 + 433$ and one gets, "I would like a room." Asking the question, "What can the microprocessor contribute towards specific teaching and learning goals in my foreign or second language program?" will lead to sound decision-making. Most likely, one will come to the conclusion that—given the normal language-classroom situation in most countries of the world—no functional use can be made of the microprocessor at this time at all.

Another example is the teletext. Of course it is possible to imagine learners who are preparing their homework in front of a television set, and whenever they need to know the equivalent of a mother-tongue word—or any other relevant information or data—they consult the electronic dictionary or another data source via telephone and television screen. This is technically possible and will soon be generally available; but is it necessary? A dictionary in the form of a book serves the same purpose, is less costly and pedagogically preferable (for a number of reasons, *e.g.*, the opportunity to learn additional vocabulary items in the process of searching for a specific vocabulary item). The teletext will—as most new technologies—play an important part in future communication systems, and learners of today will most probably live with it as we do now with telephone or television. This does not mean, however, that new technologies in the media field qualify in each and every case as instructional tools as well.

THE TEACHER'S ROLE

How can mistakes of the past be avoided in the future, and what does the teacher have to know and do so that the students can profit from media use?

The most important prerequisite is a teacher who is thoroughly informed about the instructional possibilities for, and the limitations of different media. This seems to go without saying; and yet the average language teacher in Europe who is being trained for teaching foreign or second languages at the secondary level has only a haphazard chance of getting to know how to use media in a systematic way. This is because this field of activity has not (yet) reached the level of an acknowledged university subject. It is covered, if at all, in lectures and seminars taught by professors who happen to be personally interested or only marginally involved in this subject area. And since prospective language teachers of today belong to a generation that has experienced media use during their own schooldays, most of them enter the profession with strong personal impressions based on their own experiences as students. Very often they only remember boring sessions in the language laboratory or lessons in which machines were used by teachers who could not handle them, *e.g.*, the presentation of a film in the last class session before summer holidays—a "present" to entertain students with no defensible instructional purpose at all. If the curriculum of these future teachers does not include an obligatory introduction to media use, they will most probably tend to neglect media altogether or misuse machinery as their own teachers had done. Therefore, any initial or in-service training program for foreign and second language teachers should concentrate on three positions which incorporate the experience of the past, and at the same time project our accumulated knowledge to future media planning and media use.

CONCLUSIONS

Position 1: *It is necessary to avoid one-sided and extreme views and practices.* This includes both obsessive overuse and total disregard of media. Teachers who feel impelled to use the tape-recorder, the overhead-projector, the slide projector, or other machines in each and every lesson they teach will most probably bore their students in the long run as much as if they worked only with textbooks and the blackboard. I remember an experimental foreign language teaching project in Germany in which television and radio were an integrated part of the language course (Gutschow, 1971). Each unit followed the same pace: it was introduced by a television film (Monday), the basic structures were practiced in the form of four-phase-drills broadcast over radio (Tuesday), followed up by textbook and workbook instruction for the rest of the week. One Monday, after three months of teaching in this way, the closed-circuit television system of the school broke down. The teachers were confronted with an unexpected situation: they had to introduce a new unit by themselves. Afterwards all of them reported that they had became acquainted with their classes in an entirely different and refreshingly new way. What they had experienced was that the students listened more intensively, they seemed to be more motivated than during the usual film presentations, and they participated in the classroom activities as they had seldom done before. All this resulted from *not* using media in a situation in which films and tapes were part of the usual teaching method. Teachers were forced to break the routine, and they discovered one of the basic laws of media use: whether machines serve their purposes well is not decided alone by the particular functions media can fulfill, but foremost by the total instructional context in which they are applied.

Position 2: *It is necessary to be wary of the attractiveness of sophisticated hardware.* Once again, the language laboratory is a good example to illustrate this point. Long before the laboratory had become generally accepted, some media specialists started to formulate demands which were supposed to make laboratory work more flexible and effective. The industry responded by building in whatever could be materialized, *e.g.*, the "stereo effect," the immediate repetition of the students' answers after they had spoken without the necessity of pressing buttons, the provision for flexible electronic connections in the laboratory so that partner and group work could be practiced, and many others. The more "extras" of this kind were advertised, the more "old-fashioned" the normal language laboratory appeared to be, although most of the extra functions were never really needed or used in everyday teaching situations. Language laboratories became more expensive, they broke down more often because of technical difficulties, and for many teachers they were instruments which they could no longer manage. In a school near Frankfurt (Germany) the language teachers refused to work with their classes in the language laboratory until the company had taken out sixty-four switches and pushbuttons from the teacher's console.

Position 3: *It is necessary for each language teacher to be thoroughly familiar with the basic media of his profession.* For a long time, only the textbook and the blackboard were regarded as basic elements in the language program. Many teachers still follow this tradition. However, since the development of communicative competence has become our general learning goal, other media are of equal importance. They fall into two categories: visual aids and audio material. In both, teachers have a wide range of items to choose from. The most important among the visuals are transparencies for the overhead-projector, slides, picture-cards, wallcharts, films and video-tapes; films and video-tapes in most cases also provide for the sound element which is normally available in the form of magnetic tapes and cassettes. "To be familiar" with these media actually means to know their functions and to be able to decide in each teaching situation which of these functions *can* and *should* be carried out by them. Although teachers alone can carry out almost all of the functions that machines perform, they need to realize that in many cases machines can perform these functions more effectively or efficiently.

Most media *forms* in the rest of this decade will be basically the same as they have been in the past; this also applies to media *functions*. Media *use* in the eighties will change, however, in the hands of informed teachers who know how to devise, apply, or modify a well-balanced, media-assisted language program.

REFERENCES

Dakin, Julian. *The Language Laboratory and Language Learning*. London: Longman, 1973.

Grittner, Frank M. *Teaching Foreign Languages*. New York: Harper & Row, 1969.

Gutschow, Harald. "Englisch im Medienverbund." In: *Der Fremdsprachliche Unterricht* 4/1971, pp. 2–15.

———. *Englisch an Hauptschulen*. Berlin: Cornelsen-Velhagen & Klasing, 1973.

Jung, Udo O. H. "Microprocessor Replaces Foreign-Language Teacher." In: alsed/FIPLV Newsletter 19. Paris: UNESCO, 1980.

Kunze, Manfred B. "Der Kommentar." In: *Praxis des Neusprachlichen Unterrichts* 2/1980, p. 123.

Mackiewicz, Wolfgang; Mindt, Dieter. "Sprachlabor und Multi-medialer Fremdsprachenunterricht." In: *Praxis des Neusprachlichen Unterrichts* 1/1974, pp. 11–18.

Pürschel, Heiner. "Medioten?" In: *Praxis des Neusprachlichen Unterrichts* 1/1980, pp. 12–13.

Schumann, John H. "The Acculturation Model for Second-Language Acquisition." In: Gingras, Rosario C. (ed.): *Second-Language Acquisition and Foreign Language Teaching*. Washington, D.C.: Center for Applied Linguistics, 1978, pp. 27–50.

Smith, Philip D. "A Comparison of the Cognitive and Audiolingual Approaches to Foreign Language Instruction." Philadelphia: Center for Curriculum Development, 1970.

Notes
on the Contributors

JAMES E. ALATIS is Dean of the School of Languages and Linguistics and Professor of Linguistics and Modern Greek at Georgetown University. Since 1966 he has served as Executive Secretary/Treasurer of TESOL. He was formerly an English Teaching Specialist with the U.S. Department of State, Chief of the Language Research Section of the U.S. Office of Education, and Fulbright Professor, University of Athens, Greece. Among his most recent publications is a chapter on TESOL in the Seventy-ninth Yearbook of the National Society for the Study of Education, "Learning a Second Language 1980"; he has edited the proceedings of the three latest Georgetown University Round Tables on Languages and Linguistics: *International Dimensions of Bilingual Education* (1978), *Language in Public Life* (1979), and *Current Issues in Bilingual Education* (1980).

PENELOPE M. ALATIS has been teaching English as a Second Language at the secondary school level in the Alexandria, Virginia school system since 1964. She has been a frequent participant in ACTFL national convention programs. As a member of TESOL since its inception in 1966, she has served on panels at the TESOL convention and in TESOL preconvention workshops from 1975–1979. She has served as consultant to Xerox Education Publications and is currently serving as a consultant to the Secondary Level English Proficiency Test Committee (SLEP) of the Educational Testing Service.

LOUIS G. ALEXANDER is probably the best known writer of textbooks on English as a Second Language in the world today, with more than a hundred volumes in print. He is an ubiquitous lecturer on language teaching and serves as a methodological consultant to the Council of Europe. His pedagogical writings have appeared in numerous journals, and his lectures on communicative language teaching at the Cambridge Summer Course in Linguistics have become legendary.

VIRGINIA FRENCH ALLEN has trained language teachers at three American universities, most recently at Temple University in Philadelphia, where she is Professor Emeritus. Assignments as a consultant in the Teaching of English to Speakers of Other Languages (TESOL) have taken her to Hawaii, Burma, Indonesia, the People's Republic of China, and various parts of Latin America. Her publications include several textbooks as well as numerous articles in professional journals.

HOWARD B. ALTMAN is Professor of Modern Languages at the University of Louisville, where he directs the graduate programs in Foreign Language Education. He has written and lectured widely on the individualization of language instruction. From 1976–79 he served on the faculty of the Summer Course in Linguistics and English Language at the University of Cambridge, and has been an American specialist and lecturer in Yugoslavia four times in recent years. His most recent publication is *Foreign Language Teaching: Meeting Individual Needs*, of which he is co-author and principal editor. He is also editing, with Peter Strevens, a new series of books in applied linguistics and language teaching for Cambridge University Press.

H. DOUGLAS BROWN is Associate Professor and Director of the Division of English as a Second Language at the University of Illinois, Urbana-Champaign. He previously held the position of Associate Professor of Linguistics at the English Language Institute of the University of Michigan, Ann Arbor. Currently, he serves as the President of TESOL. He has written numerous articles on second language acquisition and psycholinguistics, and has published a textbook on the theoretical foundations of language teaching, *Principles of Language Learning and Teaching*.

CHRISTOPHER J. BRUMFIT is Lecturer in English as a Foreign Language at the Institute of Education, University of London. He previously served as Education Officer in Tanzania and Lecturer in Linguistics at the City of Birmingham (England) College of Education. He has published numerous articles and, most recently, a book entitled *Problems and Principles in English Teaching*.

MARINA BURT is Executive Director and President of Bloomsbury West, Inc., a non-profit research and services corporation which focuses on language learning and education. She was Senior Research Associate at the State University of New York at Albany, Lecturer at Stanford University, and Instructor of Linguistics at the Massachusetts Institute of Technology. She is author of *From Deep to Surface Structure: An Introduction to Transformational Grammar*; co-author of *The Bilingual Syntax Measure* and *The Gooficon*; and co-editor of *Viewpoints on English as a Second Language* and *New Directions in Second Language Learning, Teaching and Bilingual Education*.

HEIDI DULAY is Director, Vice-president and Treasurer of Bloomsbury West, Inc., a non-profit research and services corporation which focuses on language learning and education. She was Assistant Professor of Puerto Rican Studies and Education at the State University of New York at Albany, Lecturer in Linguistics at Stanford University, and Instructor of Education at Harvard University. She was formerly Assistant Director of Research for Bilingual Children's Television. She is co-author of *The Bilingual Syntax Measure* and *Why Bilingual Education? A Review of Research.* She is co-editor of *New Directions in Second Language Learning, Teaching and Bilingual Education* and *Viewpoints on English as a Second Language.* In addition, she has written numerous articles on psycholinguistic factors in the process of becoming bilingual.

REINHOLD FREUDENSTEIN is Professor of Education and Director of the Foreign Language Research Information Center (IFS) at Marburg University, Federal Republic of Germany. He is a member of the Executive Board of FIPLV (Fédération Internationale des Professeurs de Langues Vivantes). He is author of *Unterrichtsmittel Sprachlabor* and editor of *Praxis des Neusprachlichen Unterrichts*, a quarterly for teachers of foreign languages, and has written numerous articles on methodology of foreign language teaching and educational technology.

FREDERICK L. JENKS is Director of the Center for Intensive English Studies and Associate Professor of Foreign Language Education at Florida State University. A former member of the ACTFL Executive Council and a past Chairperson of the Southern Conference on Language Teaching, he has served as editor of *American Foreign Language Teacher* and currently edits a series of books on language teaching, *Foreign and Second Language Educator*, for Heinle and Heinle.

HELEN L. JORSTAD is Associate Professor of Second Languages and Cultures at the University of Minnesota and a former member of the Executive Council of ACTFL. She has published numerous articles, especially in the areas of language teacher education and language testing. Recent publications include "Objectives for New Programs: A Thematic Approach in Second Language Learning," "The Education and Reeducation of Teachers," and "Student Evaluation of Peer-Group Microteaching as Preparation for Student Teaching."

STEPHEN D. KRASHEN is Associate Professor and Acting Chairman of the Department of Linguistics at the University of Southern California. He was formerly Director of ESL, Queens College of the City of New York, and Postdoctoral Fellow at the Neuropsychiatric Institute, UCLA. He is author of *Second Language Learning and Second Language Acquisition*, and has co-authored *The Human Brain*, and *The Second Language* (forthcoming). His other numerous publications are in the area of the processes of second language acquisition.

ROBERT LADO retired in 1980 from his position as Professor of Linguistics at Georgetown University, where he had formerly served as Dean of the School of Languages and Linguistics. Previous positions include Director of the English Language Institute at the University of Michigan and Fulbright Professor at the University of Madrid. His numerous publications include *Linguistics Across Cultures, Language Testing, Language Teaching: A Scientific Approach*, and *ESPAÑOL: Lengua y Letras*. He is co-editor of *Intensive Course in English*, associate editor of *Current Trends in Linguistics, Vol. IV*, and author of the *Lado English Series*.

BERNICE J. MELVIN is Associate Professor of French at Austin College (Sherman, Texas), having previously taught at the University of Texas at Austin and the University of Minnesota. She has collaborated with Wilga Rivers on various publications and has recently published her own article entitled "Recent Research in Memory and Cognition and its Implications for Foreign Language Teaching" in *Studies in Language Learning*.

ROBERT L. POLITZER is Professor of Education and Romance Linguistics at Stanford University. He was formerly Professor of French and Romance Linguistics at the University of Michigan and Assistant Professor at Harvard. He was the recipient of a Guggenheim fellowship in 1956. His writings on applied linguistics and foreign language education include *Linguistics and Applied Linguistics: Methods and Aims*, and (with Frieda Politzer) *Teaching English as a Second Language*. He was the recipient of the first Paul Pimsleur Award for Research in Foreign Language Education presented by ACTFL.

WILGA M. RIVERS is Professor of Romance Languages and Coordinator of Language Instruction in the Department of Romance Languages at Harvard University. She was formerly Professor of French at the University of Illinois at Urbana-Champaign and Visiting Professor at Teachers College, Columbia University. She has served as a Consultant Panelist to the National Endowment for the Humanities and was a Rockefeller Foundation Consultant in Bangkok. Her research on the applications of psychology and linguistics to language teaching and language teaching methodology includes, in addition to numerous articles, *The Psychologist and the Foreign-language Teacher, Teaching Foreign-language Skills*, and, most recently, she has co-authored *A Practical Guide to the Teaching of English as a Second or Foreign Language*.

H. H. STERN is Director of the Modern Language Centre at the Ontario Institute for Studies in Education. He has previously taught at the University of Hull and the University of Essex, both in England, and has served with the UNESCO Institute for Education in Hamburg. His publications include *Languages in Primary Education, Languages and the Young School Child, Modern Languages in the Universities: A Guide*, and *Perspectives on Second Language Teaching*. He has co-authored a number of research reports, including a large-scale study of the teaching of French in Ottawa, *Three Approaches to the Teaching of French*.

RENZO TITONE is Director of the Centro di Linguistica Applicata in Rome. He is Professor of Educational Psychology and Applied Psycholinguistics at the University of Rome, and was formerly Professor of Methodology at Salesian University, Rome, and Professor of Applied Linguistics and Psycholinguistics at Georgetown University. He is author of numerous books and articles on applied linguistics and psycholinguistics, including *Psicolinguistica Applicata*, *Teaching Foreign Languages: An Historical Sketch*, and *Problems in Educational Psychology*. He is editor of the *Rassegna Italiana di Linguistica Applicata* and President of the Association of Teachers of English to Speakers of Italian.

G. RICHARD TUCKER is Director of the Center for Applied Linguistics in Washington, D.C. He was formerly Professor of Psycholinguistics at McGill University, Montreal. He has been a project specialist with the Ford Foundation at English Language Centers in Southeast Asia and in the Middle East. His published research studies in language learning and teaching in both monolingual and bilingual settings include co-authoring *The Bilingual Education of Children* and *English Language Policy Survey of Jordan*.

REBECCA M. VALETTE is Professor of French and Education and Director of the Language Laboratory at Boston College. She has served as Fulbright senior lecturer in Germany. Her research concerns in modern language testing and methodology have led to the publication of *Modern Language Performance Objectives and Individualization*, and *Modern Language Testing*. She has produced many texts for French instruction and co-authored *Classroom Techniques: Foreign Languages and English as a Second Language*.

HENRY G. WIDDOWSON is Professor of English as a Foreign Language at the Institute of Education, University of London and holder of the only Chair in EFL in Great Britain. He serves as one of the editors of *Applied Linguistics*. His numerous publications include *Stylistics and the Teaching of Literature*, *Teaching Language as Communication*, and *Explorations in Applied Linguistics*.

A Selective Bibliography of Mary Finocchiaro

Mary Finocchiaro is not one to be contained on paper. This most extensive bibliography of the books, articles, and texts she has produced in her long and still fruitful career reveals only one dimension of her professional activity as a wise and enthusiastic teacher who has always spearheaded productive thinking in the development of language pedagogy. At the same time, Mary has interpreted innovations with common sense, humanity, and a sharp focus on the practical concerns and needs of the classroom teacher. She has long poured her prodigious energies into the revitalization of second language teaching. Undaunted by time or place, she has shared her insights with teachers throughout the world. Since Mary cannot visit every language teacher in the world personally—although she may yet come very close to doing so—this bibliography is intended not only to bear witness to her scholarship and dedication, but also to provide a wider readership with access to an indispensable collection. Here one must add that it is an injustice to reduce to so dry a format as a formal bibliography a series of writings which are as penetrating, vibrant and delightful as Mary herself. The publications listed below reflect her intellectually honest and unfaddish approach to language teaching and language learning. We have appended this bibliography in the interests of the profession to which Mary has dedicated her life.

J.E.A., H.B.A., P.M.A.

The Gallo-Italian Dialect of Nicosia. Columbia U. Ph.D. Thesis. New York: King's Crown Press, 1950.

"A Suggested Procedure for the Teaching of English to Puerto Ricans." *High Points.* New York City Board of Education. May 1949: 60–66.

"Impressions of Puerto Rico." *High Points.* New York City Board of Education. February 1951: 5–11.

"Minority Groups in the Community." Bulletin issued by the New York State Department of Education. April 1951.

Puerto Rican Bulletin. A Newsletter for the Junior High School Division. New York City Board of Education. 1950–52.

La Vida Diaria (with Theodore Huebener). New York: Noble and Noble, 1952.

"Helping Puerto Ricans Achieve Status." *Strengthening Democracy.* May 1953: 4–5.

"Our Schools Meet the Challenges of a New Migration." *High Points.* New York City Board of Education. March 1953: 29–34.

Source Materials and Texts for the Teacher of English as a Second Language (with the cooperation of Aileen Traver Kitchin). Bureau of Curriculum Research, New York City Board of Education, 1953.

"A Checklist for Supervisors." *The New York Supervisor.* Fall 1954: 23–27.

"A New Challenge in Education." *Teacher Education News and Notes.* Division of Teacher Education, New York City Board of Education. October 1954: Vol. VI, no. 1.

Our School, Home and City (with Theodore Huebener). New York: Noble and Noble, 1955.

"Puerto Rican Newcomers in Our Schools." *High Points.* New York City Board of Education. June 1955: 37–59.

"Puerto Rican Newcomer." *American Unity.* January 1956: 12–17.

"A Language Program for Foreign-born Students." *High Points.* New York City Board of Education. February 1957: 15–29.

Manual of Useful Spanish for Correctional Personnel. Department of Correction with the cooperation of the Commonwealth of Puerto Rico Department of Labor Migration Division, 1958.

"Teaching English as a Second Language." *The English Teachers' Magazine.* Tokyo: The Taeshukan Publishing Co, Ltd.
Part I Vol. VIII, no. 3 (June 1959)
Part II Vol. VIII, no. 4 (July 1959)
Part III Vol. VIII, no. 5 (Aug 1959)
Part IV Vol. VIII, no. 6 (Sept 1959)

American English For All the World. St. Louis: Webster Publishing Co., 1960.

Children's Living Spanish and *Children's Living Spanish Picture Dictionary.* New York: Crown Publishers, Inc., 1960.

Living Languages (Spanish) for Children. New York: Crown Publishers, Inc., 1960.

French by Sight, Sound and Story (with Mario Pei). New York: David McKay, 1962.

"An Alternative to the NDEA Institute" (with David Weiss). *The Modern Language Journal.* Vol. XLVII, no. 4 (April 1963): 147–149.

"English Teaching Seminars: Another Approach." *Linguistic Reporter.* Vol. V, no. 2 (April 1963): 2–4.

English as a Second Language: From Theory to Practice. A Synthesis of Lectures and Demonstrations given between 1960 and 1964 for the U.S. Department of State. New York: Regents Publishing Co., 1964.

Teaching Children Foreign Languages. New York: McGraw-Hill, 1964 (rev. ed).

Welcome, Amigo (with Theodore Huebener). New York: Noble and Noble, 1964.

"The Supervisor's Role in Curriculum Development." *On Teaching English to Speakers of Other Languages. Series I.* Papers read at the TESOL Conference, Tucson, Arizona, 1964. Edited by Virginia French Allen. Champaign, Illinois: National Council of Teachers of English (1965): 105–109.

Educator's Vocabulary Handbook (with Harold J. McNally). New York: American Book Company, 1965.

Bilingual Readiness in Earliest School Years: A Curriculum Demonstration Project. Project F. New York: Hunter College, 1966.

"The Challenge of Overseas Seminars." *On Teaching English to Speakers of Other Languages. Series II.* Papers read at the TESOL Conference, San Diego, California, March 1965. Edited by Carol Kreidler. Champaign, Illinois: National Council of Teachers of English (1966): 65–69.

English for Today. Our Changing World (with William Slager). New York: McGraw-Hill, Inc., 1966.

"Secondary School Composition: Problems and Practices." *TESOL Quarterly.* Vol. I, no. 3 (September 1967): 40–46.

"Teaching the Spanish-speaking Child in New York City." *On Teaching English to Speakers of Other Languages. Series III.* Papers read at the TESOL Conference, New York City, March 1966. Edited by Betty Wallace Robinett. Washington, D.C.: TESOL (1967): 58–63.

Advanced Living French. New York: Crown Publishers, Inc., 1968.

Learning to Use English. 2 vols. Montreal: Centre Educatif et Culturel Inc. (1968). (Publisher in the United States: New York: Regents Publishing Co., 1966).

Let's Learn Language. New York: McNally Publishers, 1968.

Bringing the School and the Community Together. Paper given at the third annual TESOL Convention, Chicago, Illinois, March 1969. ERIC Document 028 419.

Teaching English as a Second Language. New York: Harper and Row, Publisher, Inc., 1969. (Revised edition of the 1958 version, *Teaching English as a Second Language in Elementary and Secondary Schools.*)

Let's Talk: A Book of Conversations. New York: Simon and Schuster, 1970.

"Random Thoughts on Teaching English as a Second Language. Linguistic-Cultural Differences and American Education." Special Anthology Issue, *Florida Foreign Language Reporter.* Edited by A. Aarons, et al. Spring/Fall 1970.

Cours Structure de Francais (with R. J. Sweet, R. Lindsay, and M. Devaux). Montreal: Centre Educatif et Culturel, Inc., 1971.

Education of Puerto Ricans on the Mainland: Overcoming the Communication Barrier. Paper delivered at the conference on the Education of Puerto Rican Children on the Mainland, San Juan, 1970. Commonwealth of Puerto Rico, Department of Education (1971). ERIC Document 043 871.

"Foreign Languages and English as a Second Language: Two Sides of the Same Coin." *High Points.* New York City Board of Education. March 1971.

"Teaching English to Speakers of Other Languages: Problems and Priorities." *The English Record.* Vol. XXI, no. 4 (April 1971): 39–46.

TESOL Presidential Report to the Membership 1971. *TESOL Newsletter.* Vol. V, no. 2 (June 1971) 1.

"English/A Key to the World." *Lingua e civiltá dei paesi anglofoni per le scuole superiori* (with Renzo Titone e con la collaborazione di Violet Lavenda). Firenze: Le Monnier 1972.

"Making ESL Programs More Effective." *Instructor.* 81, 6 (1972): 89–91.

"Teaching English to Speakers of Other Languages: Problems and Priorities." *The Language Education of Minority Children; Selected Readings.* Edited by Bernard Spolsky. Rowley, Mass.: Newbury House Publishers, 1972 (reprinted with permission from *The English Record* 21:4 (1971): 39–47).

The Foreign Language Learner. A Guide for Teachers (with Michael Bonomo). New York: Regents Publishing Co., 1973.

Selections for Developing English Language Skills (with Violet Lavenda). New York: Regents Publishing Co. (rev. ed. of 1966 version), 1970, 1973).

Learning to Use English. New York: Regents Publishing Co., 1974.

"What Makes a Good EFL Teacher?" London: Educational Times Supplement. May 1974.

English as a Second Language: From Theory to Practice. New York: Regents Publishing Co., 1974.

"Myth and Reality: A Plea for a Broader View." *English Teaching Forum.* Special Issue, The Art of TESOL. Vol. XXII (1975). (Also published in *The Art of TESOL.* Selected articles from the *English Teaching Forum,* Part I. Compiled and edited by Anne Newton. Washington, D.C.: English Teaching Forum (1975): 34–40; reprinted with permission from the *TESOL Quarterly* Vol. V, no. 1 (March 1971): 3–17).

"Visual Aids in Teaching English as a Second Language." *The Art of TESOL.* Selected articles from the *English Teaching Forum,* Part II. Compiled and edited by Anne Newton. Washington, D.C.: English Teaching Forum (1975): 263–6 (reprinted with permission from *The American Book Company English as a Second Language Bulletin.* Vol. I, no. 5 (1966)).

Hablemos Español. New York: Regents Publishing Co., 1976.

"The Crucial Variable in TESOLD: The Teacher." *The Human Factors in ESL.* Edited by James E. Alatis and Ruth Crymes. Washington, D.C.: TESOL (1977). (Also published in *On TESOL '74.* Selected papers from the eighth annual TESOL Convention, Denver, Colorado, March 1974. Edited by Ruth Crymes and William E. Norris. Washington, D.C.: TESOL (1975): 39–58.)

"Developing Communicative Competence." *English Teaching Forum,* Vol. XV, no. 2 (April 1977).

Growing in English Language Skills. Steps to Communicative Competence (with Violet Hock Lavenda). New York: Regents Publishing Co., 1977.

L'insegnamento dell'inglese. Traduzione di *English as a Second Language* a cura de Biancamaria Tedeschini Lalli. Firenze: La Nuova Italia Editrice, 1977.

"Migration Today: Some Social and Educational Problems." *Viewpoints on English as a Second Language.* Edited with Marina Burt and Heidi Dulay. New York: Regents Publishing Co. (1977): 205–218.

"Classroom Practices in Bilingual Education." *Georgetown University Round Table on Languages and Linguistics 1978. International Dimensions of Bilingual Education.* Edited by James E. Alatis. Washington, D.C.: Georgetown University Press (1978): 517–526.

"Notional Functional Syllabuses: 1978 Part III." *On TESOL '78. EFL Policies, Programs, and Practices.* Selected papers from the twelfth annual TESOL Convention, Mexico City, April 1978. Washington, D.C.: TESOL (1978): 24–32.

"Role-playing in the Language Classroom." *Glottodidactica.* An International Journal of Applied Linguistics. Poznan: Uniwersytet Im Adamu Mickiewicza w Poznaniu. Vol. XI (1978): 25–31. (Also in *Zielsprache Englisch.* Munchen: Max Hueber Verlag. Vol. III (1977): 1–6.)

"Teaching Learners of Various Ability Levels." *English Language Teaching Journal.* Vol. XXXIII, no. 1 (October 1978): 1–12.

"The Functional-Notional Syllabus—Promises, Problems, Practices." *English Teaching Forum.* Vol. XVII, no. 2 (April 1979): 11–20. Expanded version in *Lingue e Didattica.* No. 37 (October 1979): 15–28.

"Motivation in Language Learning." *CATESOL Occasional Papers.* Number 5 (Fall 1979): 18–24. Preliminary version published in *English Teaching Forum.* Vol. XIV, no. 3 (July 1976): 4–8.

"Myth and Reality in Bilingual Education Programs." *Bilingual Education and Foreign Language Teaching Today.* Edited by Renzo Titone. Milano: Oxford Institutes Italiani (1979): 121–139.

"Notional Functional Syllabuses." *Rassegna Italiana di Linguistica Applicata.* Quadrimestrale a cura del Centro Italiana di Linguistica Applicata. Gennaio-Agosto 1979 anno xi, n. 1–2: 11–22.